D1871336

Philosophy of Education

Philosophy of Education

Editor

M.L. Dhawan

ISHA BOOKS
DELHI-110 033

Philosophy of Education

ISBN: 81-8205-151-7

© M.L. Dhawan

All rights are reserved. No part of this book may be reproduced in any manner without written permission.

Published in 2007 in India by
Isha Books,
B-63, Ist Floor, New Gupta Colony,
Near DDA Market, Delhi-110 009
Phone : 9212142040
Email : ishabooks@hotmail.com

Printed at : Rajdhani Printers, Delhi

Preface

A philosophy of education is the set of beliefs, ideas, and expectations a teacher has about the learning process. Individual philosophies of education vary in how reality and knowledge are understood, and each has its own implications for applications to educational systems. In application, a teacher may incorporate elements from many philosophies of education into his or her curriculum. Preservice teachers are frequently encouraged to identify and develop their own philosophy of education statements. Teachers who do not have a philosophy of education statement might not establish or attain well-defined goals and objectives for their students' education.

The present book aims to familiarize the reader with the most important perennial questions in philosophy of education. It combines both a historical overview of world education and a balanced treatment of leading educational philosophies. It explores the ideas and views of famous Indian and western philosophers, theologians, and educationists with distinctive theories of education and methods of teaching. It emphasizes both the importance of contexts and situations in the development of educational ideas as well as those features of educational theories that transcend particular historical contexts.

This work is an integrated and comprehensive approach to education, philosophies, philosophers, the child, the teacher, the curriculum and different problems of education. Researchers historians, educationists, philosophers and general readers can derive benefit out of it.

Editor

CONTENTS

1

Meaning of Philosophical Inquiry and Need for Philosophy of Education

The philosophy of education classroom, like the school classroom is strongly democratic and dialogical. In this way the energies of students will be engaged, their values respected, and their insights made available to fellow students and to professors. It is surprising how often professors of education advocate democracy for schools and yet do not practice it with their own students. If professors believe in a democratic approach to inquiry they should model it theirselves, so that the students understand what they mean and are given the opportunity to develop a democratic pedagogy which they can in turn employ in schools.

As Richard Rorty says:

> ...the intellectual...is just a special case - just somebody who does with marks and noises what other people do with their spouses and children, their fellow workers, the tools of their trade, the cash accounts of their businesses, the possessions they accumulate in their homes, the music they listen to, the sports they play and watch, or the trees they pass on their way to work.

Philosophers are simply living life like everyone else, working on the same problems as everyone else, but using a distinctive language (often more distinctive than need be). In this respect, the postmodernist attitude is the same as the hermeneutic attitude, on Gadamer's interpretation. As Dieter Misgeld expounds Gadamer's position:

> Hermeneutics...is a mode of inquiry that refuses to legitimate any disposition on the side of those inquiring to exempt themselves from what is topical in the inquiry.... [I]f inquiry is itself a situated activity, just as much as what one studies, the conduct of life of those inquiring comes to be an issue as does the relation of inquiry to their lives.

POSTMODERNISM

Postmodernism is not just a philosophical movement: it is found also, for example, in architecture, the graphic arts, dance, music, literature, and literary theory. As a general cultural phenomenon, it has such features as the challenging of convention, the mixing of styles, tolerance of ambiguity, emphasis on diversity, acceptance (indeed celebration) of innovation and change, and stress on the constructedness of reality.

Philosophical postmodernism, in turn, does not represent a single point of view. There are progressive postmodernists and conservative ones, postmodernists of "resistance" and postmodernists of "reaction," strongly reform-minded postmodernists and others who concentrate on pricking bubbles. There are bleeding hearts and loose cannons. There is constant debate among so-called postmodernists about how a true postmodernist should approach life and inquiry and hence what qualifies as postmodernism.

The names most often associated with postmodernism are those of Jean-Francois Lyotard, Jacques Derrida, Michel Foucault, and Richard Rorty. Theoretical approaches most commonly seen as postmodernist are deconstruction(ism), poststructuralism, and neopragmatism. However, a case could be made for adding other names, e.g., Nietzsche, the later Wittgenstein, Winch, Heidegger, Gadamer, and Kuhn; and other theoretical approaches, e.g., perspectivalism, postanalytic philosophy, and hermeneutics. Even the critical theory of Jurgen Habermas, with its affinity with hermeneutics and its communicative ethics, has clear postmodern elements, despite Habermas's insistence that he is furthering the project of modernity rather than rejecting it.

Overlap can be found not only between contemporary theoretical approaches but also between these and ones of earlier historical periods. This is the view of Lyotard who, according to John McGowan, holds that "postmodern and modern cannot be distinguished from each other temporally...they exist simultaneously, referring to two different responses to modernity." Rorty takes a similar position, questioning whether the shifts associated with postmodernism "are more than the latest moments of a historicization of philosophy which has been going on continuously since Hegel."

Further, Rorty thinks that these changes were "pretty well complete in Dewey." He does not see Foucault, for example, as any more radical in the postmodern manner than Dewey. He says: "I do not see any difference between Dewey and Foucault on narrowly philosophical grounds. The only difference I see between them is the presence or lack of social hope which they display."

There is of course something odd about seeing Hegel, Nietzsche, or even Dewey as postmodernists, given that they wrote within the modern era and in many ways expressed its spirit. Some writers prefer a more chronologically correct definition of postmodernism. John McGowan, for example, sides with Frederic Jameson in expressing the view that "postmodernism as a temporal term designates a (very recent) historical period that is to be identified by a set of characteristics that operate across the whole historical terrain."

And in terms of the history of philosophy, these are entirely new developments exaggerates the extent to which human thought and behavior change, and leaves us wondering how people in earlier centuries could have been so dense as to be completely taken in by the ideas of Plato, Descartes, and Kant. Accounts of postmodernism abound today in the literature of both general philosophy and educational theory.

Reality

Postmodernists have helped us see that reality is more complex than we had imagined. It does not exist objectively, "out there," simply to be mirrored by our thoughts. Rather, it is in part a human creation. We mold reality in accordance with our needs, interests, prejudices, and cultural traditions. But reality is not entirely a human construction, "made by us, not given to us," as postmodernists have claimed.

A corollary of this interactive view of reality is that there is no sharp fact-value distinction. All factual statements reflect the values they serve, and all value beliefs are conditioned by factual assumptions. There is again a difference of degree which enables us to talk of "facts" and "values." But what we call facts are only somewhat less value-determined: they are not independent of values. This ties in with Foucault's postmodernist notion that knowledge and power cannot be separated, since knowledge embodies the values of those who are powerful enough to create and disseminate it. Foucault has perhaps an overly conspiratorial view of knowledge, but the link with people's interests which he identifies cannot be denied.

Because reality is in part culture dependent, it changes over time, as cultures do, and varies from community to community. Knowledge is neither eternal nor universal. Once again, however, we should not exaggerate this point, as postmodernists have done. There are "enduring interests" and "tentative frameworks" which point to a degree of continuity;

and there are some commonalities (again qualified) from culture to culture and probably across the whole human race.

To deny continuity and commonality where it in fact exists, as postmodernists tend to do, is just as irrational and unpragmatic as to see knowledge as eternal and universal. It betrays an absolutist attachment to such values as innovation, originality, and diversity. Furthermore, it can have unfortunate practical consequences, since it leaves people without an adequate basis for daily living. It is one thing to reject the idea of a fixed, universal foundation to reality, quite another to claim that no useful guidelines can ever be identified.

Taking note of the postmodernists' cautions, however, we should be careful with generalizations: they can be deceptive. Behind a general formulation such as "all humans are rational" or "people pursue pleasure" there is usually a great diversity of realities and interpretations. We should try to become more aware of this, and also more often explicitly qualify claims with words such as "some," "many," "most," "sometimes," "often." But even qualified generalizations are of great value in everyday life.

Metaphysics

Postmodernism is often seen by its proponents as bringing an end to metaphysics, ontology, epistemology, and so forth, on the ground that these types of discourse assume a fixed, universal reality and method of inquiry. Precisely because we live in a changing, fragmented, "postmodern" world, we need whatever stability we can find. And inquiry into general intellectual, moral, and other patterns - limited and tentative though they may be - is a legitimate form of "metaphysics."

An irony of the postmodernist movement is that, despite itself, it is centrally concerned with what we can say of a general nature about reality. Postmodernists believe they have put an end to metaphysics and have thrown the ladder away after reaching their foundationless perch. But in fact their writings are full of general assumptions about culture, human nature, values, inquiry. As Landon Beyer and Daniel Liston observe, postmodernist analyses are paradoxical, containing "standpoints without footings" and "talking about nothing."

The Self

Postmodernism has rightly questioned the idea of a universal, unchanging, unified self or "subject" which has full knowledge of and control over what it thinks, says, and does. It has shown that the self is strongly influenced by its surrounding culture, changes with that culture, and is fragmented like that culture. To a degree, it is not we who think, speak, and act but the culture which thinks, speaks, and acts through us. In many ways Rorty is correct when he describes "the moral self" as "a network of beliefs, desires, and emotions with nothing behind it...constantly reweaving itself...not by reference to general criteria...but in the hit-or-miss way in which cells readjust themselves to meet the pressures of the environment."

It is an exaggeration, however, to maintain that because the self is limited, conditioned, and contingent in this way it has no significance, identity, or capacities. Individuals may be no more important than cultures, but neither are they less so. Individuals are just as unified and characterizable as communities, and they have considerable (though not unlimited) capacity for self-knowledge, self-expression, and self-regulation. There is no basis for emphasizing culture or community to the neglect of individuals.

And the same may be said for specific groups within a larger culture: ethnic groups, gender categories, socio-economic classes, and so on. There is a tendency among postmodernists to emphasize these categories to the neglect of individuals. But in fact two individuals of the same national background, ethnicity, gender, religion, or the like may differ greatly. And two individuals who differ in all these respects may turn out to be "kindred spirits" who can have a close friendship, even a good marriage, and agree on most major matters. Individuals are only in part identifiable in terms of the various categories to which they belong.

Inquiry

Postmodernist insights require a major shift in our conception of inquiry. No longer should we see ourselves as seeking to uncover a pre-existing reality; rather, we are involved in an interactive process of knowledge creation. We are developing a "working understanding" of reality and life, one which suits our purposes. And because purposes and context vary from individual to individual and from group to group, what we arrive at is in part autobiographical; it reflects our "personal narrative," our particular "site" in the world.

To some extent, then, we must question the notion of expertise. In particular fields, some people do know more than others; but the difference, insofar as it exists, is usually one of degree. So-called "experts" are often heavily dependent on "non-experts" for input if they are to arrive at sound insights; and since each individual or group's needs and circumstances are different, "expert knowledge" cannot be simply applied; it must be greatly modified for a particular case. The interaction between expert and non-expert, teacher and taught, is often best seen as a dialogue or "conversation" (to use Rorty's term), in which there is mutual influence rather than simple transmission from one to the other.

The knowledge arrived at, too, is more ambiguous and unstable than we had previously thought. It refers to probabilities rather than certainties, average effects, better rather than the best; and it is constantly changing as each individual or group gives a particular interpretation to it, reflecting distinctive needs and experiences. And as postmodernists have pointed out, language is well adapted to this constant "play" of interpretation. Words are not tied to fixed concepts or referents; they depend for their meaning on a whole system of words within which they are embedded, a system which changes over time and varies from one speech community or language user to another.

Inquiry must also be approached "pragmatically." We should not insist that reality, including human nature, take a certain form but rather accept what emerges. If altruism, for example, has to be based in part on feelings of group solidarity, then we must acknowledge that: there is no point clinging to a rationalistic view of moral motivation that cannot work.

Once again, however, we should be careful not to exaggerate these points. Postmodernists have often attacked notions of reason, means-end thinking, theory, teaching. But in fact there is a place for them, in a modified form. We must employ reason as well as feelings, intuitions, direct social influence, and so forth. We must think in means-end terms to some extent if we are to know what we want in life and how to achieve it. Theory, understood as a loose interconnection of qualified generalizations, is crucial for daily living. Teaching, so long as it is largely dialogical, is both possible and necessary. And so on. All of these can cause problems if they are understood too strictly and taken too seriously; but without them we would quite literally be lost.

We must also qualify the notion of a "pragmatic" approach to inquiry. While there is no external foundation to reality, no "traditional Kantian backup," as Rorty says, there are internal continuities which serve as important reference points. It is possible and necessary, then, to develop "theory" which explains particular phenomena in terms of these continuities. Postmodernists often display an "easy pragmatism" which, while claiming to be open and tolerant, is merely superficial, since it fails to develop and use theory of this kind; its doctrines thus become dogmatic assertions, without explanation or justification.

Forms of Scholarship

One of the slogans of postmodernism is that "there is no center," and in particular there is no central tradition of scholarship (namely Eurocentric, middle- class, predominantly male) of which other traditions - Native American, Afro-American, Islamic, feminist, working class, for example - are mere colonies. Insofar as we study traditional Western scholarship, we should be wary of its white, middle-class, male bias; and we should approach it as equals, expecting to contribute as much as we learn. This is in line with the view of knowledge and inquiry noted earlier.

The bias in favour of particular ethnic, class, and gender interests is only part of the picture. Terms such as "Eurocentric" and "patriarchal" are bandied about too much, as though they described everything that an individual or group does, and as if every error that is made is due to the bias in question. As noted earlier, people of different races, genders, religions, or whatever may have a great deal in common. There is enormous scope for people of different categories to learn from each other's scholarship.

None of this means, however, that we should regard the Western scholarly tradition as the central one to which others merely contribute or add footnotes. Rather, white, middle-class males should just contribute along with everyone else, and any new, common tradition should be pluralistic scholarship, not simply a modification of the "mainstream."

The radical democracy of postmodernism leads in this direction, but it gets waylaid because of its excessive preoccupation with cultures and speech communities. Every individual should be seen as the center of a scholarship - her or his own - comparing notes on equal terms with other individuals, groups, and traditions.

IMPLICATIONS FOR EDUCATIONAL PRACTICE

There are many implications of the foregoing for educational practice, but space permits me only to outline a few of the main ones. To begin with, students in schools from an early age should be helped to see how ideas and institutions are tailored to suit people's values and interests: how, for example, a picture book or novel expresses the distinctive needs and background of the author; or how TV programming promotes life-styles which benefit commercial enterprises; or how the health professions tend to favour males over females; or how the school curriculum reflects the values of certain sectors of society. This need not involve use of technical language, or be particularly confrontational: such study can be a rather straightforward and enjoyable aspect of the school day. But unless we foster this kind of cultural-political understanding, we are supporting our students' continued perception of the world as value-neutral, unproblematic, and unchangeable.

Surprisingly, Rorty questions engaging in this kind of problem posing in schools. He maintains that "lower education" (primary and secondary) "is mostly a matter of socialization, of trying to inculcate a sense of citizenship." It "should aim primarily at communicating enough of what is held to be true by the society to which the children belong so that they can function as citizens of that society. Whether it is true or not is none of the educator's business, in his or her professional capacity." However, to me this is an extraordinary and inexplicable betrayal of the main thrust of postmodernism. How can a society succeed in constantly "breaking the crust of convention," as Rorty advocates, when all its school teachers and all its young people up to the age of eighteen are involved in single-minded reinforcement of convention? And how will this affect the self-image and well-being of young people who, as every parent knows, begin systematically to question our conventions from about the age of two?.

At the same time as we encourage the questioning of accepted "realities," however, we must help students find "foundations" for their lives, if of a less permanent kind. Lack of a sense of stability and direction is one of the major problems of contemporary culture and is a factor in today's reactionary trends in religion, politics, education, and other spheres. If we do not acknowledge this need, our anti-foundationalist teaching may backfire and at any rate may cause students (and parents) considerable distress. We should work with students (and parents, as far as possible) in a dialogical manner, identifying outlooks which are an appropriate combination of old and new elements. Students need to find enduring values (e.g., relational, aesthetic, occupational) and ideals (e.g., pluralistic, global, ecological) which do not contradict their experience of reality but at the same time provide an adequate basis for everyday living.

The postmodernist emphasis on concrete, local concerns is important and should be applied in education: school studies are often too abstract and of little apparent relevance. But learning should combine both the concrete and the general. The learning of isolated facts and skills can be equally boring and meaningless. It is often through the drawing of broader connections between phenomena and the exploration of their value implications that learning comes alive. And study of this more "theoretical" kind is necessary if students are to build up a comprehensive worldview and way of life that will give them the security, direction, and meaning they need.

Another set of implications for schooling has to do with the democratic and dialogical emphasis of postmodernism, its questioning of the motives of authorities and its downplaying of the role of experts. We must think increasingly in terms of "teachers and students learning together," rather than the one telling the other how to live in a "top-down" manner. This is necessary both so that the values and interests of students are taken into account, and so that the wealth of their everyday experience is made available to fellow students and to the teacher.

Of course, the extent to which the teacher may be regarded as an expert varies from subject to subject. In science and mathematics, for example, a teacher may well know considerably more than most of the students in the class, while in values and family life this is less obviously the case; and with respect to a particular values topic, e.g., bullying in the school yard, a student may well know more than the teacher.

But even where the teacher does have greater knowledge, we should question excessive use of a teacher dominated method. Lyotard has pointed out the extent to which students today at the postsecondary level can learn from computerized data banks, which he calls "the Encyclopedia of tomorrow;" and the same point could be made with respect to the elementary and secondary levels. Increasingly, teachers must help students "learn how to learn," using such technology. One great advantage of self-directed inquiry is that through it students are more actively involved in determining what they learn and why, and thus are able to give expression to their distinctive interests and needs.

In democratizing education, then, we should not simply dismantle all structures and hope that something happens, but rather try to create structures that give students the support they need and allow them to make a significant input and have optimal control over their learning. While schooling should as far as possible be dialogical, it should not be a mere pooling of ignorance. To be effective, dialogue requires strong input of many kinds: information, examples, stories, feelings, ideas, theories, worldviews, and so on. The point about a democratic approach is not that structure and content are unnecessary, but that students (and teachers) should have a major say in how their learning is structured and what content is made available to them.

CRITICAL DOGMATISM IN PHOLOSOPHICAL EDUCATION

Critical dogmatism is quite common in educational philosophy. Critical work is, for example, carried out by means of a definition of what counts as education. Such a definition is used to evaluate educative practices and theories, which can then turn out to be, for example, non-educative or indoctrinary. Critical dogmatism can also be found in the work of those educational philosophers who see themselves as children's advocates. Here, the basis for critique is the conviction that the child represents a value of its own; a value that must be respected in educational theory and practice. A third example is the work of those educational philosophers who take "emancipation" to be the general criterion for the evaluation of educational theory and practice..

As Hans Albert has expressed in his "Münchhausen trilemma," any attempt to articulate foundations - and in critical dogmatism the criterion founds the critical operation - leads "to a situation with three alternatives, all of which appear unacceptable." The trilemma forces one to choose between (1) an infinite regress, because the propositions that serve as a fundament need to be founded themselves; (2) a logical circle that results from the fact that in the process of giving reasons, one has to resort to statements that have already shown themselves to be in need of justification; or (3) breaking off the attempt at a particular point by dogmatically installing a foundation.

Albert argues, that the only possible foundation of critique is a dogmatic foundation, so that the only possible form of critique is dogmatic critique. Of course, this conclusion raises some problems. If dogmatism appears at the heart of the critical enterprise, the critical operation seems to be immediately subverted. How can critique be effective - or even more: How is critique possible - if its ultimate foundation is merely conventional?

Critical dogmatism is in trouble once it is acknowledged that the criterion itself can only be installed dogmatically. This is not to suggest, that the application of such criteria has never had any positive effects or that any critical work in educational philosophy along these lines has been in vain. But we should be aware of the paradoxical character of this style of critique.

Although this brings critical dogmatism into a difficult position, it does not mean that the possibilities for critique as such are thereby exhausted. What has been argued so far, is the paradoxical character of critique as the application of a criterion that is itself beyond critique. There is, however, a critical style which claims that it can circumvent the paradox of critical dogmatism. This is transcendental critique.

Transcendental Critique

Transcendental critique has its roots in the emergence of the scientific worldview. From then onwards, philosophy could no longer claim to provide knowledge of the natural world (physics), nor of a more fundamental reality (metaphysics). Philosophy thus lost its role as a foundational discipline. It was Kant who put philosophy on a new track -the transcendental track - where it became the proper task of philosophy to articulate the conditions of possibility of true (scientific) knowledge.

Kant's program was almost immediately criticized for the reflexive paradox it contained. It was Hegel who pointed out the problematic character of the attempt to acquire knowledge about the process of knowledge acquisition. The reason why Kant did not perceive this paradox had to do with the framework of the philosophy of consciousness in which he operated. For Kant, the "Ich denke", was the "highest point, to which we must ascribe all employment of the understanding, even the whole of logic, and conformally therewith, transcendental philosophy."

The work of Karl-Otto Apel can be seen as a rearticulation of transcendental philosophy that tries to circumvent this "dogmatic element" in Kant's position by making a shift from the philosophy of consciousness to the philosophy of language. The main difference between Apel and Kant lies in Apel's recognition of the fact that all knowledge is linguistically mediated. While Kant assumed that the acquisition of knowledge is basically an individualistic enterprise, Apel argues that our individual experiences must be "lifted" to the level of a language game in order to become knowledge. The link between experience and language is, however, not established automatically. The question of the validity of our individual experiences has to be answered by means of argumentation. Because argumentation only makes sense within a language game, within a "community of communication," Apel concludes that this community is the condition of possibility of all knowledge.

Apel's "linguistic turn" results in the recognition of the a priori of the community of communication. Because we can never get "before" the actual use of language in a specific community of communication, any reflection on language can only take place in a specific language game or community of communication. The pragmatic dimension is therefore the most basic dimension of language, for which reason Apel refers to his position as transcendental pragmatics.

Although Apel establishes a strong link between transcendental pragmatics and really existing communities of communication - a maneuver which seems to give his project a strong conventionalistic basis - he introduces a critical element that is meant to enable transcendental pragmatics to go beyond convention. This element is the ideal community of communication or the transcendental language game.

Apel claims that a participant in a genuine argument is at the very same time a member of a concrete community of communication and a counterfactual ideal community of communication, a community which is, in principle, open to all speakers and which excludes all force except the force of the better argument. This community "is, at least implicitly, anticipated in all human actions claiming to be meaningful and it is explicitly anticipated in philosophical arguments claiming to be valid."

Any claim to intersubjectively valid knowledge therefore implicitly acknowledges this ideal community, as a "meta-institution" of rational argumentation, to be its ultimate source of justification. Communication would lose its meaning when one no longer aims at this ideal. The idea of the ideal community of communication provides a criterion which makes critique possible. What distinguishes Apel's position from critical dogmatism is that this criterion is not installed dogmatically but by means of a process of reflexive grounding. With respect to this process Apel claims that he can circumvent the dogmatic implications of the Münchhausen trilemma.

The first thing that has to be acknowledged, is that the first and the third option of the Münchhausen trilemma (infinite regress and dogmatism) hang together. Both are connected to Albert's contention that the process of foundation must necessarily be understood in terms of deduction. If we talk about foundations in a deductive style, that is, if we raise the question of the "foundation of the foundation," it is clear that we enter an infinite regress which can only be stopped arbitrarily. Apel admits that if we understand foundations in this sense, we will never find them. But this does not mean that we should give up the idea of foundation as such, only that we need another way to bring foundations into view.

Apel starts from the recognition that the conditions of possibility of argumentation have to be presupposed in all argumentation (otherwise they would not be conditions of possibility). But if this is so, then it follows, that one cannot argue against these conditions of possibility without immediately falling into a performative contradiction, that is, a situation where the performative dimensions of the argument contradict the propositional content. From this, Apel concludes that all contentions that cannot be disclaimed without falling into a performative contradiction, express a condition of possibility of the argumentative use of language. The principle of performative consistency is therefore the criterion which can reveal the ultimate foundations of the argumentative use of language, that is, those propositions that do not need further grounding, because, so Apel argues, they cannot be understood without knowing that they are true.

Although Apel articulates the way in which the ultimate foundations of the argumentative use of langua?e can be revealed, he does not say much about what these foundations actually are. Yet, it is not difficult to see that what the application of the principle of performative consistency can bring into view are the foundations, or, so we could say, the "meta-rules" of all argumentative use of language. These meta-rules, which include such things as the contention that all communication aims at consensus, that all communication rests upon the validity of claims to truth, rightness and truthfulness, and that these claims can in principle be redeemed, outline the ideal community of communication.

Apel's program tries to argue for the possibility or articulating criteria for critique non-dogmatically. More than just another style of critique, Apel suggests that critical dogmatism - at least in so far as it concerns the dogmatic choice for rationality - is an untenable position, because "any choice that could be understood as meaningful already presupposes the transcendental language game as its condition of possibility." From this it does not follow that every decision is rational, but it does follow that a decision in favour of the principle of rational legitimation of criticism is "rational a priori," because "reason...can always confirm its own legitimation through reflection on the fact that it presupposes its own self-understanding of the very rules it opts for."

These remarks reveal that the criticality of transcendental pragmatics is motivated by rationality. After all, the "sin" of the performative contradiction is a sin against rationality, and it is for this very reason that the contradiction has to be avoided. Rationality therefore gives transcendental critique its "right" to be critical. This becomes clear when we look at the way in which the transcendental style of critique is applied in educational philosophy.

In a more strict sense, we can see this style of critique at work in discussions about critical thinking and education. Here the work of Harvey Siegel stands out as a continuous attempt to spot the performative contradiction in any challenge to rationality. In a wider sense, the critical potential of the idea of performative contradiction is used as a form of internal critique, where the main critical work consists of a confrontation of a position or argument with its (often implicit) conditions of possibility.

Transcendental critique presents itself as a "stronger" conception of critique than critical dogmatism, primarily because it claims to be able to articulate its choice for rationality non-dogmatically. Compared to critical dogmatism, transcendental critique indeed is a more sophisticated critical program. But transcendental critique is not (yet) the last word about critique.

Deconstruction

Jacques Derrida sees the history of Western philosophy as a continuous attempt to locate a fundamental ground which serves both as an absolute beginning and as a center from which everything originating from it can be mastered and controlled. Since Plato, the origin has always been defined in terms of presence. This "metaphysics of presence" includes a hierarchical axiology in which the origin is designated as pure, simple, normal, self-sufficient, and self-identical, in order then to think in terms of derivation, complication, deterioration, accident, and so forth. This is "the metaphysical exigency," that which has been "the most constant, most profound and most potent."

Derrida wants to put this metaphysical gesture into question. He acknowledges that he is not the first to do so. But against Nietzsche, Freud, Heidegger, and all other "destructive discourses" that wanted to overcome metaphysics, Derrida argues that we can never make a total break. "There is no sense," he argues, "in doing without the concepts of metaphysics in order to shake metaphysics. We...can pronounce not a single destructive proposition which has not already had to slip into the form, the logic, and the implicit postulations of precisely what it seeks to contest."

While Derrida definitely wants to "shake" metaphysics, he acknowledges that this cannot be done from some neutral and innocent place outside of metaphysics. Derrida wants to shake metaphysics, to put it simply, by showing that metaphysics is itself always already shaking, by showing the impossibility of any attempt to fix being through the presentation of a self-identical, original presence.

One way in which Derrida articulates this impossibility and its predicaments, is through the "notion" of difference, which he articulates in discussion with the structuralist semiotics of Ferdinand de Saussure. Contrary to the idea that language is a naming process, attaching words to things, Saussure argues that language is a structure where any individual element is meaningless outside the confines of that structure. In language there are only differences. These differences, however, are not differences between positive terms, that is, between terms that in and by themselves refer to things outside the system. In language there are only differences without positive terms.

First of all, the idea of differences without positive terms entails that the "movement of signification" is only possible if each element "appearing on the scene of presence, is related to something other than itself." What is called "the present" is therefore constituted "by means of this very relation to what it is not". This contamination is a necessary contamination: For the present to be itself, it already has to be other than itself. This puts the non-present in a double position, because it is the non-present which makes the presence of the present possible, and yet, it can only make this presence possible by means of its own exclusion. What is excluded thereby, in a sense, returns to sign the act of its own exclusion. And it is this apparent complicity, which "outplays the legality of the decision to exclude" in the first place.

If this is what deconstruction can bring into view, we can already get an idea of its critical potential, because at the heart of deconstruction, we find a concern for the "constitutive outside" of what presents itself as self-sufficient. This reveals that deconstruction is more than just a destruction of the metaphysics of presence. Deconstruction is first and foremost an affirmation of what is excluded and forgotten. An affirmation, in short, of what is other.

There is, however, a complication which concerns the question of how deconstruction can bring that what is excluded into view. For if it is the case that in language there are only differences without positive terms, then we have to concede that we can no longer articulate the differential character of language itself by means of a positive term (like, for example, "differentiation"). Difference without positive terms implies that this "dimension" must itself always remain unperceived, for strictly speaking, it is unconceptualizable. The "play of difference," which is "the condition for the possibility and functioning of every sign, is in itself a silent play".

If we would want to articulate that which does not let itself be articulated and yet is the condition for the possibility of all articulation - which we might want to do in order to prevent metaphysics from re-entering - we must acknowledge that there can never be a word or a concept to represent this silent play. We must acknowledge that this play cannot simply be exposed, for "one can expose only that which at a certain moment can become present". And we must acknowledge that there is nowhere to begin, "for what is put into question is precisely the quest for a rightful beginning, an absolute point of departure". All this is expressed in the new word or concept - "which is neither a word nor a concept" but a "neographism" - of difference.

The reason why Derrida introduces that "what is written as difference" is not difficult to grasp. Although "the play of difference" is identified as the condition of possibility of all conceptuality, we should not make the mistake to think that we have finally found the real origin of all conceptuality. The predicament is this: because we are talking about the condition of possibility of all conceptuality, this condition cannot belong to that which it makes possible (the "order" of conceptuality). Yet, the only way in which we can articulate this condition of possibility is within this order. Because the condition of possibility is always articulated in terms of the system that is made possible by it, it is, in a sense, always already "too late" to be its condition of possibility.

At this level, the critical potential of deconstruction returns in an even more radical way. The point here is, that because conditions of possibility are always already contaminated by the "system" that is made possible by them, this "system" is never totally delimited by these conditions. Difference is therefore a quasi-transcendental or quasi-condition of possibility, because, as John D. Caputo aptly describes, it "does not describe fixed boundaries that delimit what can happen and what not, but points a mute, Buddhist finger at the moon of uncontainable effects."

Deconstruction thus tries to open up the system in the name of that which cannot be thought of in terms of the system (and yet makes the system possible). This reveals that the deconstructive affirmation is not simply an affirmation of what is known to be excluded by the system. Deconstruction is an affirmation of what is wholly other (tout autre), of what is unforeseeable from the present. It is an affirmation of an otherness that is always to come, as an event which "as event, exceeds calculation, rules, programs, anticipations."

Deconstruction is an openness towards the unforeseeable in-coming (l'invention; invention) of the other. It is from this concern for what is totally other, a concern to which Derrida sometimes refers as justice, that deconstruction derives its right to be critical.

2

Meaning and Nature of Education

Education encompasses teaching and learning specific skills, and also something less tangible but more profound: the imparting of knowledge, good judgement and wisdom. One of the fundamental goals of education is to impart culture across the generations. Education begins the minute a baby is born and is life-long. Education may even begin before birth as evidenced by some parents playing music or reading to the baby in the womb in the hope it will influence (educate) their child before birth. For some, the struggles and triumphs of daily life are far more instructive than formal schooling. Family members have an educational effect which is quite profound — often more profound than they realize — though family teaching techniques may be highly informal.

Formal education occurs when society makes a commitment to educate people, usually the young. Formal education can be systematic and thorough, but the sponsoring group may seek selfish advantages when shaping impressionable young scholars. Life-long or adult education has become widespread. Many adults have given up the notion that only children belong in school. Many adults are enrolled in post-secondary education schools, both part-time and full time, where they are often classified as non-traditional students in order to distinguish them administratively from young adults entering directly from high school.

Computing devices can change when and where we learn. This is the computer based or networked learning structure, in which people contribute to each others' education. It is defined as online education (a subset of distance education), the European Graduate School as a University operates during the summer. it serves as a meeting point for people that has participated in online forums through the academic year, this methodology is a break to the traditional educational system.

In education, a core curriculum is a curriculum, or course of study, which is deemed central and usually made mandatory for all students of a school or school system. Core curricula are often instituted, at the primary and secondary levels, by school boards, Departments of Education, or other administrative agencies charged with overseeing education. At the undergraduate level, individual college and university administrations and faculties sometimes mandate core curricula, especially in the liberal arts. But because of increasing specialization and depth in the student's major field of study, a typical core curriculum in higher education mandates a far smaller proportion of a student's course work than a high school or elementary school core curriculum prescribes.

In our times, education is ubiquitous. We are offered education for today, education for yesterday, education for tomorrow, education for adjusting, education for earning, education for marriage, even education for feeling and, finally, education for death. Education is offered for all the days, in all the ways, at all the times, everywhere, and every place, for everyone of every age, in every season.

In an aberrant Goyaesque displacement of reality, the fantastic, indeed, astonishing caption written directly under the picture of education in the modern world reads—Man exists for Education, not Education exists for Man! Instead of shaping the values of our culture, our educational institutions shamelessly reflect the shallow values of a materialistic, consumer-oriented society. These are the dreadful, empty values of the comfortable, the crowds standing on every corner, gathering in hotel lobbies, clamoring at sports arenas, and moving through transportation terminals, all mistakenly believing that everything can be learned, which means that everything must be taught, which means that everything must be funded, which means that everything is of equal value, which means everyone must receive a degree.

Our huge, impersonal educational bureaucracies are almost wholly concerned, indeed obsessed, with means; means that are so highly developed, so superior, so effective that there is almost a total disregard for ends. Man doesn't exist for education; education exists for man, for his personal and spiritual awakening, development, and fulfillment. In our society it often seems that only the specialist has credibility, that only the specialist is allowed to speak up, and that only the specialist has any standing or any rights. Overspecialization dehumanizes man and ultimately stupefies because it selfishly removes reality from the life of man and causes minds to distrust the very idea of truth and wisdom, which causes man to give up any hope of personal wholeness, intellectual integration or spiritual unity.

The scientific, "measurable" and "observable" conception of man, although possessed of its own values, can "neither primarily found nor primarily guide education, for education needs primarily to know what man is, what is the nature of man and the scale of values it essentially involves. The aim of education is the conquest of internal and spiritual freedom to be achieved by the individual person, or, in other words, his liberation through knowledge and wisdom, good will and love. It is to be a good citizen and a man of civilization. What matters above all is the inner center, the living source of personal conscience in which originate idealism and generosity, the sense of law and the sense of friendship, respect for others, but at the same time deep-rooted independence with regard to common opinion." If these powerful, moving and noble words are to become a lived reality, the making and education of a man and the preparing of a citizen is best accomplished through the study of the humanities.

Teachers, next to parents are the most important people in our society—most important than anyone else. Teachers, do not seek the "strut and trade of charms across the ivory stages" of the academic world, but rather slips your hands under, then lift and gently wrap the arms of your students around the truths of the ages and work only for the "common wages of their most secret hearts." Students, when you cross the threshold of this your new home so beautifully proportioned and so reverently restored, remember it was done not only to reflect the integrity of its architecture, but also to remind you that whenever you are here, you are the light of our world, the hope of your university, your teachers and friends and, indeed, the very embodiment of hope for our civilization. As you stand at the hearth of the fireplace in your new library and gaze into the glowing, radiant fire, we hope you will see the curling embracing flames of wisdom and beauty and truth and that you will not only warm your hands, but every fiber of your being, with the eternal verities of the humanities.

Through his intellect man is called to become "the light of the world," but it is through his heart that man is called to become "the salt of the earth." To become fully human, you must become "the light of the world, the salt of the earth."

Through much of classic history, we can see arguments on what constitutes a good and solid education. Plato wrote in The Republic his version of the educated masses. In his vision, all children begin life and schooling the same. Over time, and through numerous tests, those who prove worthy are separated from those less likely to succeed. These chosen are slowly and methodically weeded until a select few remain to compose the ruling class. Others, as suitability is ascertained, are tracked into their state-chosen career be it warrior, serf, or craftsmen. Although no historical human culture ever directly copied this system, its ideal has influenced the thinking of educated people after Plato.

As pure and simple as Plato's ideals may sound, they do not fit well within the democratic and capitalistic system of the United States of America. American education has been equally influenced by two separate ideas. One, that education should promote the public good which is best expressed by a commitment to educational equality. Second, that the public is entitled to pass their societal privilege on to their descendants by giving their children educational advantages that will allow these same children access to the best jobs and career paths. Paradoxically, a large number of Americans appear to hold both ideals of education at the same time.

The belief that schooling should serve all regardless of social background and give all an equal chance at an education that will lead to a potentially high social class is widespread throughout American culture. (And, at least at the beginning of Plato's vision of education before differentiation begins to occur, in sequence with The Republic.) In brief, this belief envisions that all inhabitants of the United States of America (citizens and aliens alike) will receive the same education. Those who are worthy, regardless of the backgrounds of the parents, will succeed and achieve great things and those that are less worthy will through their own efforts select their own less than spectacular destinies.

This is a powerful idea that is held by those dedicated to the egalitarian ideal of The Declaration of Independence that all men are created equal, by those who are in the working or surviving classes who believe that providence has delivered what they deserve, and to those who are in high positions who believe the educational system has justified their own status. This attempt to provide for an education for all is evident in the American conscience since before the founding of the American republic. This can be seen in the colonial Massachusetts of the 17th Century.

Colonial law provided for penalties for communities that failed to provide for public education. Although not everyone benefited from this education (Indigenous Americans, girls, and the rural poor for example), a belief that an education should be provided as public good had already developed. Several scholars have taken note of democratic equality. Cohen and Neufield wrote that, "In addition to citizenship training and equal treatment, the goal of democratic equality has taken a third form, and that is the pursuit of equal access." Labaree wrote that, "Equal access has come to mean that every American should have an equal opportunity to acquire an education at any educational level." These same scholars convincingly trace the development of this vision of equality in America from the development of public elementary schools, the rise of public high schools, and finally the realization of nearly universally access to higher education.

Unfortunately, universal school attendance creates a problem. Can schools be both equal and excellent at the same time? The answer of the American public appears to be no. By attempting to serve everyone equally, the school serves no one excellently it is believed. Democratic equality creates a problem. Vast numbers of diverse students with various backgrounds have different educational needs. Further, many of the students have no strong desire to be in school. This creates a need to find ways to make school attractive to these students.

The end result is that the school of today focuses less on the core academic subjects of the past and more on courses that will meet the special needs and interests of a highly diverse student body. Many students can challenge themselves and receive excellent college preparatory work if they desire. However, a student can also avoid "hard" courses and still receive a diploma. Teachers themselves have responded to the student body by teaching classes that the students will find acceptable. This allows the teacher to ccexist with their students in a peaceful arrangement.

Democratic equality believes in the obligation to take, retain, and instruct all possible students. This unfortunately appears to lead to a water-downed curriculum. As more and more students are educated, the likelihood that members of lower social classes will be educated increases. This can cause problems from elitist views. In Mark Twain's The Adventures of Huckleberry Finn, one white citizen refuses to vote because in Ohio blacks are allowed to vote. The white citizen figures that if blacks can vote, then voting is not that important. The same view can be seen in education. W. E. B. DuBois wrote in his essay "Of the Coming of John" of what happened when a black man came back to his hometown after receiving a college education. Both blacks and whites rejected his new views. However, to whites the black John represented a devaluing of the college education. If a black person can have a college degree they reasoned, then having a college degree most not have much value.

Democratic equality also creates another problem. When everyone is attending school, a large number of people receive high school diplomas. This means that the high school diploma is no longer a scarce resource. As such, it is not valued as highly by society. This leads to several consequences. First, the student in high school is less likely to value the high school diploma, which creates motivation problems for the schools. Secondly, it leads to a form of educational arms race where people try to acquire higher levels of education to distinguish themselves. Wrote Cohen and Nuefield, "In effect, the competitive zeal for higher education debased the value of the high-school diploma, just as the zeal for high school had earlier deflated the value of an elementary education."

The earlier mentioned idea of an educational arms race ties neatly into the second great idea that has driven American education which is the belief that individuals can use education to better themselves and their children. Many individuals want to better themselves. Countless more want to see their children do well. These people see education as one way to achieve this. Thus, the private ambition can and does lead to a pursuit of inequality. Wrote Labaree, "The aim of pursuing education is for the individual student to accumulate forms of educational property that will allow the student to gain an advantage in the competition for social positions."

The idea that individuals want different things from education than what society wants the individual to get out of education is not a surprising idea. Amy Tan in her novel *The Joy Luck Club* convincingly shows how some parents can create means other than schooling to educate their children. In the United States today these alternative or additional attempts at education can be seen for example in the churches and in the home schooling movement.

People attempt to use education to better themselves and their children at the expense of others through several methods. First, as mentioned previously, the student continues to acquire education to such a point that their education distinguishes them. If most of the work force has an undergraduate degree, they will earn a master's degree to gain an advantage. Second, they will send their children to private schools that are perceived as better than public schools due to smaller class sizes and an emphasis on core academic subjects. Third, parents will move into more expensive neighborhoods where the public schools are seen as better. In theory, these "better" schools are open to all. In reality, they are limited to those well off enough to be able to afford to live within their district boundaries.

Nearly everyone believes that public education for all is important. Education will continue to be hotly debated in the future. The United States may someday find a way to reconcile the two different educational rationales but such reconciliation will have to address America's commitment to both democracy and capitalism. As it stands, American schools are doing an amazing job of educating a large mass of diverse students and providing people with the opportunity to better themselves and advance in society.

The historical development of civilised humanity may be compared to a river which but seldom fills the entire breadth of its bed. According to the fall of the ground it drives the bulk of its energy now to this side, now to that; sometimes whole stretches of land between the two banks remain unwashed by the waters; then again it presses forward with might and main, making use of all its possibilities towards expansion.

This change of energy in the stream of life may be traced in particular in the change which takes place with regard to educational aims insomuch as we become conscious of them. Later on, educational aims of a chiefly economic or political, or learned or aesthetic nature, branch off from the religious source which still comprises existence in its entirety. Their intrinsic value, too, changes, of course, with the general situation of the times and with the specific will to life of the generations. Yet there is something typical in them, or they could not be given such general names. In Germany today people expressly profess the aim of education to be political.

If we would understand the main issue of this idea, we should have to comprehend the essence of what is political. Carl Schmitt, the leading expert in political law, has termed the contrast friend-enemy to be the original phenomenon on which are based all political groupings. Doubtless this contrast pervades all forms of culture which stand out in the life of the Nations as a whole as being definitely political. But the problem must be pressed further: why are people each other's friends or enemies?

The friend-enemy relation of men may mean a mere horizontal relation between groups and individuals. What is originally political, however, comprises vertical relations, the tendency to be at the top and not at the bottom. In other words: the will to power as a fundamental fact of men living together, indeed even as a vital root of individual life, is the main issue of what is political. The State is only a complicated form of balancing the different powers, and, finally, the highest collective power emanating from, or, vice versa, forging a national unit. At all times the education of man to become a political personality—an ideal which appears very frequently and most emphatically in the history of the human mind—has meant a development of the will to power in one sense or another. It is subject to all the laws of structure and happening which pervade the sphere of power. It presupposes in the individual as the centre of his life, so to speak, a disciplined will which is ennobled in the school of obedience towards the ethical art of commanding.

This discipline of the will, however, that is, self command as a preliminary condition of commanding others, sends forth its ray in various directions as soon as it is practised in the sphere of political life as such. For in that case a State-supporting personality is to be formed, who, in the highest stage of perfection, may some day rise to a personality commanding the State.

There is sufficient evidence in the history of education that a State-supporting personality may appear in many varieties. In his original form he is the able bodied man ready to defend the State, his Country, and his Folk, thus contributing his share towards the physical power of the State. However, the State is never an expression of power alone, but, at the same time, a structure regulated by law. It is power partly through law and in the shape of law. On the other hand, law itself is a particular manifestation of power and a system of the distribution of power, of a collective guarantee of duties and rights (spheres of liberty). So there is another variety of the political personality, namely, the legal personality, a fact which becomes most evident in the ancient Roman conception of the personality.

Finally, history teaches us that, apart from the display of military power, the art of rhetoric has always been an essential political expedient, particularly in the domestic fight for power between rival groups. In spite of Plato, philosophy has not managed to become the organising power in political life. Rhetoric, which in ancient times struggled against it for centuries to win the first place in education, has certainly taken precedence in political matters, The third variety, therefore, of the political personality is the rhetorical personality, if we mean by this that type of human being who develops and uses the power of speech expressly as a political expedient.

Thus the educational ideal of the political personality is split up into the three primary types of the military personality, the legal personality, and the rhetorical personality. All three have their peculiar history. The soldier, the jurist, the orator of today are different from what they were in the Attic democracy of the fourth century, in the Rome of the Emperors, or in the so called Renaissance period. Naturally they all absorbed an ever-increasing portion of the scientific and technical tradition of their time. They all formed themselves and changed according to the structure of the political organism in whose service they stood, and which they supported. In their primary type, however, as special original phenomena of what is political, they remain what they were throughout the ages.

The political personality, as he is meant to be the ideal of education in Germany today, bears a peculiar mark of his own. We are experiencing a renewal of our Folk which goes back to the vital biological roots of the successive generations and of the individual. We are, further, passing through a process which is going to recast and reverse our national strata, at the same time bringing about a fundamental change in our social structure. The new form demands a decisive discipline of the will for its basis, which we have found to be the general foundation of what is political. This discipline begins with the health of the body and the instincts, rising to a defensive capacity, to a type of man which should never be termed warlike or menacing, because its intention is to realise the eternal form of soldierly attitude in the entire sphere of life, not in a professional military sense.

The spirit of self sacrifice, a readiness to serve and a consciousness of being deeply connected with the Nation as a whole—these are the fundamental virtues which are to support the State. So there is a superpersonal ideal background to the entire system of education: a feeling of responsibility towards the Nation and the State, manifesting itself in deeds and not only in words. Everything depends on clearly distinguishing this ideal from a collectivism which we find in Russia, and which is definitely rejected by the German mind.

Turning away from individualism does not mean a depreciation of the individual. After the Napoleonic period, Pestalozzi, one of those who discovered that each Folk has its national individuality, most emphatically stressed the fact that education is not based on the collective existence of the human race, nor that this can be its aim. All true education is applied to the individual, but today this is the case in a very special sense. Education does not take the individual as an isolated being whose vocation is mere self preservation, not even as a being whose chief aim would be mere self realisation, but it means the individual as a future responsible representative of superindividual values and their moral consequences. The individual as such is indispensable, it is true; he is indeed the only representative that we know of which is superindividual.

For a generation, a Nation, even a State, only live as long as they make the whole of their individuals now living the vessel of their values and representatives of their spirit. National education, also national education with a political aim, never penetrates to the masses unless it has reached the individual first. Mass education is a term which gives rise to misunderstandings; the moral focus of the will, of decision, of even discipline, always rests with living souls in whom the divine spark must first flare up, if it is intended to kindle the great fire of the common spirit.

Collective responsibility consists of many small responsibilities. The national language, for instance, does not exist by itself, it only exists through the medium of those who take part in the community of language and who are, in their small part, responsible for the purity, spirit, and growth of the language. The entire culture of a Folk, which it has acquired in the course of history, is only alive if it lives through individual souls who are conscious of their responsibility in the successive generations. The same is the case with the State.

The catchword education of the political personality means neither the mass being nor the individual without a soul. In its last interpretation, it rather implies that we are beginning to mean by soul something more than what is in the body, and by personality something more than self-sufficiency and self-seclusion. The soul itself is the point of intersection of the spiritual stream; it widens with the duties it fulfils, conscious of its own responsibility. The political personality is one which takes part in the spiritual connections. Apart from all this, the soul is ever and alone that point in life where there is a connection with God.

For to whom should we feel thus responsible, if not to God? The personality is the individuality chosen by the spirit to be its representative, thus ceasing to cultivate, in its narrow sphere, a misunderstood autonomy. It is the name of a person conscious of moral ties and obligations. The term political personality must therefore be based on an ethical ideal, which the best representatives of the Nation have anticipated in former times. Today it is perceptibly and effectively being appropriated by a youth that is ready and eager to accept real responsibility.

GOALS OF MULTICULTURAL EDUCATION

Pluralism and multiculturalism come from the same source - liberal political and educational theory - but they lead in different directions and represent distinct social visions. Pluralism seeks a society in which people from different cultural formations and orientations are allowed, if they wish to do so, to express their way of life within a separate cultural sphere, and are treated as equal individuals in a common public sphere. Pluralism wants equality of opportunity in the public sphere and freedom of association in the cultural sphere.

Unlike the assimilation position, pluralism does not seek to destroy past memories and to obliterate cultural diversity. It does, however, allow for the dissolution of that identity should an insufficient number of individuals choose to pursue it. For the pluralist, society has no special obligation to maintain or support cultural structures. It must simply maintain the individual conditions which make choice possible. It must assure, for example, that children are not brainwashed or indoctrinated and that they develop an awareness of various alternative forms of life and the skill required to assess them.

Thus unlike the assimilation position, pluralism is not hostile to cultural expression, but there is, as one commentator puts it, a certain quality of benign neglect. In contrast, multiculturalism values cultural difference and authenticity, and seeks to maintain it in ways that are not solely dependent on the momentary interests of individuals. Indeed, one concern of multiculturalist theory is that access to dominant, hegemonic, and unchallenged cultural forms may work to the disadvantage of local cultural affiliation. Multiculturalism thus differs from pluralism in a number of ways.

First, it holds that the public is already cultural. Its business is carried out in English, not French, not German, not Spanish; its institutions are shaped by the traditions of some groups and not others, and its educational and employment benefits are distributed unequally according to factors of ethnicity, race, and social class. Unlike pluralists, multiculturalists do not envisage even the possibility of a culturally neutral public sphere. Their ideal of cultural fairness is not to maintain a wall of separation between culture and public, but to assure that no group dominates the public sphere in a way that serves to exclude from it the bearers of other cultural forms. Hence, the public sphere is viewed as an arena for cultural negotiation where the goal is inclusion, culture and all. The public looks more like an open bazaar than a Whig courtroom.

Second, whereas pluralism allows cultural identity to flourish, the multicultural ideal encourages it to do so. In other words, benign neglect is not sufficient for the multiculturalist. Nor is it adequate to exhibit cultural diversity simply to teach lessons about the inclusive and benign character of the American nation - that is, as a means to a larger national goal. American policies of exclusion are as important to expose as are its policies of inclusion. Hence multiculturalism seeks to give expression to the experiences of cultural groups, not from the point of view of some abstraction called "the American nation," but from the point of view of the members of different racial, and ethnic groups, or from the view of people with different sexual orientations.

Third, whereas freedom of association and equal opportunity are the dominant principles informing pluralism, affiliation and cultural recognition are the principles that inform multiculturalism. Multiculturalists argue that these values are in fact the preconditions of individual growth that undergird liberal ideals. Multiculturalism hence views individuals as part of collectivities that provide meaning to their lives, and it seeks ways to support these collectivities.

Equality of educational opportunity is intended to compensate for inequalities of opportunities that arise as an indirect result of other liberal commitments. For example, as a result of the commitment to individual choice, liberal society is also committed to allowing private wealth to be used to benefit one's own offspring. Other social systems might challenge this benefit on the grounds that it continues even after death when a person no longer has any wishes at all, and is not around to worry whether past wishes will be honoured.

However, extending the commitment beyond the life of the original creator of the wealth serves certain important social purposes. By acknowledging that living people have interests that extend beyond their own individual lives, and that serve to give their lives meaning, it provides certain constraints on state authority; it serves as an incentive for long term projects, and it contributes to a sense of extended responsibility.

Yet if this right remains unchecked, there are serious indirect social costs. One of them is that if these advantages go unaddressed, they distort the development and rewarding of talent. Less talented members are advanced over more talented ones because family background provides advantages that overwhelm relative deficits in talent. Equal opportunity seeks to mitigate this advantage by holding that children have a right to receive an education that is consistent with their capacities regardless of the circumstances of their parents.

The second principle, freedom of association, is a social and a political reason, and it is critical to maintaining democratic societies. This reason holds that individuals have rights to form whatever friendships, alliances, and interest groups they wish as long as in doing so they do not hinder the right of others to do the same. This principle requires schools to provide children with the capacity to understand the implications of the social choices they make. Under this conception of education, children are not to be treated as if they were destined to relive the lives of their parents.

Nevertheless, "understanding the implications of different lifestyle choices" includes the choice to maintain the same political, cultural, and religious associations as one's parents. Because "having a choice," entails having alternatives to that which one chooses, this principle requires that children be introduced to ways of life that are different from that of their parents, and that they be taught about the diversity of human cultures.

The third principle, individual growth, is a person-directed reason. Individual growth holds that children have a right to develop their talents and tastes in whatever way their inclinations and capacities allow, constrained only by the need for others to do the same. This principle requires the schools to challenge children in ways that they might not experience at home or in the community, and to expand their understandings and broaden their horizons.

All of these reasons have a social correlate. If individual children are to be granted equal opportunity - the right of free association and personal growth - they must also learn that it is important for others to have these rights too. This correlate is important because it is essential for stabilizing these principles within the fabric of the liberal democratic state. If children are not taught that the rights they have for themselves are rights that should be extended to others, then the principles are not workable.

Aims of Multicultural Education

Many liberals object to the multicultural project in the following way: If pride means having a favourable attitude towards one's own group - an attitude which also sets one apart from others - then one of the implications of this goal is that one should act on one's attitudes by favouring members of one's own group. But why, it may be asked, should anyone outside of that group be expected to support this goal, and how does this implication fit with the goal of public education in terms of the need to develop universal standards and meritocratic institutions? In other words, how can the development of cultural pride be justified as a goal for public school education?

Moreover, given that cultural pride is designed to advance the solidarity of particular subcultures, this, the critic continues, will short change those individual students who find subcultural identity confining and limiting. An exclusive emphasis on cultural pride will lead children to think of themselves in one-dimensional terms and will inhibit the tendency to explore other dimensions, including other cultural dimensions of the self. If cultural pride leads to this result by cutting off contact with members of other groups who have expanded interests, then the result will be to inhibit growth and development.

Similarly, some forms of multiculturalism are bad for the nation as a whole, especially if they overemphasize points of difference with other groups and under-emphasize points of similarity. Instead of thematizing all citizens as related to one another through the nation as a whole, the emphasis on cultural pride devolves into an emphasis on cultural exclusivity and national disunity.

The goal of respect brings similar questions: For example, there is an ambiguity in the notion of cultural respect. One side of this ambiguity negates individual autonomy and freedom, while the other side negates the special status that multiculturalism gives to culture. To see this ambiguity, consider the question: What are we respecting when we respect another culture? We might be respecting the culture as such - as a pattern of collective practices and meanings - or we might be respecting people's rights to express their traditions in the way they choose. If, on the one hand, cultural respect is respect for cultures as such, we seem obliged to filter out information that might lead to cultural disrespect.

Yet this seems inconsistent with notions regarding the free flow of information, and may inhibit a child's ability for personal growth and independent judgment. If, on the other hand, cultural respect is really another form of respect for the individual, then we should not be obliged to teach about any particular cultures; rather, we should simply be obliged to teach about the need to respect individual choice.

The final goal of multicultural education - to inform children about other cultures - also presents problems of interpretation and execution. Information is not neutral. It serves certain purposes and issues from certain centers of experience and not others. The question that needs to be addressed is: What should be the educational aim of such information? Critics are concerned that the information will be filtered in such a way as to highlight only the positive features of the cultural group while overemphasizing the negative factors in the nation's response to those groups. They fear that this will serve to undercut national identity.

Multicultural Education in a Liberal Society

Cultural Pride: If cultural pride simply means teaching children to feel partial towards members of their own cultural group, then there is no justification for using public resources to advance this goal within the public schools, and people may justifiably ask.

Schools are justified in affirming the merits of certain groups when at least two conditions prevail. The first is where the meanings and practices of the group are not working in the way that they should, and where members are excluded from full participation in the larger society because of cultural factors. This single condition, however, is not in itself sufficient to call forth a program that seeks to develop cultural pride.

When this single condition exists, the school needs only to develop programs that will help the child learn better the ways to interact with people in the larger society. This may include, for example, bilingual programs. However, the aim of these programs is not primarily to help the child maintain proficiency in her own language, but to use her own language as a bridge into the teachings of the host nation. The presence of this condition alone is not sufficient to justify the introduction of units that are specifically aimed at providing the child with a more favourable view of her own culture, but it is a necessary condition for it.

The second condition involves a prevailing explanation for these failures that target the local cultural practices, meanings, and interpretations themselves. Hence rather than seeing the problem in terms of a mismatch between local and officially privileged national practices, this explanation views it as a problem strictly with the local practices and with those who maintain them.

These explanations are often the lingering effects of oppression and they need to be corrected by a clearer understanding of the reasons for the development of certain practices, meanings, and interpretations. And, since many of these reasons are bound to involve the history of oppression, there will be oppositional factors that are involved in the reexamination. What then appears to the outside observer to be an exclusive emphasis on developing a favourable attitude towards one group is in reality the result of a pedagogical reinterpretation of a cultural rupture.

Cultural Respect: This brings us to the second goal of multicultural education - the requirement that we respect other cultures. This goal too is not as unproblematic or as benign as it may initially appear. Why should we respect other cultures, and what does it really mean to do so?

The question of tradition and traditional culture provides a way in which to open up this question and to examine the issues involved. In the modernist literature, traditional culture is described as backward looking, authoritarian, and fatalistic.The issues of tradition describe traditional societies as depicted in the sociological tradition:

> The tradition-informed way of life is hierarchically differentiated: both within particular traditions, and with regard to how other ways of life are evaluated. Little or no validity is accorded to those who might speak with their own, out-of-place voice. Identities are inscribed, rather than being at stake for discursive controversy. Indeed, the authorial taken-for-grantedness of identities preclude the necessity of questioning those discourses which serve to legitimate the order of things.

Now some may object to the accuracy of this as a description of what we take as traditional cultures, and may properly view it as overly general. However, suppose that this description of traditional culture is accurate for at least some set of cultures that are called "traditional," then what would respect mean and what, if any, grounds could be provided to the school for teaching children respect for these cultural forms?

Multiculturalism is not respect for cultural formations under any and all conditions. Rather, it is respect for such formations under the background of modern social conditions. Under these conditions, certain possibilities for choice are present which were not present under earlier situations in which traditional social forms dominated.

Today, traditional cultures exist within a social context in which the members share a certain political and social space with members of other traditional societies, and with people who are unambiguously modern. Hence, respect is not asked for a cultural group that dominates its members thought and action without alternative forms available; rather, respect is asked for traditional cultures whose members are almost always at the edge, and who are constantly renewing or rejecting the hegemonic dominance of their cultural authority.

Now to understand the concern for cultural respect in this way is in fact to understand it as an element within a modern, liberal framework, and not as an element within a traditional framework. It is a way of celebrating and preserving opportunities for choice, even opportunities that, once chosen, constrain choice in the way that some traditional groups do.

Yet this suggests too that the standard description of traditional cultural groups noted above is not completely accurate either. A traditional group that exists within the context of modernization is different than one that stands alone. In the latter, there is little awareness of other possibilities, and hence choice outside of that tradition is but a remote possibility. Within the context of modernization, however, traditional culture is itself an object of choice, and its members must renew their identity within such a framework.

Thus, part of what it means to respect traditional culture must be answered in terms of the meaning of such respect within the context of modernization, and this is likely different than simply respect as such. It is a respect grounded within the liberal tradition of individual choice. This is a minimal conception of respect. We are not respecting a tradition as such, but the availability of a tradition given a situation in which the individual has the possibility to choose otherwise. Respect here requires an understanding of the role that culture plays in the development of a self. Our culture has much to do with how we become the persons we are. It not only provides the scaffold for our development, it also provides the initial conditions - the other who is the same as us - for self recognition. It allows us to think of ourselves in Glover's term, as an "I," and to understand that this "I" entails a certain unity of consciousness - that it is a person.

Cultural Information: The final goal of multicultural education - to inform children about other cultures - also presents problems of interpretation and execution. Information is not neutral. It serves certain purposes and issues from certain centers of experience and not others. The question that needs to be addressed is: What should be the educational aim of such information? There are a number of different answers to this question depending on whether one is focusing on political or educational concerns, and on whether one is concerned with questions of equity or with questions of personality and growth.

The difference can be seen in terms of the contrast between the dyad domination/subordination and the dyad advantaged/disadvantaged. The former assumes that an inequality exists because certain rights are denied, while the latter also assumes an inequality, but is inconclusive with regards to the reason for the inequality, and leaves open the issue whether any given disadvantage is the result of a morally impermissible act. Disadvantages can have many different causes - some of which may be morally neutral, and others morally impermissible.

Consider, for example, the fact that almost all Americans speak English, and only a relative few speak Russian or Japanese. This means that in this country, native speakers of English will have large advantages that native speakers of Russian or Japanese will not have or will need to work harder to obtain. People who wish to become lawyers will have an advantage if they are raised either in the United States or England rather than in the former Soviet Union, and the advantage will have as much to do with habits of thought as it will with language differences. The same would hold for children raised in the United States or England who wished to practice law in Russia.

Culture matters, and it provides those who are favored with positions within the dominant culture with certain advantages that those raised in other cultures do not have or will have to struggle to obtain. Those who think that by itself this is somehow wrong or unjust have a burden of proof to satisfy. This seems obvious except for those who mistakenly believe that societies can be culturally neutral, or those who believe that any inequality, regardless of its cause or its reason, is unjust. What is unjust is if these inequalities remained unaddressed over a number of generations, or if people are blocked from living adequate lives because they were culturally different.

When children learn about other cultures under the advantaged/disadvantage dyad, the object is to show that the society is open to many different people, and that the root to achievement has many different origins. This was the lesson that most European immigrants learned, and it is the program that pluralists, as opposed to multiculturalists, still advocate.

Under this model, there is a nesting of cultural goals within national ones, and the view is presented that, despite pressures to the contrary, merit should be (and largely is) a dominant consideration in social advancement. Yet to teach children only this message, and to teach it in a way in which it were advanced as the truth of American society is problematic because it ignores the reality of another dyad - domination/subordination - a dyad which certainly describes the historical situation of African Americans and some other non-European peoples.

For many African and Native Americans, the domination/subordination script fits their historical experience more closely than does the advantaged/disadvantaged script. Nevertheless, while each of these scripts is adequate to a certain range of historical experience, either may be used in ways that inhibit educational possibilities. This is especially so if used to provide a deterministic cast to future choices. When used in this way, they seem to require students to program their future lives on the experiences of their parents and grandparents.

Moreover, neither script is adequate to contain the many facets of an individual's identity. People belong to cultural or racial groups, but they are also identified by their sex, and by their class position within those groups, and increasingly they are identified by their sexual orientation. These other facets of identity should not invalidate these scripts, but they should provide different centers of experience from which to find additional meaning.

Teachers can help students develop higher order multicultural thinking skills by exploring with them the various stories about cultural and national identity as scripts which they can validate, challenge, and negotiate. For example, at some point in their educational career, students should be able to understand how the advantaged/disadvantage script relies on a certain conception of national identity which the domination/subordination script rejects. The domination/subordination script can be examined in terms of the way it shifts the status of some Europeans from disadvantaged to dominator by reclassifying them from a national to a continental identity.

Hence, Greek-Americans, Italian-Americans, etc., who once viewed themselves as the victims of Anglo-Americans are re-categorized under the oppositional script as "Americans of European background." When self-understanding is trumped in this way, by another person's self understanding, then education calls for a dialogue over difference. At the higher levels, multicultural skills involve learning how cultural identities of different kinds, including one's own, are scripted, and how such scripts may be rewritten to give voice to alternative experiences.

THE DICHOTOMY OF LIBERAL VERSUS VOCATIONAL EDUCATION

Despite the fact that hardly anyone since Socrates has seriously held that it is possible to settle interesting philosophical problems by establishing strict definitions, the drawing of significant conceptual *distinctions* is arguably still the main stock-in-trade of professional philosophers. The trouble is, however, that since conceptual distinctions are apt to atrophy in the form of dualisms on the one hand, or are liable to generate problem cases on the other, it is also not uncommon to encounter attitudes of some distrust and hostility among philosophers towards distinction making.

While in contemporary mainstream philosophy, the day-to-day business of fine distinction-making continues unabated among philosophers, it is also true that numerous traditional distinctions, enshrining what many have come to regard as unacceptable dualisms, have come under heavy fire in recent times. One particularly good example of this philosophical iconoclasm is the assault mounted by philosophers broadly located in the pragmatist tradition on the empiricist distinction between the *analytic* and the *synthetic* — a distinction nowadays commonly denounced as useless for any significant practical philosophical purpose.

Yet it is also possible to argue, as other contemporary philosophers have shown, that it is not that the analytic-synthetic distinction serves no real philosophical purpose but that its purpose has been obscured by the failure of past philosophers to separate it from other quite different distinctions — between the *necessary* and the *contingent*, the *a priori* and the *a posteriori*, and so on. From this perspective, the real problem might well be not that a distinction has been drawn for no good purpose, but that insufficient distinctions have been drawn in circumstances where there are actually grounds for several.

Indeed, the distinction between the liberal and the vocational was considerably reinforced in the heyday of analytical philosophy of education when educational philosophers such as Richard Peters and Israel Scheffler first applied the tools of conceptual analysis to the confusions and muddles of educational discourse and distinction making was very much the order of the day. Many of those distinctions and the dualisms to which they gave rise, however, have lately come under serious attack from those who follow in the pragmatist and deeply anti-dualist tradition of John Dewey and, unsurprisingly, the distinction between liberal and vocational education has been a principal target. But, whilst it is possible to sympathize with the sentiments underlying these criticisms, I wish to explore here some reasons for believing that they might be misplaced.

One problem of major theoretical and practical proportions which continues to dog educational theorists and policy makers is that of curriculum differentiation. Essentially this is the difficulty of devising an appropriate content for education — a program of variously valued knowledge and skills — which is apt for distribution over a given population of learners heterogeneous with regard to individual differences of ability, aptitude, interest, values, aspirations, social circumstance, cultural background and so forth. In particular, of course, this is a pressing problem for state-maintained systems of schooling which are charged — in the name of some overall conception of social justice — with providing something like a common and equal educational experience for all.

The problem usually surfaces at two main levels — at the level of individual needs and at that of social requirements. First, then, the problem may be seen as one of what it is right and proper to do in terms of the best educational interests of the individual. On the one hand, it seems *prima facie* fair that all children should be afforded opportunity of access to all the recognized benefits of education and unfair that any child should be denied exposure to any part of what is generally acknowledged to be of educational value; on the other hand, however, it also seems unfair that some children should be required to persist in the learning of that for which they have little taste or aptitude — and it seems, on evidence, that the academically oriented curriculum of traditional liberal education affords not inconsiderable difficulties for the many non-academically minded citizens of most human societies.

But, secondly, the problem also has economic, social and political dimensions in the context of state maintained education since it is rightly supposed that schooling exists not merely for the benefit of the individual but also for the common good; thus, it may well seem of importance to provide students with precisely those learning experiences which will best equip them for the occupational lives they are destined to lead after school. From this perspective, however unfair it may appear to limit the academic experience of certain non-academically inclined children, it is clearly wasteful of national and social resources — as well as against their personal inclinations — to require their initiation into academic disciplines which do not interest them to the exclusion of practical and vocational subjects which do and which also contribute to meeting the urgent needs of industry, service and commerce. All this adds up to the problem of whether we should provide the same sort of educational experience for all or a different sort of educational experience for each with regard to some such distinction as that between liberal and vocational education.

A PLETHORA OF DISTINCTIONS

It would be tedious to recount the full history of this issue and the various strategies which have been suggested over the course of two millennia to address it. Historically, it probably assumes urgent significance during the nineteenth century in debates in Britain and other western European cultures about the character and content of mass popular education — precisely in the light of explicit attempts by philosophers and social theorists to formulate a distinction between academic or liberal education and vocational preparation. In particular, the issue loomed large in relation to the elaborate psychometric program of the first half of the twentieth century which culminated in the U.K. in the separate provision of different kinds of education for allegedly different intellectual categories of children on the basis of academic selection at eleven years of age.

However, analogues of the liberal-vocational distinction invariably bedevil debates surrounding educational policy making in most developed societies. They continue to turn up, for example, in the interminable wrangles between conservatives and elitists, who are invariably sympathetic to alternative schooling and curricula for different sorts of children, and liberals and egalitarians who argue, on the basis of this or that notion of justice, for a common curriculum as the right of everyone.

However, the very fact that the debates and issues in question are liable to be characterized in a wide variety of ways, considered alongside the generally unilluminating nature of their outcomes, should alert us to the possibility that perhaps rather *different* questions are at issue here, so that the way to wisdom regarding the true problem might lie through distinguishing more clearly what the relevant questions are. From this point of view, Richard Pring, in a number of important recent publications, gets off to an excellent start in his own treatment of these issues both by way of his general perception of the urgent need for some basic conceptual geography in this area and in his recognition that a substantial amount of confusion may have been engendered by the illegitimate conflation of a set of rather *different* distinctions.

These include, for example, education and training; theory and practice, the academic and the vocational and what is of intrinsic rather than instrumental value. However, it is disappointing that having insightfully recognized the pressing need for better conceptual geography in this area, Professor Pring seems, by and large, inclined to a strategy of soft-pedaling these distinctions rather than taking them as seriously as I believe he should.

Indeed, the strategy to which Pring seems inclined is the more familiar one of denouncing these distinctions in favour of some kind of pragmatic reconciliation or resolution of them. Indeed, he directly invokes the authority of John Dewey, that great archenemy of philosophical dualisms, in this connection. We are thus invited to recognize that the problems engendered by the liberal-vocational dichotomy may disappear if only we can come to see that theory is implicit in intelligent practice, that training can also be educational, that vocational activities can be pursued for their own sake, and so on.

But whilst all this may well be true it can also be doubted whether any significant dualism is resolved by these considerations — apart, that is, from the illegitimate one which follows from the wrongful conflation of different and separate distinctions; indeed, Pring is himself forced to fall back on a serious use of the distinctions in order to make the points that vocational training *can* be educational, theory *can* be inherent in practice and so forth.

For the truth is that the distinctions which Pring and others seem to want to blur in the interests of resolving awkward philosophical or educational dualisms have significant implications for our understanding of the function of schooling in relation to the proper educational and other development of young people. As such, they are not so easily disposed of by this casual sleight of hand.

Hence, although it may be true that vocational training *can* be pursued for its own sake, it is also important to recognize that there are other non-instrumentally valuable goals which have negligible vocational implications and to which we rightly feel that *all* children should have access. And whilst it may be true that practical learning is at least as important for many purposes as academic learning it is also arguable that at the heart of *education* lie certain forms of understanding which are in an important sense inherently theoretical or academic to the significant exclusion of the practical.

EDUCATION AND SCHOOLING

There are all sorts of philosophical, political and practical reasons why people may be reluctant to embrace this more complex picture there can be little doubt that much error and confusion inevitably follows from a failure to do so. In fact, it would appear to be blatantly equivocal between the idea of an education which takes the practical aspects of knowledge acquisition seriously — learning science more by doing experiments perhaps than taking notes — and that of learning practical or vocational activities in a way which focuses more on the understanding of principles than on the acquisition of skills. It is clear, however, that although these two interpretations are, in practice, quite compatible, they can function in quite different ways and on opposite sides in arguments between those who assert the primacy of liberal education and those who regard vocational training as the most important role of formal schooling.

The former interpretation, of course, construes the practical aspects of learning an academic discipline as only a *means* to understanding it more effectively and it is quite compatible with observing a sharp distinction between education and vocational training. The second interpretation, however, sees education as available just *as much* through practical and vocational pursuits as through traditional academic disciplines and is compatible with the view that for some children vocational learning may provide a legitimate alternative to or substitute for the learning of traditional subjects.

However, this seriously confuses the issue to the extent that it suggests this improved conception of vocationalism might for some children count as an education which is in some substantial sense the equivalent of what their more academic peers will be getting through the traditional educational disciplines. For no matter how principled one might try to make an initiation into hairdressing skills it is patently disingenuous to suggest that this might provide some sort of educational substitute for disinterested non-vocational development of a young person's understanding of his own culture and traditions.

The principal failure here, of course, is to distinguish between two quite different issues and considerations — that of whether we are properly providing children with the right sort of *education* and that of whether we are properly preparing young people for a life of work beyond school. This issue is confused on a well nigh cosmic scale in arguments between what one might call *instrumentalists* and *non-instrumentalists* about the nature of education and schooling; the former claim that the main purpose of schooling is to prepare young people for the adult life of post-school work and social relationships and the latter insist that education is exclusively concerned with the initiation of children into those intrinsically valuable forms of knowledge which can assist them to understand their own personal, cultural or universal predicament.

The proper way out of this impasse, of course, is to recognize that although the instrumentalist is largely right to assert what he does of schooling and the non-instrumentalist is quite correct about education; both of them would be quite wrong if they put matters the other way around. In short it would *not* be true to say that education is primarily about equipping young people with life skills or that schooling is exclusively about the initiation of individuals into a personal understanding of themselves and the world for its own sake.

In short, the instrumentalist confuses education with schooling and the non-instrumentalist confuses schooling with education. If we clearly recognize, however, that schooling are conceptually separate (albeit practically related) enterprises and that education is only *one* of the many purposes of schooling then we may come to see that the problem is not so much of seeing how vocationalism might be made educational or education vocationalized but of how to do justice to both education *and* vocational training within a coherent overall conception of the diverse purposes of institutionalized schooling.

DISTINCTIONS AND DUALISMS

To acknowledge that in relation to the school curriculum there is room for the claims of both instrumentalists and non-instrumentalists is essentially to recognize that it is proper for people to require quite different benefits from the experience of schooling and that there are therefore quite different reasons for including various subjects and activities in the conventional state curriculum. Thus, one can hardly deny that human agents do require both theory and practice for the successful pursuit of their projects; they do engage in activities and pursuits for their own sake as well as for instrumental reasons; and they require, in the interests of a more general education, some initiation into a personal appreciation of what is worth living for as well as some of the vocationally useful skills which might assist them to earn their living.

These distinctions are by no means identical, as Pring himself observes, but it is precisely on this account that each of them is necessary for a clear understanding of education and schooling; they interrelate and cut across each other in markedly different ways in diverse curriculum subjects and activities and they serve to identify the various purposes for which different activities are standardly included in school curricula.

To be sure, there are certain regrettable dualist tendencies in Peters's thought — clearly apparent in his exclusive identification of education with intellectual reflection, his denial that practice has much to contribute to a principled understanding of the world, and that practices have anything more than instrumental value, and so forth — which call for proper philosophical resistance; but we should not let this obscure our view of certain significant insights at the heart of his account.

Thus, while in the course of recognizing that education concerns the acquisition of knowledge and understanding we need to remember that knowledge has its practical as well as theoretical aspects, we may also be wise to bear in mind that not all sorts of knowledge are centrally implicated in educational development. As Peters argued, education concerns the acquisition of the sort of knowledge which is capable of affording a broad intellectual and explanatory perspective on the world and one's place in it, rather than the mere know how of practical skills.

Of course, practice may indeed serve or contribute to the promotion of such explanation and understanding in precisely the way that scientific experiment can contribute to scientific knowledge or the movements of the dancer express the meaning of the dance; but the practical skills of experiment or dance are by no means self-explanatory and it is not hard to see how they might well be acquired in the absence of real understanding. Again, various sports and games may well be performed only for their own sake if that means for no other purpose than the sheer enjoyment of them, but this certainly does not mean that they are educational ends in themselves in the way that history or science are; for whereas rational reflection on nature or inquiry into the human past are well nigh paradigm cases of what it means to have one's understanding of the world substantially enlarged, it is less plausible to claim that hockey or netball contribute comparably to any educated appreciation of the human natural, cultural or social predicament.

This is certainly not an attempt to downgrade the non-educational aspects of human development or to argue that practices and skills of negligible educational significance have no legitimate place in the school curriculum. For although such practices and skills may have little to contribute to the educational development of an individual (however much their performance may entail the grasp of practical rational principles) they may yet play an indispensable part in schooling with regard to programs of vocational training, so-called leisure education and elsewhere.

What should be apparent from all this, of course, is that although any human activity or enterprise whatsoever can be viewed as having theoretical *and* practical aspects, as amenable to study in *either* academic *or* vocational terms or as pursuable for its own sake *or* as a means to an end, it is above all crucial to see why, in the light of these distinctions and some coherent conception of the aims of schooling and education, a range of diverse school subjects have traditionally been included in the school curriculum.

What seldom seems to be done with regard to so-called curriculum theory, however, is precisely to consider the various possible reasons for teaching this or that subject in its particularity rather than as part of some general story about what school subjects ought to be contributing to the educational or other development of pupils. Hence, the familiar non-instrumentalist account of the school curriculum canvassed by the new liberal educational philosophers of the sixties tended to assume, or was often taken to assume, that for a subject to be worthy of curricular inclusion it must be shown to have genuine educational value. Likewise, some subsequent officially prescribed curricula would seem to imply that for a subject to be considered worthwhile, it must be susceptible to instrumental justification by reference to various extrinsic economic, social or political benefits.

RENDERING UNTO GOD AND CAESAR

Instead what is needed is more attention to what particular school subjects or forms of knowledge have in their quite distinctive ways to contribute to the human development of young people, consistent with ensuring that their due entitlement to education *and* various forms of training is not unfairly unequal where it should be equal or unfairly equal where it need not be so.

To start with, in response to vocationalist skepticism about the value of academic subjects we could ask whether we might ever decently propose that we should dispense in the context of schooling — at least in the case of some children — with their substantial initiation into the sorts of activities which non-instrumentalists argue to be of intrinsic educational value, such as science, history, literature, art and mathematics. These, of course, are precisely the forms of knowledge and understanding which liberal educationalists insist that no one should be denied access to if they are to become civilized and rational members of society. Put thus, however, it should be clear from what has been said so far that we are here faced with several categories of educational activity rather than just one.

As regards history and literature, for example, we are clearly dealing with activities which have genuine intrinsic value from an educational point of view but practically negligible utility or instrumental value. When it comes to the various forms of scientific study, of course, we are faced with activities which have *both* educational and instrumental value in view of their contribution to our understanding of the natural circumstances of human life *and* their obvious technological implications for and applications to a wide range of problems which may also have vocational import for the future of many children in schools. For various reasons we cannot fully explore here, however, it is arguable that substantial scientific understanding is not as crucial as substantial understanding of history for the development of an educated appreciation of their cultural identity on the part of *all* children, and so a proper strategy might be to go for a minimum of general science for everyone and more vocationally oriented specialist programs of pure and applied science for those whose particular abilities and interests take them in that direction.

What, then, should we say of mathematical education? Non-instrumentalists, of course, make much of the intrinsic educational value of mathematics and of its being concerned with considerably more than the promotion of mere numeracy. But again we should beware of assuming that because it is possible to make sense of mathematics as an intrinsically worthwhile form of human understanding it is thereby appropriate to teach it as such to *all* children; for if mathematics is also an activity for which a certain natural flair or ability is required — as has often been maintained — then it may well be that mathematical *education* can never be a realistic option, as it would be hard to claim of history, for those who lack the necessary intellectual requirements.

In that case we may have to accept that it is no more realistic to entertain any substantial degree of mathematical understanding as a valid goal of educational development for all children than it is to entertain musical appreciation and performance as educational goals for those on whom nature has bestowed a so-called tin ear. But to recognize that a serious conceptual understanding of mathematics is beyond the reach of very many children is quite consistent with endorsing a strong instrumentalist line on the importance of a thorough school training for all in basic mathematical skills on the common sense grounds that basic numeracy is an urgent requirement for the day to day practical purposes of all members of society.

What has already been said in relation to music would also seem to apply to painting and dance and to many other arts for which a particular flair is required; whilst there is room here for an initiation into the basics, particularly at the primary level, it would seem that a freedom to choose according to ability or interests should enter the picture fairly soon at the secondary stage of education. A distinction which might be of considerable significance here, of course, is that between appreciation and participation in these art forms since it would appear to make sense to try to promote appreciation on a rather wider scale than training in the actual skills of performance.

Once again, however, it seems possible to conclude on the basis of common experience that whilst there are considerations and circumstances of physical or other kinds which might interfere with a person's appreciation of either music or painting there are also no arguments here of the sort to which we might appeal on behalf of the indispensable educational benefits of literature for requiring the exposure of *all* children to other fine arts.

It is also likely that there are no compelling educational grounds for requiring the initiation of children into certain physical sports and games — although there may be valid reasons, if these are empirically sustainable, for including such activities in the school curriculum on the extrinsic grounds of their potential for the promotion of health and fitness. But arguments based on the alleged value of such activities for the development of moral, spiritual or aesthetic understanding or appreciation are at best highly contested and more than likely simply confused.

We should also say a little, to conclude this very truncated survey of the content of the conventional school curriculum, about the value of a whole range of kinds of knowledge and skill of a primarily instrumental nature — domestic, craft, and technical skills of various kinds. Here again, the relevant distinction may well be between the basic skills of everyday coping such as elementary home economics, computing or woodwork, to which it is reasonable to introduce *everyone* to some degree, and such higher specialist vocational competencies as electronic engineering or commercial and business skills which may be relevant only to those who wish to pursue eventual careers in such areas.

To be sure, each of these observations stands in need of considerably more by way of detailed and substantial argument; my main point is that the overall tendency of the argument should not be in the direction of some general ideological defence of *either* liberal education *or* vocational preparation *or* of some dubious resolution of the two, but towards a better recognition and appreciation of what the various distinctions which underlie what some have seen as an unacceptable dualism have to reveal about the structure and complexity of human needs and interests and the capacity and potential of both schooling and education to satisfy them. Young people do not need secretarial skills or business studies *instead* of history or biology; in at least some cases (but not all) they require *both*.

Again, they may not need electronics if they have no wish to pursue a technological career and it may not be necessary to require their initiation into the conceptual complexities of mathematical understanding if they have no recognizable aptitude for it. On the other hand they do require the skills of numeracy even if they have trouble mastering them and some substantial knowledge and appreciation of history, geography and literature irrespective of whether they have any real taste for such studies.

SOME PHILOSOPHICAL CONSIDERATIONS IN THE MODE OF INFORMATION

The "information" in the last decade of the twentieth century is that we are entering the age of information and that our social and cultural life will become restructured as we "evolve" into the information society. The notion of information is also an important building block for the "reform" literatures which are guiding changes in western educational systems, and is presented as a fundamental key not only to economic success, but also to social success.

While the reform literatures have emphasized the importance of information, the necessary acquisition of skills related to information and, in particular, skills related to the electronic media and electronic communication, this has not been cited in a context of an explicit total rethinking of the form that this education will, should, or may take, but seems to be a continuation, though an extension of what has preceded. Thus electronic communication and electronic information are treated as being extensions of traditional print literacy in particular, but also of oral literacy.

In general the "advance" of electronic communication and the move from the printed word to electronic language are not treated as being philosophically problematic in the educational literature. There are a number of philosophical issues here. First, there is a poverty of the concept of knowledge inherent in talk of information. This will be discussed initially. Second, there are a number of other philosophical issues: the availability of information: power and authority; and the nature of the self, among others. Given the emphasis on information in current educational documents, these philosophical issues, in so far as they impinge upon education, need to be explored. Finally I develop a critique of this approach to electronic communication.

Knowledge

In this section it is my intention to examine the espoused philosophy, and the account of knowledge underlying the curriculum "reforms." In the central philosophy of the proposals for the national curriculum, with what are called the Principles, the Essential Learning Areas, and the Essential Skills, there is a stunning lack of concern with basic and fundamental questions about the nature of knowledge and pedagogy.

Central to a consideration of curricula are questions about what counts as knowledge, how it is defined and controlled, and whose knowledge is selected for inclusion - who decides and on what basis? What counts as important knowledge also defines what is seen as not worth knowing and, consequently, the interests of different gender, class and ethnic groups may be unequally represented in what is, and what is not, included in the curriculum offered. Reference is made to sound learning theory, to the needs and requirements of groups and society, to the essential knowledge which will allow individuals to take their place in society, and to succeed in a modern competitive society, but no consideration is given to whether the nature of knowledge determines how we can think, and whether our approach to education and pedagogy ought to be influenced by those considerations.

The term "knowledge" essentially to explain other definitions or principles. In the nine major principles said to underlie the curriculum, "knowledge" does not occur in any of the formal wording of the principles. In other words knowledge is not considered important enough to occur in the wording of any one of the principles which "give direction to the curriculum in New Zealand schools.". It is used as part of the definition of "learning areas" and occurs again in relation to the curriculum, but as "curriculum" has already been defined in terms of learning areas, this is merely tautologous and does not represent any new principled approach to knowledge as being crucially important. Knowledge is not mentioned at all in the four pages devoted to skills.

In effect knowledge has been replaced by skills and learning. Everything which might have been seen as obtaining knowledge - an object of an activity - seems to have moved into an activity mode, where what is important is a process. Knowledge, in the sense of knowing that something is the case, has been replaced by knowing how, with the explicit emphasis on getting skilled; and learning as process has replaced knowing some thing in the notion of learning areas, in getting skilled, and in the area of attitudes and values, where it is an attitude towards learning (as a process) that is valued and not an attitude towards knowledge (as something known). It is the processes, the ever ongoing learning and reskilling processes, that are seen as of paramount importance.

In part this is because the outcome is no longer knowledge but instead information. And because it is (merely) information it has to be continuously "relearned," readjusted and restructured to meet the demands of the consumer in the service information industry. It is the consumer who determines quality (truth?) in the information industry. Hence the necessity to value "learning." and life long "learning."

When we search the curriculum document under the skills section, what we find are skills related to information retrieval and dissemination. Students are also meant to have problem solving skills which, on the face of it, seem the normal liberal educational set of critical skills as it is said, e.g., that fact should be distinguished from opinion. But even that "endeavour" rests in the mode of information, and on the schema of skills outlined would amount to testing bits of information against other bits of information because the fundamental concepts are in the information mode. At best there is a demand for quality of information in the cry for fact, but quality of information will be decided by the consumer not the provider. It is the consumer in the information industry who decides truth/quality.

But this notion of information and the skills necessary for problem solving and decision making in the mode of information are needed in electronic communication. But more is needed. In order to understand what this might be we need a form of critical theory that is able to decode the new linguistic dimensions of electronic writing and new forms of social interaction that will accompany it.

Other Philosophical Issues

According to Poster:

> The prospect of instant universal information, introduced by electronic media, clearly has profound effects upon society, the extent of which are still to be determined. But the conquest of space and time by electronic media augurs more for institutions and for theory than a mere returning of practices and ideas to new communicational frequencies.

For example when information is readily available on a scale never previously envisaged, it seems that it is not being freely disseminated. There is a politics of control which may deny access, or permit it only to those who have the technology and the assets to purchase information. In principle information is available to anyone, with traditional barriers of space and time obliterated by electronic communication. Why restrict access?

There are a number of related issues here concerned with the fragility of social networks, the breakdown of traditional authority structures associated with oral and written communication, new ways of exercising power relationships through these different forms of knowledge, and new ways of constituting the self, in the new realm of electronic communication.

Consider the form of face to face social network associated with oral communication. Compare it with the written word where the authority of the speaker - who that person is - is different from the authority of the author, and contrast both of these with the information encoded in the pixels on the electronic screen. The social networks associated with oral and written communication can become very fragile in electronic communication because of the introduction of say a virus, which may bring about a breakdown, or require the complete shutdown of the network. The information encoded by an emitter can be transformed on receipt by the recipient. Unwanted information can appear on the screen and this may be irrelevant, contradictory, intemperate, abusive or even obscene.

It is not just that the social networks are tender, but that the roles of speaker or author are instantly reversible, and not subject to the same social conventions that govern oral and written communication. Further, authority structures become tenuous. Both the authority that accompanied oral communication - that of who the speaker is - and the authority of written communication - where the notions of truth, evidence, and of being an authority are important - became tenous. But the authority to control what is said also becomes tenuous. If unwanted communication cannot be controlled then traditional notions of being in authority become very tenuous. Of course a "solution" to this is to control emitters and emittees so that they are passive senders and receivers.

This requires a particular "education" which concentrates on processes or activities as opposed to content, and emphasizes information as opposed to knowledge. What counts as good or authoritative information is checked, in the mode of information, against other information assembled or transmitted by an emittee suitably "educated." If content has been replaced by process, and if knowledge and understanding have been replaced by skills and information, then there is no way out. It is as if one is enclosed in a circular system like a dictionary, where one can stay within the words without needing to check the reality or points of reference with the real world. It is knowledge and understanding which provides the way out of the information "dictionary" and it is this which is being lost, if not denied, in the new forms of education.

But knowledge should not be dissociated from power. Insofar as new forms of knowledge and therefore power are implicit in the age of information, so too we should expect new forms of subjectivity in the mode of information. It is in the writings of Michel Foucault, among others, that we meet with the notion that subjects are constituted.

A notion of the self which underlies the reform literatures is that of the free autonomous chooser. According to Foucault, the Enlightenment notion of personal autonomy did not provide freedom. Furthermore, Foucault's bio-power, with its emphasis on the body, does not seem very appropriate in relation to electronic communication. Foucault introduced the term "bio-power" as follows:

> The disciplines of the body and the regulations of the population constituted the two poles around which the organization of power over life was deployed. The setting up, in the course of the classical age, of this great bipolar technology - anatomic and biological, individualizing and specifying, directed towards the performances of the body, with attention to the processes of life - characterized a power whose highest function was perhaps no longer to kill, but to invest life through and through.

Bio-power is exercised on the body, carries a specifically anatomical and biological aspect, and is exercised over individuals as members of a population, first, so that their sexuality and individuality are constituted in certain ways, but second, so that this connects with issues of national policy. Thereby docile and healthy bodies can be inserted into the machinery of production so that populations can be adjusted in accordance with economic processes.

Foucault discusses in considerable detail how the requisite techniques and technologies for the exercise of bio-power were developed. These can be classified as technologies of domination and technologies of the self. Technologies of domination act essentially on the body, and classify and objectify individuals. The key to technologies of the self is the belief, now common in Western culture, that it is possible to reveal the truth about one's self. By telling the truth about one's sexuality, where the "deepest" truth is embedded in the discourse and discursive practices of sexuality, individuals become objects of knowledge, both to themselves and to others.

In telling the truth, one knows oneself and is known to others in a process which is both therapeutic and also controlling. Eventually, according to Foucault, we learn how to do these things to ourselves. He refers to the conjoint effects of these two technologies as governmentality.

In the reform literatures students, parents, etc. are presumed to be persons not merely capable of deliberating upon alternatives, and choosing between alternative educational programs according to individual needs and interests, and the qualities of programs, but it seems to be presumed that it is part of the very nature of being human to both make, and want to make, continuous consumer style choices. But the notions of autonomy needed to make choices, and the notions of needs and interests, presuppose that such choices are the student's (or chooser's) own, that as choosers they are independent, and that needs and interests have not been manipulated or imposed in some way upon them.

It is not just that the individual should become an autonomous chooser, but also that this connects with wider government policy and economic theory. The autonomous chooser becomes a unit in an enterprise and in consumer driven market totality. These changed notions can and should be understood as involving changes in the forms that governmentality takes. But the power involved is not the bio-power of Foucault introduced above.

Bio-power was directed at and through the body, at the health and sexuality of the individual, and through that, at populations. This new form of power, which can be called busno-power, is directed at the subjectivity of the person, not through the body, but through the mind, through forms of educational practice and pedagogy which shape through busnocratic rationality, choices in education and the subjectivities of autonomous choosers. Education, embedded in the frameworks of busno-power and busnocratic rationality, is the first step in the individualizing and totalizing functions of busno-power.

Busnocratic rationality is developed from the notion of technocratic rationality, but rather than there being a sharp distinction between values and means, values permeate this form of "rationality" throughout, especially at the very micro-level. In the Age of Information, and in relation to identity, the new self will be decentered and dispersed, as in post-structuralist theory, without spatio-temporal and bodily constraints. But, furthermore, the physical body has nothing to do with identity in electronic communication. It is almost as though the self has become invisible.

It is not just that the self can "transport" itself spatio-temporally, but it is almost that there is no self other than the self-reflexive signs of electronic communication - the pixels on the screen. But as the emitter's information can be obliterated almost immediately by the changing of the pixels in the process of receiving and transmitting information, then so too can the self be obliterated because of the self reflexive character of language in this new mode of information. At best, the self is in continuous instability as pixels change in the flow of information between emitter and emittee, who are also in constant "reversal" of roles. It seems as if the self becomes obliterated or unidentifiable in the flux, maze and buzz of information. But, because there is nothing other than the flux, the self cannot be obliterated, because in order for that to happen, it had to first exist and that is not possible in the flux of information.

But if the self is not identifiable, in principle, this poses problems for traditional authority structures and governance.

THE CRITIQUE OF INFORMATION

Mark Poster is an analyst who recognizes the importance of a study of electronic languages which does not merely look at technologies, machines and the new efficiencies brought about in communication. According to Poster, "an adequate account of electronic communications requires a theory that is able to decode the linguistic dimension of the new forms of social interaction." He argues that traditional critical theory is inadequate for the task.

Poster advocates, as a step in that direction, the concept of the mode of information which is, he says, a play upon Marx's notion of the mode of production. But as he defines the concept, it is more than this, for it bears close resemblances in two important ways to the mode of production. First he notes that it provides an historical category which divides and periodizes the past, but, second, it provides a metaphor for how certain activities are privileged. For Marx, of The German Ideology, the concept of the mode of production served both of these purposes.

Poster's definition of the concept of the mode of information is then, "By mode of information I similarly suggest that history can be periodised by variations in the structure in this case of symbolic exchange, but also that the current culture gives a certain fetishistic importance to 'information.'"

With this definition he then designates three important periodizations of forms of symbolic exchange: first there is face to face and orally mediated exchange; second there are written exchanges mediated by print; and finally, electronically mediated exchanges. These are not to be seen as progressions, or improvements. But is the third stage just an extension of the second, and thereby just another form of printed exchange? Poster's major claim is that it is not.

His two main arguments are concerned with meanings and the self in each of the three stages. Meaning, in the first stage of meaning, is characterized by symbolic correspondences; in the second stage, by representation; and in the third stage, by simulation. Poster accepts that language shapes both the individual and societies. Therefore, corresponding to these three stages of meaning, he talks of three stages of the self: in the first stage, the self is seen as established in face-to-face relations through a position of enunciation, as the person who speaks; in the second stage, the self is constituted as being personally/ rationally autonomous and as the author endowing meaning to the printed page; and in the third or electronically mediated stage, the self is decentered, dispersed, and has multiple "identities." Although still essentially in the second stage of the mode of information, a number of post structuralist writers, including Foucault, have emphasized these themes.

Poster states some cautions, however. The stages are not to be "found" in the documents of each epoch, but instead are to be imposed by the theory to attain knowledge - here the test must be the value of empirical studies informed by the concept of the mode of information. Nor are they consecutive or sequential, as elements of all are in the present. Contrary to what many technically minded enthusiasts may believe, the third stage is neither privileged nor more progressive. The study of electronic communication cannot therefore be reduced to narrowly conceived questions of technology and efficiency.

Poster argues further that these matters and the restraints or enhancements upon them can govern with striking force the shape that societies take. For him, technicist approaches do not approach the heart of the matter, "the configuration of information exchange," or as he calls it, "the wrapping of language." He argues that the configuration of language is an analytically autonomous realm of experience, especially with the rapidly changing modes of electronic communication that not only alter, but restructure networks of social relations and constitute subjects in very different ways from the personally autonomous agent of the second stage and any representational view of language. Changes in the wrapping of language then alter the way meanings are derived, restructure social relations, constitute the subject in different ways, and alter the relations between subject and the world.

But Poster's point is that even where language might be considered as having a representational function, the relation between word and thing has become tenuous. To illustrate the loss of the referent in ordinary everyday use he uses the word "money," tracking its referent from precious metals, to banknotes and, finally, to a configuration of oxides stored on a tape in a bank's computer department. This shows that the referential notion has become tenuous, and that in fact, words no longer stand for things, but come to stand in the place of things. This can be called the self referential function of language and it permeates the new forms of electronic communication.

Language is being wrapped differently by new configurations in electronic communications: there is the distance between addresser and addressee which imposes different relations from say face-to-face oral communication; there are new relations between message and context; and there are differences in the ways in which senders and receivers may represent themselves. This new wrapping of language imposes in turn new relations between science and power, between the individual and both society and the state, between authority and the law, between family members, and between consumer and retailer. There are immense philosophical implications here for education.

There are physical differences between the "print" of electronic text and the printed words of books. The pixels or picture elements of electronic text can be blown up, separated, and manipulated so that they no longer resemble the words or letters of print. Furthermore, we have come to believe that the letters and words of printed text are unmediated in that they just stand for thought. Yet there is clear evidence historically that words and text of the printed text had to be mediated, and that they were not a transparent window into thought.

Nor can there be an interaction between the reader and the printed text. The reader of print can write on the text (if it is owned), but it changes the text, perhaps in ways in which the author and owner of the printed text (protected by copyright which is itself unclear in relation to electronic texts) would not wish, and it is not part of the printed text. The critical comments and the interpretations are not in the text, or even part of the text, but the beginnings of texts about texts. Similarly, if a director of a Shakespearean play changes the ending quite dramatically - MacBeth is not defeated say - then it is not MacBeth.

However, in electronic text, the author or reader can alter, amend, or add to the text. The author can continuously update a text as his or her position shifts and changes. Or a number of scenarios to a text can be provided by the author so that the reader can interact and choose the desired scenario. Or the reader can shift text, add text, combine texts, or play with texts in ways that are possible with electronic text but not with printed text. In film, music and electronic media in general, the notion of "no final cut" has almost become commonplace. Will this become the same in philosophical and/or academic texts?

Poster argues that an outcome may be that social life in part becomes the positioning of subjects to receive and interpret these electronic messages. Clearly this has important bearings on what has been said above about the emphases on information and electronic communication in relation to the educational reform literature, and the absence of knowledge and a critical examination of the mode of information.

The message given by Foucault, among others, is that language has an important capacity for constituting us as subjects. By distancing emitter and emittee, electronic communication disturbs relations normally conceived between speaker and hearer, or between writer and reader, and thus reconstitutes both subjects and their relations to symbols. Indeed, for a subject in electronic communications, there seems no longer to be a material wor'd as normally represented by language, but just a flow of electronic language. Instead of a real world behind the language, we have instead a simulated world with simulcra and no real objects.

3

EDUCATIONAL IMPLICATIONS OF SCHOOLS OF PHILOSOPHY

According to Aristotle:

> "In modern times there are opposing views about the practice of education. There is no general agreement about what the young should learn either in relation to virtue or in relation to the best life; nor is it clear whether their education ought to be directed more towards the intellect than towards the character of the soul.... And it is not certain whether training should be directed at things useful in life, or at those conducive to virtue, or at non-essentials.... And there is no agreement as to what in fact does tend towards virtue. Men do not all prize most highly the same virtue, so naturally they differ also about the proper training for it."

Aristotle's statement made so many years ago gets to the heart of the intent of educational philosophy. Educational philosophy poses such questions as:

— What knowledge is of most worth? (in other words, what should we teach?)

— What should be the aims of education?

— How do people learn?

— What should the relationship between teacher and learner look like?

There are 6 philosophical perspectives on education: essentialism, perennialism, progressivism, existentialism, reconstructionism, and critical pedagogy.

ESSENTIALISM

Essentialism refers to the "traditional" or "Back to the Basics" approach to education. It is so named because it strives to instill students with the "essentials" of academic knowledge and character development. The term essentialism as an educational philosophy was originally popularized in the 1930s by the American educator William Bagley. The philosophy itself, however, had been the dominant approach to education in America from the beginnings of American history. Early in the twentieth century, essentialism was criticized as being too rigid to prepare students adequately for adult life. But with the launching of Sputnik in 1957, interest in essentialism revived. Among modern supporters of this position are members of the President's Commission on Excellence in Education. Their 1983 report, A Nation at Risk, mirrors essentialist concerns today.

(American) essentialism is grounded in a conservative philosophy that accepts the social, political, and economic structure of American society. It contends that schools should not try to radically reshape society. Rather, essentialists argue, American schools should transmit the traditional moral values and intellectual knowledge that students need to become model citizens. Essentialists believe that teachers should instill such traditional American virtues as respect for authority, perseverance, fidelity to duty, consideration for others, and practicality.

Reflecting its conservative philosophy, essentialism tends to accept the philosophical views associated with the traditional, conservative elements of American society. For example, American culture traditionally has placed tremendous emphasis on the central importance of tile physical world and of understanding the world through scientific experimentation. As a result, to convey important knowledge about our world, essentialist educators emphasize instruction in natural science rather than non-scientific disciplines such as philosophy or comparative religion.

The Essentialist Classroom

Essentialists urge that the most essential or basic academic skills and knowledge be taught to all students. Traditional disciplines such as math, natural science, history, foreign language, and literature form the foundation of the essentialist curriculum. Essentialists frown upon vocational, lift-adjustment, or other courses with "watered down" academic content.

Elementary students receive instruction in skills such as writing, reading, measurement, and computers. Even while learning art and music, subjects most often associated with the development of creativity. the students are required to master a body of information and basic techniques, gradually moving from less to more complex skills and detailed knowledge. Only by mastering the required material for their grade level are students promote to the next higher grade.

Essentialist programs are academically rigorous, for both slow and fast learners. The report A Nation at Risk reflects the essentialist emphasis on rigor. It calls for more core requirements, a longer school day, a longer academic year, and more challenging textbooks. Moreover, essentialists maintain that classrooms should be oriented around the teacher, who ideally serves as an intellectual and moral role model for the students. The teachers or administrators decide what is most important for the students to learn and place little emphasis on student interests, particularly when they divert time and attention from the academic curriculum. Essentialist teachers focus heavily on achievement test scores as a means of evaluating progress.

In an essentialist classroom, students are taught to be "culturally literate," that is, to possess a working knowledge about the people, events, ideas, and institutions that have shaped American society. Reflecting the essentialist emphasis on technological literacy, A Nation at Risk recommends that all high school students complete at least one semester of computer science. Essentialists hope that when students leave school, they will possess not only basic skills and an extensive body of knowledge, but also disciplined, practical minds, capable of applying schoolhouse lessons in the real world.

PERENNIALISM

Perennial means "everlasting," like a perennial flower that comes up year after year. Espousing the notion that some ideas have lasted over centuries and are as relevant today as when they were first conceived, perennialism urges that these ideas should be the focus of education. According to perennialists, when students are immersed in the study of those profound and enduring ideas, they will appreciate learning for its own sake and become true intellectuals.

The roots of perennialism lie in the philosophy of Plato and Aristotle, as well as that of St. Thomas Aquinas, the thirteenth-century Italian whose ideas continue to shape the nature of Catholic schools throughout the world.

Perennialists are generally divided into two groups: those who espouse the religious approach to education adopted by Aquinas, and those who follow the secular approach formulated in twentieth-century America by such individuals as Mortimer Adler and Robert Hutchins. We will be concentrating here on this second branch of perennialism. It strives above all to develop our capacity to reason and regards training in the humanities as particularly essential to the development of our rational powers.

Similarities to Essentialism

While Hutchins and Adler regard perennialism as a badly needed alternative to essentialism, the two philosophies have many similarities. Both aim to rigorously develop all students' intellectual powers, first, and moral qualities, second. Moreover, both advocate classrooms centered around teachers in order to accomplish these goals. The teachers do not allow the students' interests or experiences to substantially dictate what they teach. They apply whatever creative techniques and other tried and true methods are believed to be most conducive to disciplining the students' minds.

As with essentialism, perennialism accepts little flexibility in the curriculum. For example, in his Paideia Program, published in 1982, Mortimer Adler recommends a single elementary and secondary curriculum for all students, supplemented by years of pre-schooling in the case of the educational disadvantaged. He would allow no curricular electives except in the choice of a second language.

The perennialists base their support of a universal curriculum on the view that all human beings possess the same essential nature: We are all rational animals. Perennialists argue that allowing students to take vocational or life-adjustment courses denies them the opportunity to fully develop their rational powers. As Plato might claim, by neglecting the students' reasoning skills, we deprive them of the ability to use their "higher" faculties to control their "lower" ones (passions and appetites).

Differences from Essentialism

Unlike essentialism, perennialism is not rooted in any particular time or place. The distinctively American emphasis on the value of scientific experimentation to acquire knowledge is reflected in essentialism, but not in perennialism. Similarly, while essentialism reflects the traditional American view that the "real" world is the physical world we experience with our senses, perennialism is more open to the notion that universal spiritual forms—such as those posited by Plato or by theological philosophers—are equally real.

Perennialists seek to help students discover those ideas most insightful and timeless in understanding the human condition. The study of philosophy is thus a crucial part of the perennialist curriculum. Perennialists regard essentialism, and its view that knowledge stems primarily from the empirical findings of scientists, as undermining the importance of our capacity to reason as individuals; that is, to think deeply, analytically, flexibly, and imaginatively.

Recognizing that enormous strides have been made in our knowledge about the physical universe, perennialists teach about the processes by which scientific truths have been discovered. Perennialists emphasize, though, that students should not be taught information that may soon be obsolete or found to be incorrect because of future scientific and technological findings. They would not be as interested as the essentialists, for example, in teaching students how to use current forms of computer technology.

Like progressivists, perennialists criticize the vast amount of discrete factual information that educators traditionally have required students to absorb. Perennialists urge schools to spend more time teaching about concepts and explaining how these concepts are meaningful to students. Particularly at the high school and university levels, perennialists decry undue reliance on textbooks and lectures to communicate ideas. Perennialists suggest that a greater emphasis be placed On teacher-guided seminars, where students and teachers engage in Socratic dialogues, or mutual inquiry sessions, to develop an enhanced understanding of history's most timeless concepts. In addition, perennialists recommend that students learn directly from reading and analyzing the Great Books. These are the creative works by history's finest thinkers and writers, which perennialists believe are as profound, beautiful, and meaningful today as when they were written.

Perennialists lament the change in universities over the centuries from places where students (and teachers) pursued truth for its own sake to mere glorified training grounds for the students' careers. University students may learn a few trees, perennialists claim, but many will be quite ignorant about the forests: the timeless philosophical questions.

PROGRESSIVISM

Progressivism's respect for individuality, its high regard for science, and its receptivity to change harmonized well with the American environment in which it was created. The person most responsible for the success of progressivism was John Dewey. Dewey entered the field of education as a liberal social reformer with a background in philosophy and psychology. In 1896, while a professor at the University of Chicago, Dewey founded the famous Laboratory School as a testing ground for his educational ideas. Dewey's writings and his work with the Laboratory School set the stage for the progressive education movement, which, beginning in the 1920s, has produced major lasting innovations in American education.

The progressivist movement stimulated schools to broaden their curricula, making education more relevant to the needs and interests of students. Its influence waned during the 1950s, particularly after the 1957 launching of Sputnik by the Soviets prompted schools to emphasize traditional instruction in math, science, foreign languages, and other defense-related subjects. In the late 1960s and 1970s, under the guise of citizenship education and educational relevance, many of Dewey's ideas enjoyed a renewed popularity that decreased again during the education reform movement of the 1980s.

Roots of Progressivism

Dewey regarded the physical universe as real and fundamental. He also claimed that the one constant truth about the universe is the existence of change. For Dewey, change was not an uncontrollable force; rather, it could be directed by human intelligence. He explained that as we alter our relationship with our environment, we ourselves are made different by the experience.

Dewey not only believed in the existence of change but welcomed it. He regarded the principles of democracy and freedom espoused in America as representing tremendous progress over the political ideas of earlier times. Nevertheless, Dewey found much that was wrong with American society, and he had little affection for the traditional American approach to education. He hoped that his school reforms would alter the social fabric of America, making it a more democratic nation of free thinking, intelligent citizens.

Dewey taught that people are social animals who learn well through active interplay with others and that our learning increases when we are engaged in activities that have meaning for us. Book learning, to Dewey, was no substitute for actually doing things. Fundamental to Dewey's epistemology is the notion that knowledge is acquired and expanded as we apply our previous experiences to solving new, meaningful problems. Education, to Dewey, is a reconstruction of experience, an opportunity to apply previous experiences in new ways. Relying heavily on the scientific method, Dewey proposed a five step method for solving problems:

1. Become aware of the problem;
2. Define it;
3. Propose various hypotheses to solve it;
4. Examine the consequences of each hypothesis in the light of previous
5. Experience; and
6. Test the most likely solution.

Progressivism in the Classroom

Believing that people learn best from what they consider most relevant to their lives, progressivists center the curriculum around the experiences, interests, and abilities of students. Teachers plan lessons that arouse curiosity and push the students to a higher level of knowledge. In addition to reading textbooks, the students must learn by doing Often students leave the classroom for fieldtrips during which they interact with nature or society. Teachers also stimulate the students' interests through thought-provoking games. For example, modified forms of the board game Monopoly have been used to illustrate the principles of capitalism and socialism.

In a progressivist school, students are encouraged to interact with one another and to develop social virtues such as cooperation and tolerance for different points of view. Also, teachers feel no compulsion to focus their students' attentions on one discrete discipline at a time, and students may be responsible for learning lessons that combine several different subjects.

Progressivists emphasize in their curriculum the study of the natural and social sciences. Teachers expose students to many new scientific, technological, and social developments, reflecting the progressivist notion that progress and change are fundamental. Students are also exposed to a more democratic curriculum that recognizes accomplishments of women and minorities as well as white males. In addition, students solve problems in the classroom similar to those they will encounter outside of the schoolhouse; they learn to be flexible problem solvers.

Progressivists believe that education should be a perpetually enriching process of ongoing growth, not merely a preparation for adult lives. They also deny the essentialist belief that the study of traditional subject matter is appropriate for all students, regardless of interest and personal experience. By including instruction in industrial arts and home economics, progressivists strive to make schooling both interesting and useful. Ideally, the home, workplace, and schoolhouse blend together to generate a continuous, fulfilling learning experience in life. It is the progressivist dream that the dreary, seemingly irrelevant classroom exercises that so many adults recall from childhood will someday become a thing of the past.

EXISTENTIALISM

The existentialist movement in education is based on an intellectual attitude that philosophers term existentialism. Born in nineteenth-century Europe, existentialism is associated with such diverse thinkers as Kierkegaard, a passionate Christian, and Nietzsche who wrote a book entitled The Antichrist and coined the phrase God is dead. While the famous existentialists would passionately disagree with one another on many basic philosophical issues, what they shared was a respect for individualism. In particular, they argued that traditional approaches to philosophy do not adequately respect the unique concerns of each individual.

Jean Paul Sartre's classic formulation of existentialism—that "existence precedes essence"—means that there exists no universal, inborn human nature. We are born and exist, and then we ourselves freely determine our essence (that is, our innermost nature). Some philosophers commonly associated with the existentialist tradition never fully adopted the "existence precedes essence" principle. Nevertheless, that principle is fundamental to the educational existentialist movement.

Just as its namesake sprang from a strong rejection of traditional philosophy, educational existentialism sprang from a strong rejection of the traditional, essentialist approach to education. Existentialism rejects the existence of any source of objective, authoritative truth about metaphysics, epistemology, and ethics. Instead, individuals are responsible for determining for themselves what is "true" or "false," "right" or "wrong," "beautiful" or "ugly." For the existentialist, there exists no universal form of human nature; each of us has the free will to develop as we see fit.

In the existentialist classroom, subject matter takes second place to helping the students understand and appreciate themselves as unique individuals who accept complete responsibility for their thoughts, feelings, and actions. The teacher's role is to help students define their own essence by exposing them to various paths they may take in life and creating an environment in which they may freely choose their own preferred way. Since feeling is not divorced from reason in decision making, the existentialist demands the education of the whole person, not just the mind.

Although many existentialist educators provide some curricular structure, existentialism, more than other educational philosophies, affords students great latitude in their choice of subject matter. In an existentialist curriculum, students are given a wide variety of options from which to choose.

To the extent that the staff, rather than the students, influence the curriculum, the humanities are commonly given tremendous emphasis. They are explored as a means of providing students with vicarious experiences that will help unleash their own creativity and self-expression. For example, rather than emphasizing historical events, existentialists focus upon the actions of historical individuals, each of whom provides possible models for the students' own behavior. In contrast to the humanities, math and the natural sciences may be de-emphasized, presumably because their subject matter would be considered "cold," "dry," "objective," and therefore less fruitful to self-awareness.

Moreover, vocational education is regarded more as a means of teaching students about themselves and their potential than of earning a livelihood. In teaching art, existentialism encourages individual creativity and imagination more than copying and imitating established models. Existentialist methods focus on the individual. Learning is self-paced, self directed, and includes a great deal of individual contact with the teacher, who relates to each student openly and honestly. Although elements of existentialism occasionally appear in public schools, this philosophy has found wider acceptance in private schools and ill alternative public schools founded in the late 1960s and early 1970s.

RECONSTRUCTION

Although reconstruction finds some of its roots in existentialism, it is primarily grounded in the work of progressivists. The commonalities are found in the beliefs that everything in the world is relative and that human beings process that world in order to understand and change it. Reconstruction differs from progressivism in the area of educational roles Unlike the perennialists, who emphasize the transmitting of the knowledge of the existing culture, and the progressivists, who emphasize evaluating the existing culture, the reconstructionists want to transform the existing culture based upon their analysis of its inequities and fundamental flaws.

They are critical of contemporary society and are viewed as social activists who address international as well as national concerns. If human beings are to become change agents, they must be equipped to do so; reconstructionists believe it is the responsibility of the school to provide them with the tools that will enable them to transform the contemporary world.

Most of the reconstructionist literature is found in the works of George Counts, Theodore Brameld, Ivan Illich, and Paulo Freire. The work of Counts provided the key issue for reconstructionism when he posed the question, "Dare the school build a new social order?" His concern that America's schools did not serve the needs of most of the children arose from the impact of the Great Depression in the 1930s and his belief that only a small, favored group was being prepared for the challenges of a technological and global future. One could argue that Counts was well ahead of his time when he wrote in 1952:

> The supreme task of the present and the coming generation in all countries, surpassing any domestic issue, is the development of the institutions, the outlook, the morality

and the defenses of a world community. All geographical barriers, including distance, have been surmounted. Retreat into the past is impossible; perpetuation of the present means chaos and disaster. He further believed that teachers play a critical role in shaping culture, for if they are interested in the lives of children—the central responsibility with which they are charged by the state—they must work boldly and without ceasing for a better social order.

Brameld championed the educational role of transforming the existing culture and the need for students to be able to establish useful goals. In his work, Education for the Emerging Age, Brameld suggested that we "give (goals or objectives) not for the sake of credits or even knowledge as such; we give them so that people of all races, creeds, classes, and cultures may realize a more satisfying life for themselves and their fellows. Knowledge, training, skill — all these are means to the end of such social self-realization."

FACES OF COMMUNICATIVE PEDAGOGY

Educators of very different times and places share a common intuition about the educational relationship. They want it to be — or at least want it to become — an equal and symmetrical relationship. For this reason they refer to this relationship using such terms as "dialogue" and "communication." There is at least one obvious reason for this intuition, grounded in the fact that the educational relationship is a relationship between human beings. The argument is that the educational relationship cannot and should not be reduced to a merely instrumental, manipulative, or what Habermas calls a strategic relationship, because this would ignore the personhood — or at least the emerging personhood — of the child. Kant has expressed the assumption behind this argument very explicitly in his second formulation of the Categorical Imperative, where he argues that, because "man exists as an end in itself," he must in all actions be regarded not merely as a means but always "at the same time as an end."

Basically, educators have taken up the challenge implied in this intuition in two different ways. On the one hand, there are those who endorse the Kantian maxim but at the same time argue that the child is not yet capable of real dialogue and real communication. For them this capacity is the very sign of adulthood and therefore it is postulated as the intended outcome of education. Education itself is presented as a kind of trajectory which sets out as manipulation and eventually develops into communication.

The other position is held by educators who do not merely want to anticipate the child's communicative and dialogical competency by treating it, for example, as a useful practical fiction. They want to acknowledge this capacity within the very process of education itself. Consequently, they treat education as real dialogue or real communication. Although the communicative conception seems to express an empirical impossibility, this has by no means prevented educators from developing, supporting, promoting and practicing some form of communicative pedagogy. The field is densely populated and contains a wide range of different options, from the dialogical pedagogy of Martin Buber and "critical-communicative pedagogy" of Klaus Schaller, through positions inspired by Socrates, Hans-Georg Gadamer, John Dewey and Jürgen Habermas, to German "anti-pedagogy" and the work of Paulo Freire.

Now the intriguing question is, Why is communicative pedagogy flourishing? Do adherents of communicative pedagogy think that they can ignore the "brute facts of child development?" If so, is there any reasonable ground for this? Or must we conclude that adherents of communicative pedagogy simply act irrationally?

Friedrich Kron reconstructs three phases in the development of the way in which the educational relationship has been theorized in German educational philosophy. The interesting thing about Kron's reconstruction is not only that it documents a trajectory from a manipulative to a communicative conception of education. He also offers a conceptual framework for specifying the exact difference between manipulative and communicative pedagogy.

Kron starts with Wilhelm Dilthey, who in 1894 declares that "the science of education has to start with a description of the educator in his relation to the educated, as what is first of all needed is a depiction of the educational phenomenon itself.". Although Dilthey acknowledges that "education is a function of society," he adds that this function can only be realized in a personal relationship between the educator and the educated. In this relationship the intentional activities of the educator are thought to coincide with the "educatibility" of the child.

Herman Nohl, a student of Dilthey, holds a similar position. For him the foundation of education is situated in the "educative community" ("Bildungsgemeinschaft") between a mature and an immature human being. This relationship exists for the sake of the child, so that he can come "to his own life and form." Where Dilthey — following Herbart — talks about educatibility, Nohl refers to the child's "will to be educated" ("Bildungswille").

Kron argues that this "classical" conception of the educational relationship —which was dominant in German pedagogy at least until the sixties — has two central characteristics. First of all, the educational relationship is characterized by a one-directional or unilateral intentionality. Education is seen as an intentional activity, but it is only the educator who has intentions, not the educated. The latter is only "educatible." The second characteristic is what Kron refers to as negative anthropology. The Dilthey-Nohl conception defines the child in negative terms. The child is not yet educated, not yet rational, not yet competent to communicate, not yet really intentional, etc. Taken together, these two characteristics depict the educational relationship as a structurally asymmetrical relationship in which the personhood of the immature child is produced by the intentional activities of the mature adult.

In the second phase — in which the philosophy of Existentialism plays a central role — the "idealized" Dilthey-Nohl conception is replaced by a more "realistic" one. The most important theoretical shift occurs with respect to intentionality: the idea of unilateral intentionality is replaced by the idea of "broken" intentionality. It is acknowledged that the educator can fail in his pedagogical activities because the child is not just "willing material." This means that the child's personhood is no longer thought to be exclusively constituted by the intentional actions of the adult. Educational authority is supplemented by educational impotence, educational love and responsibility by fear and despair. This has repercussions for the anthropological underpinning of education.

In a sense, educator and educated are in the same anthropological position. Kron calls it a "radical equality of opportunity" in that the child and the adult are both "thrown into existence." Although the two central characteristics of the first phase are undermined, representatives of the second phase do not come to a theoretical articulation of their position. The reason for this is very well expressed by Otto Bollnow, who argues that the fallibility of education can only be existentially experienced; it cannot be put into theory.

This does happen, however, in the third phase, where the leading paradigm is Symbolic Interactionism. From this perspective education is no longer understood as manipulation of the behavior or the behavioural dispositions of the child; education is considered to be a process of social interaction, constituted by the interpretive actions of all participants. This entails a crucial theoretical shift, as the educational relationship is now understood as a two-directional or bilateral intentional process. This also has anthropological implications, because the child is no longer seen as, by definition, deficient. Bilateral intentionality entails a positive anthropology.

Kron's reconstruction offers a conceptual framework for specifying what is at stake in the shift from a manipulative to a communicative conception of education. In terms of this framework it is a shift from unilateral to bilateral intentionality and, correspondingly, from an negative to a positive anthropology. While in the first position, the personhood of the child is thought to be dependent upon the intentional activities of the educator, the second position envisages education as a process constituted by the intentionality of both the educator and the educandee.

THE ETHICAL VARIETY OF COMMUNICATIVE PEDAGOGY

Although Kron gives a clear idea of what is at stake in a communicative conception of education, one crucial distinction within the field of communicative pedagogy remains invisible. A fine example of the ethical variety has recently been given by Nicholas Burbules in his book Dialogue in Teaching. Burbules characterizes his book as a description and a defence of a particular educational ideal, namely, dialogue.

Dialogue is described as "a particular kind of pedagogical communicative relation: a conversational interaction directed intentionally towards teaching and learning," which implies that not every interaction between human beings counts as dialogue. Burbules stresses that dialogue is "non-teleological" in that it has no pre-determined outcome. Also, dialogue "tends toward a decentered and non authoritarian view of learning," as it is not aimed at changing other people but at effecting a change in and by the participants themselves. The communicative foundations of dialogue are found in the fact that language, reason, morality and our social organization — and here Burbules refers to Bakhtin, Vygotsky, Habermas and Dewey — are thought to be thoroughly dialogical and relational in character.

Although Burbules argues for a dialogical type of education, he is well aware that there is no guarantee that the practice of education will ever conform to this educational ideal. Dialogue might therefore best be understood as a kind of "critical reference point." Crucial for Burbules's position is his claim that it is not an unrealistic or utopian reference point.

The benefit of communicative norms such as dialogue...is not that they represent abstract ideals to which we should aspire, but that they exemplify implicit values that we actually do hold, that are latent in the practices in which we are actually engaged. In this, they function as reminders of standards that are necessarily implied by what we do and by what we say we want.

Elsewhere in his book, Burbules stretches this argument a bit further when he writes that according to Habermas the essential feature of communication towards understanding is that it entails an implicit commitment to certain standards...that can be invoked by either partner in conversation.

Throughout his book Burbules stresses that dialogue depends upon "the commitment that joins interlocutors in an ongoing communicative relation." Therefore, successful dialogue involves a willing partnership and cooperation in the fact of likely disagreements, confusions, failures and misunderstandings. Persisting in this process requires a relation of mutual respect, trust, and concern — and part of the dialogical interchange often must relate to the establishment and maintenance of these bonds.

This shows that the dialogical relation is not exhausted by a cognitive interest; the "affective qualities of concern and commitment that draw us into dialogue" and "the capacity of dialogue to involve us and carry us beyond our intentions" are all aspects of the dialogical relation.

As Burbules's point is that dialogue depends upon "a commitment to the process of communicative interchange itself," it does not come as a surprise that the development and fostering of such a commitment is taken as a crucial step towards a dialogical educational practice. Here Burbules introduces the notion of "communicative virtues," which include such qualities as "tolerance, patience, an openness to give and receive criticism, the inclination to admit that one might be mistaken, the desire to reinterpret or translate one's own concerns...the self-imposition of restraint in order that others may have a turn to speak, and...the willingness to listen thoughtfully and attentively."

Burbules sees the relationship between the communicative virtues and dialogue as a reciprocal one. Whether dialogue will happen, depends upon the communicative virtues of the interacting partners; but it is precisely by means of dialogue that these virtues are developed. On the one hand, this means that the communicative virtues constitute "significant educational aims in their own right." On the other hand, it implies that education itself is a process of "initiation" into dialogical relationships. This is thought of as a "bootstrapped process," because for Burbules it makes no sense to wait for ideal conditions to happen. "We improve by imitating, practicing, and experimenting in the midst of real-time activities."

There can be no doubt that Burbules's position is a specimen of communicative pedagogy. Dialogue is not something to happen after the child has been educated; education itself should be dialogical. Further, Burbules defines dialogue in terms of a bilateral intentionality, which suggests that it is backed by a positive anthropology. Burbules's position a specimen of the ethical variety of communicative pedagogy is twofold. First it should be noted — and this is by no means meant as a disqualification of Burbules's position — that he only gives a "description and defence" of a particular educational ideal. Burbules's point is that we ought to educate in a dialogical way.

THE EMPIRICAL VARIETY OF COMMUNICATIVE PEDAGOGY

While the ethical variety argues that education should be dialogical or communicative, the basic claim of the empirical variety is that education is communication. The difference is not a merely verbal one. What lies behind these claims, are two different anthropological presuppositions, or, to be more precise, two different conceptions about the relationship between subjectivity and intersubjectivity. While the ethical variety understands intersubjectivity as grounded in subjectivity, the empirical variety understands subjectivity as grounded in intersubjectivity.

The ethical variety of communicative pedagogy rests upon an intentional conception of human (inter)action which has its theoretical roots in what Habermas refers to as the tradition of the philosophy of consciousness. This tradition takes the individual, conscious subject as the unproblematic unit of analysis and explains social interaction — including educational interaction — as an achievement of the interacting partners. In this tradition, the individual subject is treated as an independent variable. In the empirical variety precisely this conception of human subjectivity is contested. From the empirical point of view, subjectivity is thought to be in need of an explanation. And the intersubjective, communicative "praxis" is proposed as the independent variable that can do so.

Within philosophy the "intersubjective turn" has, amongst others, been taken by John Dewey, George Herbert Mead and, more recently, by Jürgen Habermas. Habermas has introduced the notion of "communicative action" to refer to the communicative praxis which precedes subjectivity. Although this matrix can be understood ontologically, that is, as the source from which subjectivity emerges, the "paradigm of intersubjectivity" at least entails a methodological rule, namely, that intersubjectivity is the explanatory entity. The claim that education is communication should be understood against this background. This means that it is meant as an alternative for those views of education based upon the — in the eyes of the empirical variety problematical —presuppositions of the philosophy of consciousness. Both positions presuppose the existence of intentional subjects. The only difference is that manipulative pedagogy denies that the child already has intentions of its own, while the ethical variety of communicative pedagogy holds that the child should be treated as having real intentions.

Although Kron is right in arguing that the difference between the two positions can be specified in terms of unilateral versus bilateral intentionality, we can now add that in both cases intentionality — and thus the existence of intentional subjects — is presupposed. From this point of view, the split is not between manipulative and communicative pedagogy, but between manipulative pedagogy and the ethical variety of communicative pedagogy on the one hand, and the empirical variety on the other.

The key question of course is what the intersubjective turn exactly implies for our understanding of education. The definitive answer to this question has not yet been given; so far there have only been very few attempts to make this connection. The first issue concerns the claim of adherents of manipulative pedagogy that education-as-manipulation is the means by which the "Palace of Communication" can and must be reached. The claim of the empirical variety of communicative pedagogy is that precisely this community is the basis for any interaction at all. In this sense community — or communication — is not only thought to precede all education, but is in fact a constitutive precondition, or what might be called a transcendental precondition, of education.

The suggestion that education has a non-intentional communicative basis, can also be clarified by means of the difference between the intention and the meaning of an act. In the manipulative account, it is presumed that the intentions behind the actions of the educator coincide with their meaning. From the perspective of the empirical variety, it is argued that there is no reason whatsoever to assume such a coincidence between intention and meaning. The meaning of an act is brought about in the communicative praxis in which this act plays a role. It is therefore (by definition) intersubjective.

Educational actions are not excluded from this, and the adherents of Kron's second phase were well aware of this fact. But neither they, nor the adherents of Symbolic Interactionism were able to articulate this intuition in a non-intentionalistic way.

Empirical communicative pedagogy, however, is able to do away with this "intentionalistic bias," by arguing that intersubjective meaning overrides subjective intention. Manipulative pedagogy simply acknowledges this and consequently sees education as a structurally asymmetrical — and paradoxical — enterprise. In the ethical variety of communicative pedagogy, the problem is circumvented. This is most clearly shown in Kron's discussion of Symbolic Interactionism, where it is argued that education has a lower limit in what is known as the "phase of stubbornness." This stubbornness is thought to be the first sign of the intentionality of the child; from there education can supposedly take off.

IDEOLOGY, INDOCTRINATION, AND LEARNING COMMUNITIES

In Educating Reason, Harvey Siegel argues for a "reasons conception" of critical thinking as the ideal of education. According to this account critical thinking is none other than the ability and the willingness to decide what to believe and how to behave on the basis of good reasons. Since critical thinking is advanced as the educational ideal, education according to this view is about becoming more rational. This account of the role that critical rationality plays in education is of great import to those who find fault with dogmatic and doctrinaire approaches to the transmission of culture, such as may be found among fundamentalist religious groups or totalitarian regimes. If there is to be a difference between education and indoctrination, between liberal and doctrinaire conceptions of cultural transmission, then something like Siegel's account must be correct.

Siegel offers four arguments in support of his "reasons conception of critical thinking" as an educational ideal, based on notions of respect, empowerment, traditions of inquiry, and democratic citizenship. Inherent in the justification that he does provide, however, is a way of thinking about the significance of critical rationality in education that is plausible, at least to those who prize liberal democracy and open society. The adoption of this approach requires a sort of "Copernican revolution" in educational thought by recognizing that we base our commitment to critical rationality on conceptions of the good life for moral persons rather than basing our conceptions of the good on rational justifications. Critical thinking, in other words, is not the educational ideal; it is a tool we use to achieve that ideal. Rationality is not the end in view; it is a means used by educators, among others, to cultivate moral personhood.

THE IDEOLOGY OBJECTION

After careful consideration of the wide variety of ways in which the term "ideology" is used in the scholarly literature, Siegel stipulates that he will regard ideology "as a general framework that shapes individual consciousness, guides and legitimates belief and action, and renders experience meaningful." The objection raised on the basis of ideology, then, is to the idea that critical thinking can be justified independently of ideological commitment, when in fact "ideological commitment is logically prior to a commitment to educational ideals....What counts as a reason depends on what one's ideology recognizes as a reason," so the objection goes. "Rationality itself...is ideology dependent."

This objection is based, Siegel argues, on the premise that ideology shapes consciousness. He dubs this doctrine "ideological determinism," because it holds that ideology rather than reasoning determines belief and behaviour. For the ideological determinist, writes Siegel, "rationality itself is a function of ideology, and what counts as good reason will depend on the ideological stance from which one evaluates reasons." Siegel responds with the following argument:

1. Suppose p is a putative reason for some thesis T.

2. Either (a) p genuinely supports T or (b) it does not.

3. Suppose T is ideological determinism.
4. If p does not genuinely support T (2b), then ideological determinism is no more plausible than its alternative.
5. If p does genuinely support T (2a), then either (a) one's ideology accepts that p genuinely supports T or (b) one's ideology does not accept that p genuinely supports T.
6. If one's ideology does not accept that p genuinely supports T (5b), then p is not a genuine reason for T which contradicts the assumption in premise 5.
7. If one's ideology accepts that p genuinely supports T (5a), then ideological determinism is affirmed which holds that there are no ideology independent reasons that genuinely support T. Since premise 1 supposes that p is such an ideology independent reason, this also contradicts premise 5.
8. Ideological determinism is therefore either arbitrary or self-defeating. It should be rejected.

In Siegel's words:

> The ideological determinist is thus in a bind. Either there exists some good reason for embracing the determinist thesis or not. If there is not, then there is no good reason for embracing that view....If there can be good reason for embracing the thesis, then the thesis is undercut, for asserting that there can be good reason to embrace it is tantamount to asserting that such good reason can be independent of prior ideological commitment - which is just what the thesis denies.....Either way the determinist goes, the determinist thesis must be given up.

The problem with this response, of course, is that it assumes precisely that which is at issue between critical rationalism and ideological determinism, namely, whether reasons are ever independent of ideology. Premise (1) already supposes that p is such an ideology independent reason. Premise (4) puts that supposition to work by assuming that if p does not genuinely support ideological determinism, then the thesis is no more plausible than the alternative. Its acceptance, in Siegel's words. "is arbitrary and without merit."

But this is just what the determinist denies. To the claim that ideological determinism is not supported by adequate reasons, the determinist might respond as follows:

> Who cares? It is you, the rationalist, who insists upon ideology independent reasons to support your theses. As far as I am concerned. my deterministic beliefs are a product of the cultural and political milieu of the late twentieth-century, Western society of which I am a part. My adherence to these views is no more a product of decisions based on reasoning than the language I learned from my parents. Whether or not they are supported by ideology independent reasons is quite beside the point. These beliefs are part of the air I breath, and any reasons I would use to evaluate my beliefs would ultimately support them since those reasons are born of the same air.

Premise (6) also puts Siegel's supposition that p is an ideology independent reason to work by claiming that it contradicts the affirmation of ideological determinism, which of course it does. But this reasoning is possible only because Siegel has presupposed that which he set out to demonstrate in the first place.

In short, the ideologist is in a bind on Siegel's account only if she already accepts the view that Siegel set out to defend, and which the determinist thesis denies, namely, that reason can be independent of ideology. In the absence of that presupposition, the determinist is stung by neither horn of Siegel's dilemma. Indeed, the assumptions of critical rationality seem plausible only to those who already accept them, which would appear to lend support to the determinist thesis.

Missing from Siegel's response to the ideology objection is a justification of rationality that does not itself depend on a prior commitment to the value of reason. This paradox of rationality is, of course, nothing new. But, in claiming that rationality is ideology dependent, the ideological determinist reminds us of this paradox; and short of some solution to it, the independence of reason from ideology is surely in doubt.

Unfortunately, critical rationality appears to fair no better in responding to the indoctrination objection. After carefully reviewing the standard approaches to indoctrination that see it as stemming from the intentions, methods, or content, Siegel follows Green in depicting indoctrination as the promotion of a non-evidential style of belief. In Siegel's words:

> If a belief is held non-evidentially - that is in such a way that it is held without regard to evidence relevant to its rational assessment...then the belief is an indoctrinated one....Indoctrination may be regarded as the collection of those modes of belief inculcation which foster a non-evidential...style of belief.

Indoctrination, then, "whatever else it may be, is anti-critical." It would be a problem for critical thinking as an educational ideal, therefore, were indoctrination to be inevitable. Yet some argue that this is precisely the case. Indeed, they claim not only that indoctrination is inevitable in general, but that the non-evidential inculcation of the value of critical thinking is inevitable in particular. In Siegel's words once again,

> If this value must be indoctrinated, the students must be unable to embrace it on its merits...Either the value of critical thinking would not...be rationally supportable; or...the student would not accept the values for reasons that...support it. Either way, the student is not valuing critical thinking critically.

In sum, if indoctrination is inevitable, then critical thinking is impossible. But is indoctrination inevitable? This is the question that Siegel sets out to answer in responding to this objection.

Siegel admits that inculcation is indeed inevitable since all societies inculcate ideas in youngsters whose rational capacities are limited by their stage of development. This having been said, as children grow intellectually, the nonrational grounds on which they base their ideas can sometimes be replaced with good reasons. Siegel calls ideas of this kind "redeemable by reasons." The difference between indoctrination and nonrational belief inculcation, then, is that indoctrinated ideas are not redeemable, inculcated ideas are. As Siegel put it, "if indoctrinated, the belief cannot be redeemable, if redeemable, it cannot have been indoctrinated."

The problem with this response arises when we ask whether critical rationality is itself redeemable by reasons. Having inculcated the child to accept the assumptions and values of critical thinking, can it be supposed that the plausibility of those assumptions and values are themselves justifiable, such that the nonrational grounds upon which the child initially based her commitment to rationality could later be replaced by good reasons?

As we have seen, the answer to these queries is yes only if one already accepts the assumptions and values of rationality. But the child who has truly imbibed the assumptions of rationality will not allow such a vicious circle in seeking to replace her nonrational grounds for this commitment with good reasons. Rather, to shed the nonrational basis of her conviction, she will require that any justification must convince, without presupposing that which it endeavors to demonstrate; and this sort of justification for rationality is again absent from Siegel's analysis.

Since Siegel offers no solution to the paradox of rationality's rationality, there is no basis for the claim that critical thinking is redeemable by reasons; and if the very process of reasoning is itself nonredeemable, there is also no basis to the belief that reasons are capable of redeeming any other commitments a child might be inculcated to adopt. In short, Siegel's distinction between indoctrination and belief inculcation collapses because rationality is not redeemable; and with the collapse of this distinction, we are left with the inevitability of indoctrination, and the consequent impossibility of critical thinking.

SIEGEL'S RESPONSE

Siegel has responded to this sort of critique. If the determinist claims that the rationalist has not properly justified his position concerning the value of reasons, Siegel argues that she has in fact already accepted the very claim for which a justification is being demanded; for the call for a justification presupposes that such a rational account is required for the rationalist position to be worthy of accent. In Siegel's words:

> The skeptic is herself asking our question. She is asking: "Why be rational?" that is, she is asking for reasons which justify the rationalist's commitment to rationality. She is suggesting that if reasons cannot be adduced which justify the rationalists's position, then that position fails to be justified and so fails legitimately to command the rationalist's respect.

Rationality, then, is self justifying according to Siegel, "in that seriously querying the justificatory status of rationality presupposes that very status. In order to seriously question the value or justificatory status of rationality," Siegel continues, "one must assume the relevance of considerations which rationally support one or another answer to the question; in so assuming, one is presupposing the rationalist's position."

If, on the other hand, the determinist does not offer such a call for a justification, then, according to Siegel, she has not in fact joined the issue with her rationalist opponent. If she simply refuses the rationalist's gambit by stating "I don't care whether or not your position or any other is justified because it is you the rationalist not I who is concerned about reasons," then there is no real dispute between them. The determinist or ideologist has not entered the debate. "What I think I've shown," wrote Siegel in private correspondence, "is that any dispute about the justificatory status of rationality will involve the disputants in a prior commitment to the value of reasons. Such a commitment is a requirement of engaging in the dispute."

Siegel agrees that if the determinist does not care to join the issue with the rationalist, there is nothing of a rational nature that the latter can do to convince her to do so. Indeed, reasons are simply irrelevant to such a person. Hence, it is unclear why Siegel holds that rationality is self justifying, when by his own account it is justified only to those who already accept its justificatory power. Put differently, rationality is self-justifying to those who already accept rationality as justified. The rationalist's arguments are convincing only to those who already accept them. Robert Ennis put it this way:

> Unfortunately, even if this ploy did work to show that the questioner is committed to rationality, it would not constitute a justification of rationality. It would only show that the questioner, by presupposing rationality, is committed to it. Suppose Siegel's enemy does not even bother to ask for the justification of rationality, but goes merrily on in his or her irrational way. Then no justification for rationality has been presented.

"The question," wrote Siegel again in private correspondence, is whether the determinist can, "establish the rightness of her view, or the wrongness of mine." But the determinist is out to establish neither the rightness of her view nor the wrongness of Siegel's, since she has in fact rejected the very utility of such categories as right and wrong. It is the rationalist, therefore, who is out to establish the rightness of his view and the wrongness of the determinist's. And this, according to Siegel's own account, cannot be accomplished unless the rightness of rationality is already agreed to in the first place.

Siegel has not shown, therefore, that there is a rational basis for the belief in the value of good reasons that can appeal to those who lie outside of a community of discourse that already accepts their value. Consequently, his responses to the ideology and indoctrination objections fail. The question remains, however, whether Siegel has not demonstrated something of value for those who function within that community of discourse.

CRITICAL THINKING RECONSIDERED

To see what Siegel has demonstrated, it will be useful to distinguish between two kinds of rationalism and two approaches to ideology. Dogmatic rationalists tend to believe that they possess absolute truth because their methods of both discovery and justification are unassailable. Since this group generally believes that there is one best interpretation of data, one best reading of texts, one best answer to most questions, provided the proper methods are employed, those who accept other interpretations, readings, or answers are viewed with suspicion and mistrust.

These dogmatic ideologists often accept a Marxian analysis which holds that their is no truth, and that what passes for knowledge is nothing more than the propaganda used to justify the actions of those in power. There is no difference between rationalism and rationalization. All versions of rationalism, therefore, are merely the ideologies of those who claim the privileges of power. Thinking that is genuinely critical will attempt to empower those denied access to such privileges by exposing the arbitrary, and where appropriate, oppressive character of these rationalisms.

Siegel's arguments against ideology and indoctrination will not convince dogmatic ideologists of the merits of critical rationality because they view Siegel's reasons conception of critical thinking as no less dogmatic than other rationalisms. It is they who will simply refuse to accept the idea that a doctrine that lacks sufficient rational support is no more arbitrary than one that does not. Dogmatic versions of both rationalism and ideology, then, are essentially incommensurable.

There are approaches to both rationalism and ideology, however, that are not dogmatic. Pragmatic rationalism shares, with its dogmatic counterpart, a commitment to the value of critical thinking in the pursuit of truth and goodness. It differs from dogmatism, however, in at least two ways: First, it tends to be committed to a more robust fallibilism. According to dogmatic rationalism, doctrines which we hold true today might be proven false tomorrow through the consistent application of appropriate methods of discovery. This view tends to be less willing than pragmatism to subject methods of discovery and justification to critical scrutiny. For pragmatic rationalism, not only truth, but also method is fallible.

Second, dogmatic rationalism tends to see rationality as an end-in-itself. Pragmatic rationalism, on the other hand; sees critical thinking as a means to more important ends. To illustrate this distinction, consider Siegel's four arguments for critical thinking as an educational ideal. According to one of these arguments, critical thinking is needed to initiate students into the community of inquirers. This argument views rationality as an end-in-view, since it claims that learning to reason is valuable because it leads to further reasoning. Here, Siegel's rationalism tends to be more dogmatic, since as we have seen, he offers no successful justification for such a commitment.

According to Siegel's other three arguments, however, critical thinking is praised because it promotes respect for persons, self-sufficiency, and democratic society. Here, rationality is not the end-in-view, it is a means to achieve moral and political ends. One could, of course, claim that these values are themselves rationally justifiable. Here, Siegel's rationalism tends to be more pragmatic. Unlike their dogmatic counterparts, pragmatic approaches to ideology have not completely abandoned the possibility of truth. Although they accept that knowledge can be used as a tool of oppression, they do not reduce it to propaganda for rationalizing the actions of the powerful.

Rather, they are concerned that those who have the power to advance their own interpretations of the universe fail to understand that all interpretations are under-determined by the facts, and that there are many ways to understand experience that are consistent with reality as it is presented to consciousness. For this reason, alternative ways of conceiving human realities and the people who adhere to them are too often not afforded sufficient respect.

Whereas dogmatic versions of rationalism and ideology appear to be incompatible, pragmatic versions of these two doctrines do not. On the contrary, they seem to share common commitments to respect for persons, empowerment, and democratic living. They differ, however, over whether critical rationality is a help or a hindrance toward these ends.

Although pragmatic ideologists sometimes argue at crosspurposes with rationalism, they do not completely reject rationality. Rather, they reject its misuse for immoral and politically undesirable ends. Hence, ideologists of this sort would not remain silent or respond with, "Who cares?" when the likes of Siegel point out that, without justification, their position is without merit. On the contrary, they see their position as making a truth claim, if also a political one; and they seek to support that claim with relevant reasons and not merely with plays for power.

In short, pragmatic rationalists and ideologists share a community of discourse that is not shared by the dogmatists; one that begins with a common conception of human beings as moral persons, and with a vision of human communities as promoting the good for moral persons. According to this conception, humans possess free will, that is, the capacity in many situations to decide of their own volition what they wish to believe and how they choose to behave. They also posses the capacity to understand their circumstances with sufficient intelligence to make decisions about beliefs and behaviors that can contribute to accomplishing the ends they deem desirable.

Because of these capacities, humans can be held responsible for the consequences of those choices; because of these capacities, it is possible to talk about whether those choices are right or wrong, and because of these capacities, human life in all of its potential is intrinsically valuable. Without people who are intelligent and free it would be nonsense to speak of values altogether.

It would not be inappropriate to refer to this as a broadly liberal conception of the human condition - although its roots in the West are to be found first in the Hebrew Bible which is too often inappropriately seen as endorsing conceptions of the good that are anything but liberal. Communities, according to this liberal conception, are capable of promoting opportunities for people to enhance their moral personhood, both as individuals and as groups, by exercising their intelligence and their free will. Communities of this type require a commitment to learning in order to enhance the exercise of free will toward desired ends. This sort of learning requires standards of rationality akin to those advanced by Siegel. It also requires traditions of inquiry that will record what has been learned for transmission across the generations.

It is within the context of this sort of community of discourse that Siegel's arguments against ideological determinism and indoctrination make sense, because pragmatic ideologists cannot duck the requirement of providing good reasons to support their position. To make this case, Siegel would have to demonstrate that liberal conceptions of moral personhood and community would be better served by means of critical thinking than unchecked ideological pluralism. At least three of the arguments he advances in defense of his reasons conception, those rooted in respect, empowerment, and democratic citizenship, are the basis for such a case.

Dogmatic rationalism tends to accept this liberal view. However, unlike pragmatic rationalism, it holds that this view is rationally justifiable rather than being the basis for the justification of rationality; it is based on reasons rather than being the basis of reasoning. As has been argued, this position cannot withstand rational scrutiny.

Dogmatic ideologists, on the other hand, tend to reject this liberal conception of the human condition because they believe that human behaviour and belief are determined by history, politics, or environment, rather than by the choices people make. People, according to this doctrine, are not moral persons: they are amoral because they cannot be held responsible for their behaviour, since it was determined by forces outside of themselves. Any discussion of good or bad behaviour is literally nonsense, in this view, since the origin of the behaviour is not a moral agent, but rather, history, politics, or environment.

Dogmatic conceptions of ideology, then, are not only incommensurable with all varieties of rationalism, they are incommensurable with pragmatic conceptions of ideology as well. Although there may be no refuting the dogmatic ideologist on rational grounds, this analysis has uncovered a choice between two clear alternatives - at least for those who believe that we are capable of choice - between an irrefutable, amoral dogmatism, on the one hand, and on the other, a community of discourse in which the possibility of moral discussion is preserved. In the former, the distinction between education and indoctrination collapses; in the latter it does not.

INTELLECTURAL FOUNDATION OF TECHNOLOGY EDUCATION

Since the colonial era,, Western institutionalized education increasingly has been put into the service of civilization-building by seeking to advance practical industrial needs. But education has not always had such an explicitly economic orientation. In the early Middle Ages, the purpose of education was conceived of primarily in terms of advancing spiritual well-being, Church- or State-sponsored occupations, and socially "proper" forms of knowledge. Only as European nations embarked upon colonial expansion did education begin to become associated with citizenship, nation-building, practical and secular knowledge, and the advancement of a technological civilization and private enterprise.

As a result, since the eighteenth century, this second school of educational thought has become increasingly dominant in educational thought and practice. Our contemporary understanding of science and technology education owes much to Enlightenment-based assumptions on the nature of civilizational advancement. These assumptions are illustrated in the writings of formative educational thinkers during the eighteenth and nineteenth centuries, especially the works of Antoine-Nicholas de Condorcet and John Dewey.

EDUCATION, TECHNOLOGY, AND CONDORCET

Throughout the Middle Ages, the Renaissance, and the Reformation, nearly all technological innovations took place on an individual craft basis; knowledge was transferred from generation to generation by apprenticeship. Significant technological advancements, such as the clock, the horizontal axle windmill, gigantic Gothic cathedrals, the printing press, and better guns and ships, were being developed outside of the universities. But these advancements, by themselves, did not cause Europeans to rethink their then-dominant understanding of human purpose in relation to spiritual perfection. Nor did the outward expansion of the market economy, which has frequently been identified as the most significant force leading to the Industrial Revolution, cause Europeans to rethink their lofty status.

The growth of the market economy is often tied closely to the growth of secular institutions, government bureaucracies, the availability of raw materials, and early trade with, later exploitation of, non-Western societies. All of these elements, it has been argued, somehow worked together to convince Europeans of the merits of industrialization; that the same development did not occur outside of Europe appears to merely reinforce this perspective. What is generally overlooked, however, is how the Europeans' growing knowledge of distant cultures helped to change their worldview of themselves and their relation to the physical world and other cultures. The Enlightenment was one result of this new orientation; another was the Industrial Revolution; and still another was a growing emphasis on the merits of technology education.

Throughout the seventeenth and eighteenth centuries, higher education in Europe and the emerging power of the United States retained a classical format. The first broadly based engineering university would not be founded until the Ecole Polytechnique was established in France in 1794. During these two centuries, however, Europeans increased their trade and colonial interactions with less technologically advanced cultures, and began to recognize their own cultural superiority in terms of technological achievements. As a result, a fundamental reorientation was beginning to take place concerning the role of technology and the purpose of education in European society.

The French Enlightenment of the eighteenth century built upon the ideas of Francis Bacon and his contemporaries. The Enlightenment was a rejection of both realism and the idea that the greatness of humankind rested in ancient knowledge. While all Enlightenment thinkers believed in certain basic principles, namely, the inherent goodness of humankind, the right to a democratic society, and that civilization must advance through technological progress to a more advanced state of being, only Jean-Jacques Rousseau and Antoine-Nicholas de Condorcet focused on education to any degree, and Condorcet was arguably the more thorough and influential of the two.

During mid-eighteenth century France, education was targeted at the elite, dominated by the Church, and unavailable for most of the population. The universities of France, as in most of Europe, still regarded law, medicine, and theology as the only relevant disciplines in the classical study framework; the Catholic Church and its cohort the French monarchy retained an ever-weakening hegemony in a declining and battle-weary French state. Great Britain was becoming a formidable power in Europe, and would further enhance its position by giving birth to the Industrial Revolution in the middle of the century.

On the other hand, late-eighteenth century France, like Germany and the United States, was becoming increasingly "backward" by comparison, and education was beginning to be seen as a way to catch up with the British. In 1791-92, Condorcet presented a plan for a universal form of education to the French Legislative Assembly, proposing a "complete national system of secular schools to provide equal opportunity for all children, free, compulsory and universal" His plan was rejected at the time, but he put in place germinal ideas for mass education that later would be used in educational planning in France, Germany, and the United States.

Condorcet, like other Enlightenment thinkers, believed that there was no limit to the learning capabilities of the human mind and that progress meant the perfection of science and technology. He also believed that all "men" are products of nature, with equal rights bestowed upon them to the moral, practical, and intellectual pursuits of reason. Human progress, in his view, rested on an individual's ability to educate and refine himself in those three areas of human action. Since colonization had proven the "superiority" of Western technology, such knowledge should be spread to all through the liberating power of education.

In 1793, Condorcet wrote his great essay, Sketch for a Historical Picture of the Progress of the Human Mind; in it, he argued that the human mind must progress from irrationality to rationality, from superstition to reason, from pre-scientific thought to scientific enlightenment. Progress constitutes ten stages of human development, or "civilization." The first stage of civilization is the "savage" tribe, dependent on hunting, fishing, crude weapons, and simple utensils, with little government bureaucracy and only a "small number of moral ideas". Condorcet viewed the African tribe as representative of this first stage of human development, while he placed European-based societies further up the evolutionary ladder:

> Will all nations one day attain that state of civilization which the most enlightened, the freest and the least burdened by prejudices, such as the French and Anglo-Americans, have attained already? Will the vast gulf that separates

> these peoples from the slavery of nations under the rule of monarchs, from the barbarism of African tribes, from the ignorances of savages, little by little disappear?

For Condorcet, as a culture moves from one stage to the next, it develops more advanced technologies and bureaucratic political systems, and exhibits more personal freedoms and democratic principles.

Condorcet's tenth stage of civilization, the last and the greatest, is marked by liberty, equality, democracy and universal education for all. Of all these social developments, education is the most significant to Condorcet because it is the key to all forms of human progress: "With greater equality of education there will be greater equality in industry and so in wealth; equality in wealth necessarily leads to equality in education: and equality between nations and equality within a single nation are mutually dependent". Thus, a "well directed system of education" will result in "progress" in its most basic form and "the absolute perfection of the human race".

Through education, the citizen of the masses might, among other things, be taught to manage their own households, to know their rights and to exercise those rights, to be empowered in the face of those who possess authority, to overcome ignorant prejudices, to use reason to overcome superstition, and to advance the technological arts. Furthermore, Condorcet recognized the need for a linkage between science and the technological arts in education:

> If we turn now to the arts, whose theory depends on [the] sciences, we shall find that their progress depending as it does on that of theory, can have no other limits; that the procedures of the different arts can be perfected and simplified in the same way as the methods of the sciences; new instruments, machines and looms can add to man's strength and can improve at once the quality and the accuracy of his productions, and can diminish the time and labour that has to be expended on them. The obstacles still in the way of this progress will disappear, accidents will be foreseen and prevented, the insanitary conditions

> that are due either to the work itself or the climate will be eliminated.

Given this faith in technology, Condorcet not surprisingly blended his understanding of education, technological progress, and reason with morality and happiness. Human reason and logic, which always work for the betterment of humankind, are responsible for keeping technological development on track. Although technological development might have limits (such as through overpopulation and the lack of food), human reason will solve those problems:

> But even if we agree that the limit will one day arrive, nothing follows from it that is in the least alarming as far as either the happiness of the human race or its indefinite perfectibility is concerned;...we can assume that by then men will know that, if they have a duty towards those not yet born, that duty is not to give them existence but to give them happiness; their aim should be to promote the general welfare of the human race or of the society in which they live or of the family to which they belong, rather than foolishly to encumber the world with useless and wretched beings.

Thus, Condorcet predicted that reason would somehow progress far enough to provide the moral grounding necessary to avoiding overpopulating the world with "useless and wretched beings." Progress, reason, science, technology, and knowledge would collapse into one unified, determining force, since these are the foundations for morality.

Finally, while Condorcet condemned the ignorant prejudices of his day, what he called the "murderous contempt for men of another colour or creed," he was a firm proponent of the civilizing mission of the West. He believed that the Europeans had a duty to civilize those "savage nations who still inhabit vast tracts of land". European missionaries and their "superstitions," he predicted, would disappear, as would the existing practices of trade and colonialism for greed and profit. Instead, enlightened, newly appointed European trade representatives would be assigned to colonial outposts to act as "liberators" to the uncivilized lands of the world; teachers to educate the ignorant:

> These vast lands are inhabited partly by large tribes who need assistance from us to become civilized, who wait only to find brothers amongst the European nations to become their friends and pupils; partly by races oppressed by sacred despots or dull-witted conquerors, and who for so many centuries have cried out to be liberated; partly by tribes living in a condition of almost total savagery in a climate whose harshness repels the sweet blessings of civilization and deters those who would teach them its benefits; and finally, by conquering hordes who know no other law but force, no other profession but piracy. The progress of these two last classes of people will be slower and stormier; and perhaps it will even be that, reduced in number as they are driven back by civilized nations, they will finally disappear imperceptibly before them or merge into them.

Cloaked in Condorcet's colorful prose, the preceding passage advances the notion of European "civilized" cultural superiority. And, although Condorcet condemned the "sacred despots or dull-witted conquerors" of the "oppressed" tribal cultures, he failed to acknowledge the impact of European tyrants. Ironically, the average European peasant was arguably no more liberated than the tribal cultures he criticized.

Condorcet's text was published and widely read after his death in 1794, and his ideas began to be put into practice in the early nineteenth century. But the Enlightenment emerged at a violent time in French and European history, and Condorcet himself was imprisoned as an aristocrat during the French Revolution and died shortly thereafter. Furthermore, the Catholic and Protestant Churches remained powerful stabilizing forces well beyond the Enlightenment and into the nineteenth century. Thus, although Condorcet and the other Enlightenment thinkers had only a minor immediate impact on education in Europe, they planted important seeds of change that would ultimately transform the theory and practice of European and American institutionalized education.

The model for what can now be called "mass" education was put into place by the four Western modernizing powers of the last two centuries: Great Britain, France, Germany, and the United States. The educational systems developed by these nations helped them to realize Condorcet's vision of education, that is, mass education with a technological orientation. Although several factors played a role in the emergence of technology education—the development of the nation-state, the expansion of the market economy, the weakness of the Catholic Church, and other tangible factors—the Enlightenment represented a more crucial repositioning of civilizational advancement. Viewed in these terms, the Industrial Revolution was both a practical manifestation of this changing orientation and a foundational moment in history which helped stimulate other nations to modernize. To illustrate these assertions, I will consider some key points in the development of technology education in the United States in the post-Enlightenment era.

Although the United States is more heavily endowed with natural resources than any of its European counterparts, its ascent to economic superpower over the last century owes much to the expansion of technology education, particularly at the university level. Since the American Revolution of 1776, one of the most dominant and recurrent themes in American educational philosophy has been the motif of Condorcet's concept of "education for citizenship," or education as the *right* of the people. Prominent educational historian R. Freeman Butts notes, "One of the most far-reaching results of Enlightenment theories of education was the development of education for citizenship". Owing much to Enlightenment thought, this theme has also been linked to other Enlightenment ideals, such as the value of natural science, progress, and technological advancement.

From its beginnings, unlike the German version of education as "enlightenment from above," educational practice in the United States exemplified the principle of "enlightenment from below"—the establishment of a universal, free, and compulsory education program under the control of public organizations. Following the American Revolution, Thomas Jefferson, a former ambassador to France sympathetic to early French Enlightenment thought, became the most formidable spokesperson for a state-supported free and universal educational system, and science was one key component of his proposed educational curriculum.

As a starting point, Jefferson introduced his plan to the Virginia legislature in 1779, where, just as Condorcet would later experience in France, it failed to receive enough votes for approval. Subsequently, American education would remain in the hands of private parties, primarily the Church, until well into the nineteenth century. But Jefferson sparked a debate around the purpose of education, and his influence closely paralleled Condorcet's in Europe. By 1818, he had successfully introduced bills that led to the founding of the University of Virginia and the reorganization of William and Mary.

American historian Page Smith has characterized the legacy of Jefferson as introducing an ongoing tension between two forms of "consciousness" that have shaped American educational theory and practice. The first, what he calls the "Classical Christian Consciousness," and what the American Constitution was based on, embodies the long-standing tradition of an ordered universe governed by natural laws and laws governing human beings as defined by God Himself. This consciousness held that "the best thought and experience of the race was a precious heritage that must be preserved as a vital part of the consciousness of the new nation". This consciousness was evident in the long-standing dominance of classical education, with its religious underpinnings and elite nature.

Conversely, the "Secular Democratic Consciousness" embodies the values of the Enlightenment and is characterized by a "faith in limitless progress through reason and science" and "the natural goodness of man once he was free from superstition/religion". The Secular Democratic Consciousness, with Jefferson as its leading spokesperson, would eventually become the predominant consciousness, in spite of the dogma of the early classical college system in America. The new consciousness was initially aided by the pragmatic, skill-oriented teachings of Noah Webster's spelling and grammar books in the late-eighteenth century, the introduction of *McGuffey's Readers* in 1836, and many other similar texts that celebrated American knowledge and sought to create "traditional American values".

McGuffey's Readers eventually sold 100 million copies and for over half a century served as the "principal reading matter" for rural America; young American's were "dazzled" with such stories as "Washington and His Little Hatchet" and "Woodman Spare That Tree". The values espoused by the *Readers* were as much Victorian as American, but they served to inspire "patriotic and moral values" and "loudly proclaimed the glories of resourcefulness and the sadness of indolence".

Yet, the Classical Christian Consciousness remained dominant in education throughout the nineteenth century, and distinct core curriculums, such as programs in engineering and science, and professional majors did not commonly appear until near the turn of the twentieth century. Smith notes that the debate between these two schools of thought "has, indeed, been continual throughout the history of the republic and goes on scarcely diminished to the this day".

Responding to Jeffersonian and pragmatic ideals, by the middle of the nineteenth century, a rising chorus of voices began calling for a public education system, voices including Horace Mann, James G. Carter, Henry Barnard, Calvin Stowe, Caleb Mills, John D. Pierce, Ninian Edwards, Calvin Wiley, and Charles F. Mercer. Foremost among these men was Horace Mann, who was one of the first to put into place a free state educational system for primary schools. Writing in 1847, Mann advanced the "natural rights" theme of Condorcet and argued that education was the "*absolute right* of every human being that comes into the world". Mann held that institutionalized, government-supported free education should be the responsibility of each successive generation. Mann's ideas were influential in moving education away from the lingering classical education for the elites to public education for the masses.

Although aspects of Enlightenment science—including the ideas of Descartes, Newton, Copernicus, Galileo, and Kepler—crept into the curriculums of traditional institutions such as Harvard beginning in the early eighteenth century, technological university-level institutions did not appear for another 100 years. Finally, in the early nineteenth century, Rensselaer Polytechnic Institute and West Point were founded. At first, these schools were regarded as less prestigious than their classical counterparts. By mid-century, however, "catching up" to the European powers became an increasing concern as "the clamor of the modernizers became more insistent, claiming that economic development, industrialization, and urbanization required more and more highly trained manpower". Soon, other initiatives were expanding the opportunities for technological university education, and by 1860, Michigan, Maryland, and Pennsylvania had established agricultural schools.

The voices of modernization reform grew increasingly stronger from then on, as industrialists pushed more fervently for political changes in higher education funding. By 1862, already twenty institutions could be accurately called "scientific schools," but these were insufficient to meet corporate needs. Industrialists' strongly lobbied Congress for more technically oriented schools, and their efforts resulted in the passage of the Morrill Act in 1862. The Act granted federal aid in support of state colleges in agriculture and engineering "in order to promote the liberal and practical education of the industrial classes in the several pursuits and professions of life".

To encourage the rapid building of these schools, a state was required to found a college within five years of the act to secure a grant. In 1890, a second Morrill Act was passed with similar guidelines. As a direct result of these reforms, by 1880 there were 85 college-level engineering schools in the country;

by 1917, there were 126. And the annual number of engineering graduates rose from 100 in 1870 to 4300 by the onset of World War I.

Beginning in the late nineteenth century, one the most powerful calls for modernization, and one that deserves special attention, came from the educational philosophy of John Dewey. Dewey, who would later be highly influential to Chinese and Japanese educators in the early twentieth century, rallied against the lingering dominance of elite and classical education. Deservedly, Dewey is often credited with leading the final assault on American religious and classical education: "As the nineteenth century turned into the twentieth century the experimentation of John Dewey and his followers made it even more difficult for advocates of a closed intellectual system and conventional body of truth to hold their own". In addition, Dewey is still regarded today as *the* proponent of democratic education and education for citizenship philosophies.

Building upon the ideals of Condorcet, Jefferson, and Mann, Dewey wrote in his 1900 essay "Schooling as a Form of Community Life" that school should be thought of as a "miniature community, an embryonic society". As such, Dewey recognized the need for a more "cultural" education, one that combined theory and practice, to help create more well-rounded, intelligent, and adaptable citizens: When the school introduces and trains each child of society into membership within such a little community, saturating him with the spirit of service, and providing him with the instruments of effective self-direction, we shall have the deepest and best guaranty of a larger society which is worthy, lovely, and harmonious.

These general themes throughout Dewey's writings have been continuously resurrected in educational thought and criticism. Dewey's thinking was, and still is, influential in helping to sustain an institutionalized Western education system that would not merely teach skills for a narrowly defined job or function, but also included education for citizenship and experience.

At the root of Dewey's pedagogy is his philosophy of science, a belief that the scientific methodology can be interpreted or translated into educational theory and practice, as well as in terms of human activity. This point has been de-emphasized in many of the more celebratory accounts of Dewey's pedagogy, but it is equally critical to understanding his broad outlook on educational purpose and progress:

> For more than fifty years Dewey was the chief apostle of modernity in American philosophy as well as in American education. He argued that schools should strive to emphasize moral goals based upon democratic civic and social experience, vocational and practical usefulness, and individual development in light of the rapid modernizing changes that were taking place in Western civilization.

Central to Dewey's thinking are the ideas of "logical" reflective thought and objectivity. Everything is subject to objective scientific scrutiny, including morality and values as well as scientific and practical affairs. In fact, working from the Enlightenment as a basis, Dewey refers to knowledge and morality as virtually identical concepts: "Actively to participate in the making of knowledge is the highest prerogative of man". For Dewey, these beliefs are *critical* to human purpose, and all stem from his firm commitment to the scientific methodology: "One of the only two articles that remain in my creed of life is that the future of civilization depends upon the widening spread and deepening hold of the scientific habit of mind"..

At a deeper level, Dewey's perspective on civilizational advancement reflects the Enlightenment bias towards progress and "civilized" versus "savage" cultures. Dewey thus might be characterized as Condorcet's interpreter:

> A savage who has been shipwrecked on a river may note certain things that serve him as signs of danger in the future. But civilized man deliberately *makes* such signs; he sets up in advance of any particular shipwreck warning buoys, and builds lighthouses where he sees signs with great expertness; civilized man institutes a weather service by which signs are artificially secured and information is

> distributed in advance of the appearance of any signs that could be detected with special methods. A savage finds his way skillfully through a wilderness by reading obscure indications; civilized man builds a highway that shows the road to it all.

Although Dewey is saying civilized man uses technology to expand the capabilities inherent in the savage, and is therefore apparently not as harsh as Condorcet, he nonetheless makes a clear distinction between civilized–advanced and uncivilized–primitive based upon relative measures of technological development.

Building "civilization" is important to Dewey, and throughout his writings there is a recurrent preoccupation with the positive aspects of functional, practical tasks—the core of his educational philosophy. For Dewey, only by engaging in and thereby experiencing functional tasks, with scientific understanding, does education become truly meaningful:

> The occupation supplies the child with a genuine motive; it gives him experience at first hand; it brings him into contact with realities. It does all this, but in addition it is liberalized throughout by translation into its historic and social values and scientific equivalent. With the growth of the child's mind in power and knowledge it ceases to be a pleasant occupation merely and becomes more and more a medium, an instrument, an organ—and is thereby transformed.

The pedagogy of Dewey boils down to what he calls the "project method," or the active intellectual pursuit of a project and its scientific basis. Linking scientific theory and technological practice is the key component in Dewey's recommendations on education. Arousing "intellectual interest" is therefore understood by Dewey purely in terms of scientific interest; the net result being that "Theoretical subjects will become more practical, because more related to the scope of life; practical subjects will become more charged with theory and intelligent insight. Both will be vitally and not just formally unified".

In the end, Dewey's legacy is as a key figure in reflecting the undercurrents of turn-of-the-century industrial America, and informing and predicting the growth of the technical disciplines in modern American education. In the twentieth century, the importance of engineering and other technical occupations is signified by the relative prestige of institutions such MIT and the California Institute of Technology. By 1913, the United States had emerged as an industrial power and had replaced Britain as the world leader in coal mining, machine tools, and chemical and automobile production. By that time, the ideal of education for citizenship was virtually inseparable, in practice, from education for practical occupations in the service of industrial needs.

CURRENT TRENDS

The gradual growth of skill-based technology education in the West grew out of an increase in the perceived need for technological advancement and the industrial power-holders need for skilled workers, especially those in engineering and related technical backgrounds. In the twentieth century, all educational disciplines (both technical and non-technical) have been increasingly scrutinized on their "use" value.

In light of the Japanese high-technology competitive advancements and apparent successes in skill-based education, it is not surprising that much contemporary educational literature calls for changes needed to fix the "failing" American education system. Often, the concern in this literature is with developing "correct" educational models that will enhance skill-based learning. Of special importance is more effectively bridging academic and industrial interests, especially in high technology. This is no better illustrated than by the 1995 educational pilot program of the Malcolm Baldrige Quality Award, an award originally designed exclusively for organizational improvement by profit-making companies.

The pilot program is headed by both industrial and university representatives and claims to have been "successfully" tested at all levels of education. The goal of the award is to stimulate educational process improvement using criteria very similar to the corporate quality award. "Education" is defined in practical terms—schools must prove their "effectiveness" through "measurable" results, and "learner-centered" education must account for the "real needs of learners":

> Such needs derive from the requirements of the marketplace and the responsibilities of citizenship. Changes in technology and in the national and world economies are creating increasing demands on employees to become knowledge workers and problem solvers, keeping pace with the rapid changes in the marketplace....A learning-centered school needs to fully understand and translate marketplace and citizenship requirements into appropriate curricula.

Given this foundation for "learning," the underlying emphasis throughout the criteria is the urgent need for building closer ties between education and industry.

It is important to recognize, however, that industrial motivations are also linked to a firm faith in technological progress. Thus, to say that technology education has merely been reduced to industrial needs, as may be exemplified most explicitly by the global proliferation of secondary and post-secondary technical institutes, is to too easily reduce the problem to industrial "interference." Furthermore, although Dewey might now argue that such an approach to education is too rigid and narrow, his definition of "creativity" also falls squarely within the scientific and technological framework—one which might be easily adapted to industrial needs. The fact remains that education and industry have nurtured each other, and it would be difficult to define the contemporary purpose of technology education solely in non-industrial terms.

RETHINKING TECHNOLOGY EDUCATION AND SOCIAL PROGRESS

Since the late Middle Ages, Western education has become widespread and institutionalized out of a historical need for skills. The process of developing and practicing mass education thus has been closely linked with the expansion of Western technological development and the pursuit of progress. Consequently, skill-based education has become critical to the survival of all disciplines, and the closer a program of study is allied to servicing the needs of our technology-driven society, the better.

Western education in the West does offer some students (usually graduate students) the prospect of engaging technology from a critical perspective. A host of humanistic philosophers and social historians in Critical Theory, Cultural Studies, Postmodernism, or other philosophy- and history-based schools of thought have brought into question Western technology and progress. But while the *practice* of technological development in modern Western society marches forward and expands into the third world, the educational attention paid to placing technology into a broader social context is paltry by comparison. Technology studies, as a specific program of study, appears to be just beyond the scope of both the technical and the non-technical disciplines, both of which remain largely content to focus on skill-based education.

Teachers of technology education, in both secondary and higher levels, are in a unique position to directly influence administration, peer, and student perceptions of the role technology in contemporary society. Technology education must seek to go beyond the transmission of the most effective and economic usage of "tools" in modern society to include critical investigations of the social purpose of technology. This means embracing a critical approach to technological issues, considering so-called humanistic and social science perspectives on the role of technology in society, and empowering all students to engage in a critical dialog around technology, progress, education, and the meaning of civilizational advancement.

CHALLENGES OF MULTICULTURALISM

Civic education, Cultural differences and mutural respect

Public schools in the United States once included Protestant prayers and readings from the King James Version of the Bible as central parts of the school day. Little or no effort was made to respect the diverse religious beliefs of non-Protestants. Catholic children were sometimes whipped by teachers if they refused to read from the King James Bible. In the same schools, history was taught largely without reference to, let alone understanding of, the experiences of American Indians, blacks, and women. And, perhaps more significantly, all subjects were taught to racially segregated student bodies, for whom even an inclusive, culturally respectful civics curriculum would have been overwhelmed by the civics lesson in white supremacy implicit in the way children were distributed among schools.

This traditional model illustrates the problem with a civic education unmodified by multiculturalism. The traditional model withheld respect from different ways of life, and denigrated the contributions of minority groups and women to American civic culture. It also taught morally skewed lessons in civic virtue. When history classes exalted the contributions of the founding fathers with scant discussion of the institution of slavery, the lives of slaves, the Underground Railroad, or the contributions of African-Americans to civic understandings, public schools failed, among other things, to teach students the civic values of democratic dissent and disobedience to unjust laws. In not teaching these democratic values, schools diminished the role of dissenters and restricted the range of reasonable political alternatives that children could understand and embrace.

These purportedly patriotic history lessons were repressive and discriminatory. They simultaneously restricted understanding of diverse ways of life and denigrated the people who lived those lives. Repression in schooling is commonly identified with banning books and punishing teachers or students for unpopular ideas. But schooling is often repressive, and more insidiously so, by virtue of what it fails to teach. A civic education is repressive when it fails to teach appreciation and respect for the positive contributions by minorities to a society's common culture.

An antidote to this traditional civics curriculum is education that aims to appreciate the social contributions and life experiences of the various groups that constitute society. Such appreciation defines one common conception of multicultural education, a conception compatible with the principles of democratic education. We are a society constituted by many cultures. It is both morally wrong and empirically false to teach students as if it were otherwise.

Some contemporary American educators, however, defend schooling that is multicultural in a different sense. They defend schools designed primarily to cultivate the separatist cultural identities of minorities and to bolster the self-esteem of students based on their membership in a separatist culture. Afrocentrism is a currently controversial instance of such a separatist multicultural perspective, but the perspective is not unique to Afrocentrism, nor is it new to American education. Some all-white schools are designed to serve a similar if less publicly criticized purpose: to teach children a sense of racial superiority, which is taken to justify racial discrimination.

The chief problem with such segregation academies from a democratic perspective is not the inaccuracy of what they teach children about the superior accomplishments of their ancestors, but their attempt to cultivate among these children a sense of superiority based on race. These schools try to teach racial discrimination, albeit for differing reasons. Democratic governments cannot prevent private individuals and associations from conveying to children a sense of superiority based on race, religion, gender, or class, but they must not support schools that convey the very disrespect that democratic education should be designed to dispel.

Some educators say that teaching disadvantaged students to identify with the superior contributions of their ancestors bolsters their self-esteem, "the favorable appreciation or opinion of oneself." But this way of cultivating self-esteem comes at the cost of undercutting mutual respect among citizens, "a proper regard for the dignity of [a] person or position." In a democracy, proper regard for the position of citizens includes the mutual recognition that all persons, regardless of the accomplishments of their ancestors, are entitled to equal political and civil liberties and fair equality of opportunity to live a good life.

Public schooling in a democracy should not therefore forswear the aim of increasing the self-esteem of disadvantaged students. That schools should not try to increase self-esteem by discriminatory means, such as crediting to particular groups of students the superiority of their ancestors. This aim is to be distinguished from recognizing and respecting the identification of individuals with particular cultures. This identification is something that public schooling can support, as a way of respecting students with different cultural identifications, and also as a way of recognizing the multitude of cultural opportunities that are open to all students as members of a multicultural society. Imagine a curriculum in which the achievements of Africa and Africans, ancient and modern, are given due place alongside the treatment of other continents and peoples, and in which the links (causal, cultural, and emotional) between the history of Africa and the history of African-Americans are made plain.

Such a curriculum taught to all students puts multicultural education in service to democratic values, not in opposition. Such a curriculum supports rather than subverts one of the most basic lessons of democratic education: that all individuals, regardless of their cultural identifications, have equal civic standing, and are honored or dishonored by their own acts, not by the acts of their ancestors.

For schools to cultivate a sense of self-esteem in students that is sustainable alongside mutual respect among citizens, schools need to help every student succeed academically. Students learn to appreciate themselves as accomplished individuals when schools help them become accomplished learners. This educational task is a lot harder than teaching students to identify with their ancestors. Educational success entails learning something that is worthy of being publicly honored as knowledge and (moral, empirical, or analytical) understanding. The fact that educational success, like self-esteem, is achieved by individuals does not mean that its attainment must be a solitary endeavor. Quite the contrary. Some of the most successful teaching occurs in cooperative and diverse learning groups. The self-esteem that is compatible with civic equality (which, in turn, is based on a commitment to treating people as equals) cannot be acquired by group identification.

We have identified two ways that schools have failed to meet the challenge of securing common values and respecting cultural differences. The traditional civics curriculum imposes a cultural singularity that is false to the pluralism of American life and disrespectful of many of its citizens. A separatist curricula also educates by exclusion by fostering a sense of superiority among some students at the cost of disparaging or degrading others. Neither response promotes mutual respect among citizens, which is still sorely lacking in our society, and many others.

Why worry about cultivating mutual respect, a positive regard for other people who are also motivated to be respectful even in the face of cultural and political differences? Why should democratic education not rest content with teaching the less ambitious virtue of toleration, simply "to live and let live" in the face of our differences? Toleration is an essential democratic virtue and a necessary but not sufficient condition of mutual respect. In a democratic society, mutual respect is a public as well as a private good. It expresses the equal standing of every person as an individual and citizen, and it also enables democratic citizens to discuss their political differences in a productive way by first understanding one another's perspectives and then by trying to find fair ways of resolving their disagreements.

Schools can teach mutual respect in at least two ways that meet the challenge of joining civic and multicultural aims to the benefit of both. Schools can create curricula that recognize the multicultural heritage of the United States as everyone's resource. belonging not only to all of us, but also to future immigrants and generations to come. In addition, schools can teach about foreign cultures in a way that is more conducive to our remaining a society of immigrants. If we are to remain a haven for political and economic refugees, we need to respect not only the diverse cultures that are already ours, but also those that are not presently represented within our borders. Recognition of foreign cultures cannot of course be comprehensive In any case, cultivating a relatively deep appreciation of a few foreign cultures is likely to be more educationally effective than conveying a superficial familiarity with many.

But appreciation of cultural diversity is not enough to teach students the civic virtue of mutual respect, nor is it the toughest task now facing most schools. Expanding the knowledge of students meets only half the intellectual and moral challenge of the democratic ideal that have been defending. The second, pedagogically as well as politically more demanding, way in which schools can cultivate mutual respect is to teach students how to engage together in respectful discussions in which they strive to understand, appreciate, and, if possible, resolve political disagreements, including those that may be partly rooted in cultural differences. Mutual respect that rests only on therecognition of cultural diversity is an incomplete democratic virtue. Recognition needs to be accompanied by a willingness and ability to deliberate about politically relevant disagreements.

A culturally diverse citizenry dedicated to deliberation strives for reciprocity in political relationships. It seeks agreement on public policies that are (as far as possible) mutually acceptable to all citizens who are bound by them. Reciprocity is a goal which is unlikely to be fully realized. As with many valuable ends, reciprocity is an aspirational ideal, one that is constitutive of the political ideal of democracy. By teaching the skills and virtues of deliberation among citizens, schools can contribute to bringing a democracy closer to its own ideal.

Even if reciprocity may never be fully realized, we can find partial ways of approaching its educational aims of cultivating an inclusive multiculturalism and a morally informed deliberation. We can find examples of promising practices in non-elite public schools in the United States. Deborah Meier's pioneering District 4 in East Harlem and California's statewide history curriculum offer models of inclusive multicultural curricula. Neither model is perfect, but both are better than what has gone before them. Meier's school is successful both by traditional measures (increased reading and mathematical achievement scores) and non-traditional measures (integration of a multiracial student body).

Like this small but significant lesson in deliberation, a multicultural curriculum dedicated to teaching deliberation would encourage students to respect each other as equal citizens, regardless of the accomplishments of their ancestors, and to take different points of view seriously when thinking about politics. The practice of morally informed deliberation engages students in according each other the mutual respect and moral understanding that is too often lacking in contemporary politics.

Teaching mutual respect among citizens in these ways is a central aim of civic education in a multicultural democracy. Bolstering self-esteem by group identification is not — not because self-esteem is unimportant or insupportable by education, but because the self-esteem that is compatible with mutual respect among citizens cannot be acquired merely by means of group identification. Just as a civic education, unmodified by multiculturalism, represses cultural differences, multiculturalism, uninformed by civic values, discriminates among citizens on the basis of their group identities. Schools can meet this challenge of multiculturalism by allying common civic values with uncommon cultural appreciations.

A democratic integration of civic education and multiculturalism can capture the partial truth in the two common perspectives by refusing to divorce the aims of civic education from those of multicultural education, at the same time recognizing that there are potential tensions between these two inter-related strands of democratic education.

"Easier said than done," a critic might reply. This integration of multiculturalism and civic education has yet to confront the challenge of accommodating religious differences. To see if democratic education can meet this challenge, we should consider a controversy in which the aims of civic education are apparently at odds with religious freedom.

In 1989, three Muslim adolescent girls went to their local public high school in Creil, France wearing chadors (head coverings that are associated with religiously orthodox Muslims). French public schools are, by law and centuries-long tradition, secular. A 1937 law prohibits the wearing of religious symbols, or at least conspicuous religious symbols, in government-run schools. Citing the 1937 law, the principal of the high school, a Catholic of Martinican origin, told the three students that they must remove their chadors in class. When they refused, the principal, supported by the school's teachers, forbade the girls to attend class.

Controversies like this one pose perhaps the toughest challenge of multiculturalism to civic education. The chador case divided not only French society, but French socialists, who consider themselves as universalist as anyone. Although the socialists could unite in criticizing reactions like those of the conservative newspaper Le Point, whose headline read "Should We Let Islam Colonize Our Schools?" and the right-wing politician, Le Pen, who urged the repatriation of all immigrants who had arrived in France since 1974, they were bitterly divided among themselves. Some socialists found themselves allied with conservatives in defending the 1937 law, while others proclaimed it unjust. The debate among socialists helps demonstrate why transcendent universalism is inadequate as a public educational philosophy, and points us to a more defensible way of posing and provisionally resolving such problems.

Socialists who supported the 1937 law argued that the veil is "a sign of imprisonment that considers women to be subhumans under the law of Islam" and should therefore not be admitted by a public educational system committed to teaching gender equality. In opposition to the law, Prime Minister Michel Rocard argued that "tolerance must be put before principle." We might say instead that religious toleration itself is a universal principle to be considered alongside the principle of teaching gender equality.. Invoking universal values alone therefore does not resolve the conflict, since religious toleration and gender equality both share the status of universal principles for the social context under consideration.

Even after we reject appeals to an exclusionary nationalism, the question therefore remains: If French public schools are committed to universalist principles, which principle should take priority in the case of conflict? Should universalists agree with Mme. Mitterand who took the position that public schools should tolerate all religious symbols, even those that express gender inequality, because teaching religious toleration takes priority over teaching gender equality? Or should they side with Gisele Halimi, a founding member of a prominent anti-racist organization, SOS-Racism, who argued that distinctively public (or civic) values, rather than private (or personal) values, should be taught in public schools? The social equality of men and women is a public value, Halimi argued. The chador is "a humiliating form of dress" symbolizing gender subordination and therefore has no legitimate place in public schools. Although each argument invokes universalist principles, they support conflicting conclusions.

The indeterminacy of universalism is not a reason to abandon it, unless particularism carries with it better moral arguments. Does particularism get the better of universalism in this conflict? Should we give up looking for mutually-acceptable values in public education, and leave education to parents or religious groups? One attraction of particularism is that it offers religious parents effective access to schools that reflect their religious perspectives. Divide school systems into streams, particularists argue, and give every major cultural group the effective opportunity to shape the schooling of its own children.

The French government could then authorize each major community, including secularists, to run its own publicly subsidized schools. French secular schools could remain strictly secular, while orthodox Catholics, Muslims, and Jews (among other groups) could send their children to subsidized schools committed to reinforcing their particular communal values. If the government subsidizes separate schooling for each group, then no group needs to compromise its particularist values for the sake of a common civic education.

Although the particularist response would require a radical restructuring of French education, it cannot be rejected on grounds that its values are foreign to French social understandings. Asked about the situation of orthodox Jewish students in France who wish to wear yarmulkes, Sabine Roitman of the Representative Council of Jewish Institutions in France responded that "Jewish students have had little trouble with the issue, because those who want to wear yarmulkes generally attend private religious schools." What about the fact that many parents, like those of the Muslim girls, cannot afford the private schools of their choice? Particularists can respond by defending public subsidies for all schools, religious as well as secular. Any adequate defense of this response would take us beyond particularism to the claim that subsidies of separate educational streams are more justifiable to citizens than public subsidy of a common civic education.

Something more is missing from this particularist perspective that a more democratic perspective provides. The particularist response to religious diversity neglects, or at least downplays, the government's role in regulating the schools that it subsidizes. The particularist response is radically indeterminate when it comes to specifying what governments must do to ensure that schools adequately educate future citizens. It is this aim of educating future citizens that justifies massive state subsidies of schooling.

So particularism cannot escape the question that it lacks the resources to answer: What may citizens reasonably expect of schools as a condition of their receiving public funding and accreditation? The silence of particularism in response to this question sustains the worry that separatist education is not designed to promote the civic values that justify public funding in the first place.

Unless schools serve civic purposes that citizens can share, their support should be left primarily to parents and private associations. Particularists who favor public support therefore should recognize that all streams of schooling must be publicly regulated to the extent necessary to ensure that they promote civic educational purposes. This recognition opens the door to giving precedence to democratic principles over and alongside particularistic purposes. Particularism, so modified, is far more defensible, but it no longer can claim the attraction of avoiding controversies over the content of civic education by ceding to each religious (or ethnic) group its own autonomous sphere of schooling. Nor is this kind of particularism easy to distinguish from a universalism that recognizes the value of religious (or ethnic) diversity.

The problems of unregulated particularism are the mirror-image of those confronting a universalism that tries to transcend particularist cultures. While transcendent universalism expects too much uniformity in the content of public schooling, separatist particularism expects too little.

Public schools are the primary institution by which a democratic society educates future citizens, preparing them to share in responsible self-government. Teaching the elements of responsible self-government — which include mutual respect for basic liberty, opportunity, and a commitment to deliberate about politically relevant issues — is a major reason for mandating and publicly subsidizing schooling for all children. These lessons are constitutive of the purposes of public schooling in contemporary liberal democracies, or aspiring liberal democracies.

Suppose we grant that teaching students the values of basic liberty, opportunity, and deliberation is a primary purpose of public education. We must still wonder whether any conception of education that recognizes this purpose can find a way of resolving the chador case and similar conflicts that pit civic education and cultural diversity against each other. Is there a way of resolving the conflict between religious freedom and a civic education that aims to educate children for the rights and responsibilities of citizenship, where religious beliefs apparently conflict with the aims of civic education?

We cannot defer as a matter of principle to religious freedom regardless of its claims against civic education, as does a particularism unmodified by civic values. Nor can we defer as a matter of principle to a civic education that would expel religious dissenters, regardless of the content of their claims against civic education, as would one version of the universalism represented by the French left — a transcendent universalism that is unmodified by particularist values. This kind of universalism in effect denies that religious freedom, like freedom of conscience more generally, is a basic liberty, necessary to the integrity of persons as we know them.

Public schools have a responsibility to teach and practice religious toleration as part of civic education. Both a universalism that respects particular values and a particularism that respects civic values can recognize this responsibility. The critical question remains: To what extent can schools teach and practice religious toleration without sacrificing civic equality and mutual respect among men and women?

We can begin to answer the question by recognizing that there are principled limits to the religious freedom that the law must respect, and therefore also limits to the religious practices that a public school must tolerate. We need to determine the substantive limits of religious toleration in a particular context of public schooling and therefore to consider in the chador case whether the wearing of conspicuous religious symbols — especially religious symbols of gender inequality in a public school classroom —exceeds those limits.

We can locate religious practices that lie beyond the legally protected realm of religious freedom and toleration. The legally protected realm excludes religious practices that conflict with other basic democratic rights and which are themselves less valuable than the particular rights with which they conflict. Examples of religious practices that may be outlawed in order to protect more valuable rights are ritual human sacrifice and the denial of essential health care to children.

In harder cases where rights conflict, we encounter more uncertainty. These conflicts must be resolved, at least provisionally, but they cannot be even provisionally resolved without our rendering some substantive judgment, which will not be neutral, among particular ways of life. The position of deferring, either to established religious practices or established state policy, is not morally neutral, nor does liberal democracy establish a presumption in favor of either position. We have no better alternative than to assess the conflict as carefully as we can and at the most specific level that public policy can handle. We cannot legitimately counterpoise teaching gender equality against protecting religious freedom in its entirety.

Instead, we need to focus on the specific aspects of gender equality and religious freedom that are at issue — that is, the school's obligation to teach students, regardless of their religion or gender, to associate as civic equals in the classroom, and the students' freedom to wear conspicuous religious symbols to school, including those that are commonly associated with gender subordination. We now must ask: Is there any way to reconcile these two apparently conflicting values? If not, which value is the more important to secure in this context?

If we recognize the school's dual responsibility — to teach the civic equality of men and women, and to respect individuals regardless of religious differences insofar as these differences are consistent with civic values — we can develop an alternative way of viewing the conflict, a principled integration of the central purposes of the two perspectives. The liberal democratic values that give public schooling its primary social purpose guide the integration. Schools should tolerate the religious difference represented by the chadors without acquiescing in the gender segregation and subordination that typically accompanies this dress in religious practice outside of schools. The French public schools could have made an educational opportunity out of the girls' wearing of the scarves in school in order to express a democratic commitment to educate all students, regardless of their gender and the religious convictions of their parents.

Schools can teach these democratic lessons in different ways, but the way in which the French government recently resolved the chador controversy is not one of them. In September 1994, the government reversed an earlier ruling by the Conseil d'Etat that would have allowed the wearing of chadors in public schools. Under the new policy, students are not permitted to wear "ostentatious religious signs" in the classroom, and chadors count as ostentatious signs. Crucifixes and yarmulkes, on the other hand, are considered discrete and are therefore permitted. Thus, Catholic boys and girls who wear crucifixes or Jewish boys who wear yarmulkes will be welcome within French public schools, while Muslim girls who insist on wearing chadors will not.

The previous ruling by the Conseil d'Etat had been more defensible on democratic grounds, though it too fell short of a fully principled integration of particularism and universalism. The wearing of religious symbols, the Conseil had said, is permissible so long as it does not involve one of the four Ps: "pressure on others, provocation, propaganda, or proselytism." The ruling raised a critical question concerning moral responsibility in an educational context: What if the wearing of chadors provokes some students to taunt the girls? The ruling suggested that discipline may be directed to the girls rather than the taunters. Yet this way of resolving the problem of provocation would be unjust to the girls, who should not be held responsible for the uncivil behavior of students who fail to respect their right to religious freedom.

Educators should be able to distinguish such uncivil behavior from another kind of reaction among students, which would be fully consistent with democratic education. The wearing of chadors might provoke criticism among some students for being a symbol of women's second-class citizenship. This criticism, in turn, might provoke the Muslim girls to respond with a defense of their tradition. These forms of civil provocation might be discomforting to all parties, but such discomfort is not unwelcome to democratic education. While multiculturalism, informed by democratic principles, encourages us to understand the value that different ways of life have for people who live them, it also exposes every way of life to civil criticism.

The democratic rationale for opening schools to the display of religious difference, along with other kinds of cultural difference, is therefore not to protect each particular way of life from criticism or even from erosion. The rationale is rather to encourage citizens to understand, appreciate, and evaluate politically relevant differences among ways of life. Because some ways of life are more open to criticism and change than others, reflection on politically relevant differences is bound to be more unsettling to some students and citizens than to others, but the non-neutrality of a democratic education is a virtue as well as a necessity.

Non-neutrality is a necessity because an educational program would be empty were it to rest upon neutrality among different conceptions of the good life. Non-neutrality, more interestingly, is a virtue because citizens should support an educational system only if it is not neutral between those ways of life that respect basic liberty, opportunity, and deliberation, and those that do not. A liberal democracy should take its own side in arguments about teaching the skills and virtues that are constitutive of its own flourishing.

Among the various responses in France to the chador case, the one that best reflects the democratic aim of integrating particularism and universalism was that of Souad Benani, a spokesperson for Les Nanas Beurs, an organization of women of North African descent. "As Arab feminists of Muslim culture," Benani said,

> we believe that fundamentalism in all its forms is dangerous and the scarf is oppressive. But it should not be used as a pretext to exclude twelve- or thirteen-year-old girls from school when it is precisely these secular schools that should offer them the opportunity to learn, grow, and make their own choices.

Informed by a larger conception of democratic education, this response does not simply defer to the religious beliefs of Muslim parents or students, nor does it claim to be transcendent in its universalism. Its guiding principles — which include basic liberty and opportunity for all individuals, and their effective freedom to deliberate as civic equals about collective choices — are arguably universal for our world as we now know it, but these principles are also importantly open-ended in their content.

Not only will their implications vary with the facts of particular societies, but the principles themselves are also legitimately subject to interpretation by the ongoing public deliberation that democratic education ideally supports. The principles of democratic education do not comprehensively specify what constitutes a good education independently of particular cultures, life projects, and democratic deliberations.

Democratic education rejects the separatist strand of particularism, which would give up on the project of educating all children for the rights and responsibilities of citizenship, regardless of their familial culture. But it respects the widest range of cultural differences compatible with teaching those rights and responsibilities. Democratic education would not force the girls to give up wearing chadors in class, but it would expose them to a public culture of gender equality in public school. This exposure gives them reasons why women should view themselves as the civic equals of men, and it opens up opportunities that are not offered by their families and religious communities. By opening up such opportunities, democratic education may lessen the likelihood that certain kinds of cultural practices will perpetuate themselves. A democratic government should not go out of its way to perpetuate cultural practices that conflict with its constitutive principles.

Some critics suggest that this position of partial accommodation is little more than a pretense of accommodation with ways of life that dissent from liberal democratic orthodoxy. "Funny-hat liberalism," it is sometimes disparagingly called Why? Because the price paid by orthodox Muslim parents for accepting the accommodationist position of democratic education may be a serious weakening of the hold of their religious convictions and inherited way of life on their children.

The critics are correct in suggesting that democratic education does not grant illiberal ways of life nearly all that they claim for themselves, nor even all that they may need in order to perpetuate themselves in their present form. Democratic education does not claim to support any cultural way of life on its own terms, or even to the extent necessary to guarantee its survival as such. Nor should it.

Cultures do not have rights to survival. People have rights to religious freedom, along with other basic liberties and opportunities, that place demands on democratic education. The right to religious freedom, as we have seen, has principled limits. Among those limits is the right of children to be educated for full citizenship in a democratic society, and the responsibility of publicly-supported schools to secure that right for students, even when it conflicts with religious commitments of their parents.

Moreover, the critics' disparagement of accommodating the wearing of chadors in public schools is not true to the experience of the Muslim parents and the girls themselves. The Muslim parents and the girls in this case preferred, and had good reason to prefer, the earlier accommodation by the Conseil d'Etat to the more recent banning of chadors. The parents argued for the right of their children, dressed in accordance with their religious convictions, to be educated as future French citizens within the public schools. They did not argue for their right to be religiously educated, as fundamentalist Muslims, in public schools.

The critics seem to assume that religious education in publicly subsidized schools is the only consistent position available to any truly religious parents. Many religious parents reasonably believe otherwise, and it is the willingness of the vast majority of citizens to draw some line of separation between civic education and religious education that permits any religiously pluralistic democracy to pursue liberty and justice for all.

The critics are therefore correct in claiming that the earlier ruling by the Conseil d'Etat did not provide the Muslim girls with a public education that conformed to their religious convictions, but the critics fail to defend their presumption that public education should be judged by its conformity with the religious convictions of parents. The critics offer no reason to reject the view that publicly subsidized education should serve distinctively civic purposes, which can be shared by a diverse citizenry, not distinctively religious purposes which divide us.

Democratic education respects religious differences that are consistent with expecting all citizens, regardless of their religious beliefs, to honor a set of civic responsibilities. Those civic responsibilities include allowing one's children to be educated for democratic citizenship. Democratic education thereby integrates particularist and universalist values. A religiously diverse citizenry can honor this integration as long as they are willing to share a society together on terms that they can justify to one another.

4

EDUCATION ACCORDING TO INDIAN THINKERS

MAHATMA GANDHI

According to Gandhiji,

> The real difficulty is that people have no idea of what education truly is. We assess the value of education in the same manner as we assess the value of land or of shares in the stock-exchange market. We want to provide only such education as would enable the student to earn more. We hardly give any thought to the improvement of the character of the educated. The girls, we say, do not have to earn; so why should they be educated? As long as such ideas persist there is no hope of our ever knowing the true value of education.

In a piece published some years ago, Krishna Kumar, Professor of Education at Delhi University, wrote that 'no one rejected colonial education as sharply and as completely as Gandhi did, nor did anyone else put forward an alternative as radical as the one he proposed'. Gandhi's critique of Western, particularly English, education was part of his critique of Western civilization as a whole. There is a story that, on arriving in Britain after he had become famous, someone asked him the question: 'Mr Gandhi, what do you think of civilization in England?' to which he replied 'I think that it would be something worth trying!'

Early life Mohandas Karamchand Gandhi was born in 1869 in Porbander on the West coast of India. He had a reasonably conventional middle class Indian upbringing. His father (Karamchand) was the senior official (dewan or prime minister) of a small Indian state (Porbandar) before moving on to be the chief karbhari (adviser) in the principality of Rajkot. He looked to his son to follow in his footsteps. Gandhi went to school, did not particularly excel at anything but learned the things that were expected of him. He married in 1882, aged 13. His wife, Kasturbai Makanji who was also 13, was the daughter of a local merchant and was chosen for him. At the end of his formal schooling he decided that he wanted to be a lawyer. To do this he had to come to England to enroll at the Inner Temple. He was called to the Bar in the summer of 1891. On his return to India, he found that he could not make a successful career as a lawyer so he moved to South Africa in 1893.

His experiences in South Africa changed his life. While he was there, he came face to face with blatant racism and discrimination of a kind that he had never witnessed in India. The humiliation he felt at the hands of officials turned him from a meek and unassertive individual into a determined political activist. He had originally gone to South Africa on a one year contract to work for an Indian law firm in Natal Province. There he took up various grievances on behalf of the Indian community and gradually found himself first as their advocate on civil rights issues and finally as their leader in a political movement against racial discrimination and for South African Indian rights.

His methods were unusual. He launched a struggle against the authorities which in keeping with his strict Hindu beliefs was based on a strict adherence to non-violence. This meant that it consisted of passive resistance - the peaceful violation of certain laws, the courting of collective arrests (he urged his followers to fill the jails), non-co-operation with the authorities, boycotts and spectacular marches. These methods were later to be perfected back in India in the fight for independence from the British Empire.

Gandhi's ideas were gradually perfected as a result of his South African experiences. Throughout his life, the ideas he formed in these first few years in South Africa were to be developed to fit various changed circumstances in the fight for Indian independence. They were, however, set within a global context of a total rejection of modern civilization. His rejection of 'modern' or Western civilization was all encompassing. He described it as the 'Kingdom of Satan' polluting everyone it touched. Modernization in the form of industrialization, machinery, parliamentary government, the growth of the British Empire and all the things that most people regarded as progress, Gandhi rejected.

In opposition to modern civilization he counter posed ancient Indian civilization with its perceived emphasis on village communities that were self-sufficient and self-governing. He was concerned with the stranglehold that Western civilization had over India. The materialistic values that the British Raj imposed on India had to be countered by the spirituality of Ancient India. Time and time again throughout his life he would return to this theme of the need to revert to what he called their 'own glorious civilization' which was far superior to anything modern society could offer.

Swaraj and Swadeshi

What Gandhi was looking for was what he called swaraj and swadeshi. These two terms taken together represent the type of society that Gandhi was looking for. Swaraj, very badly translates as independence/autonomy/home rule/self rule. Swadeshi can be translated as self-sufficiency or self-reliance.

Swaraj for Gandhi was not simply a question of ousting the British from India and declaring independence. What it implied was a wholly different type of society. He did not want the British to be replaced by Indians doing exactly the same. If that was all they achieved, they would not have achieved true freedom but merely the same type of government run by a different set of men. He wanted the value system and life style of the British Raj to be done away with and totally replaced by a simpler, more spiritual, communal life. This new type of society, reflecting the old values of pre-colonial days, was to be based on the village. He stated that:

> [I]ndependence must begin at the bottom. Thus every village will be a republic ... having full powers. It follows, therefore, that every village has to be self-sustained and capable of managing its affairs. Thus, ultimately, it is the individual who is the unit. This does not exclude dependence on and willing help from neighbours or from the world... In this structure composed of innumerable villages, there will be ever-widening, never-ascending circles. Life will not be a pyramid with the apex sustained by the bottom.

Gandhi's vision for a new India entailed that 'every religion has its full and equal place'. (He was totally opposed to the partition of India). Equally, 'there would be no room for machines that would displace human labour and that would concentrate power in a few hands'.

In his Collected Works there is a passage, written in 1942, that amplifies his ideas on the role of the village. He states that 'my idea of village swaraj is that it is a complete republic, independent of its neighbours for its own vital wants, and yet interdependent for many others in which dependence is a necessity'. He continues:

> Thus every villages first concern will be to grow its own food crops and cotton for its cloth. It should have a reserve for its cattle, recreation and playground for adults and children. Then, if there is more land available, it will grow useful money crops, thus excluding ganja, tobacco, opium and the like. The village will maintain a village theatre, school and public hail. It will have its own waterworks, ensuring clean water supply. This can be done through

> controlled wells or tanks. Education will be compulsory up to the final basic course. As far as possible every activity will be conducted on the co-operative basis. There will be no castes such as we have today with their graded untouchability. Non-violence with its technique of... non-cooperation will be the sanction of the village community. There will be a compulsory service of village guards who will be selected by rotation from the register maintained by the village. The government of the village will be conducted by a [council] of five persons annually, elected by the adult villagers, male and female, possessing minimum prescribed qualifications. These will have all the authority and jurisdiction required. Since there will be no system of punishments in the accepted sense, this [council] will be the legislature, judiciary and executive combined to operate for its year of office.

Gandhi was quite certain that any village could become such a republic straight away without much interference even from the colonial government because he beleived that their sole effective connection with the villages was the collection of village taxes. All that was needed was the will to do it. He referred to his ideal state as one of 'enlightened anarchy in which each person will become his own ruler'. It is interesting to see that throughout his writings on the autonomous self-sufficient village communities we see echoes of the anarchist lifestyles proposed by such writers as Tolstoy or Thoreau in the nineteenth century.

On education Given Gandhi's values and his vision of what constituted a truly civilized and free India, it was not surprising that he developed firm views on education. Education not only moulds the new generation, but reflects a society's fundamental assumptions about itself and the individuals which compose it. His experience in South Africa not only changed his outlook on politics but also helped him to see the role education played in that struggle. He was aware that he had been a beneficiary of Western education and for a number of years while he was in South Africa he still tried to persuade Indians to take advantage of it.

However, it was not until the early years of this century, when he was in his middle thirties, that he became so opposed to English education that he could write about 'the rottenness of this education' and that 'to give millions a knowledge of English is to enslave them ... that, by receiving English education, we have enslaved the nation'. He was enraged that he had to speak of Home Rule or Independence in what was clearly a foreign tongue, that he could not practice in court in his mother tongue, that all official documents were in English as were all the best newspapers and that education was carried out in English for the chosen few. He did not blame the colonial powers for this. He saw that it was quite logical that they would want an elite of native Indians to become like their rulers in both manners and values.

In this way, the Empire could be consolidated. Gandhi blamed his fellow Indians for accepting the situation. Later in his life he was to declare that 'real freedom will come only when we free ourselves of the domination of Western education, Western culture and Western way of living which have been ingrained in us .. . Emancipation from this culture would mean real freedom for us'.

As we have seen, Gandhi had not only rejected colonial education but also put forward a radical alternative. So what was this alternative? What was so radical about it?

First of all, I need to say a word about Gandhi's attitude to industrialization. He was, in fact, absolutely opposed to modern machinery. In his collected works, he refers to machinery as having impoverished India, that it was difficult to measure the harm that Manchester had done to them by producing machine-made cloth which, in turn, ruined the internal market for locally produced handwoven goods. Typically of Gandhi, however, he does not blame Manchester or the mill owners. 'How can Manchester be blamed?' he writes. 'We wore Manchester cloth and this is why Manchester wove it'.

However, he notes that where cloth mills were not introduced in India, in places such as Bengal, the original hand-weaving occupation was thriving. Where they did have mills e.g. in Bombay, he felt that the workers there had become slaves. He was shocked by the conditions of the women working in the mills of Bombay and made the point that before they were introduced these women were not starving. He maintained that 'if the machinery craze grows in our country, it will become an unhappy land'. What he wanted was for Indians to boycott all machine-made goods not just cloth. He was quite clear when he asked the question 'What did India do before these articles were introduced?' and then answered his own question by stating 'Precisely the same should be done today.

As long as we cannot make pins without machinery, so long will we do without them. The tinsel splendour of glassware we will have nothing to do with, and we will make wicks, as of old, with home-grown cotton and use hand-made earthen saucers or lamps. So doing, we shall save our eyes and money and support swadeshi and so shall we attain Home Rule'. Within this context of the need for a machine-less society, Gandhi developed his ideas on education. The core of his proposal was the introduction of productive handicrafts in the school curriculum.

The idea was not simply to introduce handicrafts as a compulsory school subject, but to make the learning of a craft the centrepiece of the entire teaching programme. It implied a radical restructuring of the sociology of school knowledge in India, where productive handicrafts had been associated with the lowest groups in the hierarchy of the caste system. Knowledge of the production processes involved in crafts, such as spinning, weaving, leather-work, pottery, metal-work, basket-making and bookbinding, had been the monopoly of specific caste groups in the lowest stratum of the traditional social hierarchy. Many of them belonged to the category of 'untouchables'. India's own tradition of education as well as the colonial education system had emphasized skills such as literacy and acquisition of knowledge of which the upper castes had a monopoly.

Gandhi's proposal intended to stand the education system on its head. The social philosophy and the curriculum of what he called 'basic education' thus favoured the child belonging to the lowest stratum of society. in such a way it implied a programme of social transformation. It sought to alter the symbolic meaning of 'education' and to change the established structure of opportunities for education.

Why Gandhi proposed the introduction of productive handicrafts into the school system was not really as outrageous as may appear. What he really wanted was for the schools to be self-supporting, as far as possible. There were two reasons for this. Firstly, a poor society such as India simply could not afford to provide education for all children unless the schools could generate resources from within. Secondly, the more financially independent the schools were, the more politically independent they could be. What Gandhi wanted to avoid was dependence on the state which he felt would mean interference from the centre. Above all else, Gandhi valued self-sufficiency and autonomy. These were vital for his vision of an independent India made up of autonomous village communities to survive. It was the combination of swaraj and swadeshi related to the education system. A state system of education within an independent India would have been a complete contradiction as far as Gandhi was concerned.

He was also of the opinion that manual work should not be seen as something inferior to mental work. He felt that the work of the craftsman or labourer should be the ideal model for the 'good life'. Schools which were based around productive work where that work was for the benefit of all were, therefore, carrying out education of the whole person - mind, body and spirit.

The right to autonomy that Gandhi's educational plan assigns to the teacher in the context of the school's daily curriculum is consistent with the libertarian principles that he shared with Tolstoy. Gandhi wanted to free the Indian teacher from interference from outside, particularly government or state bureaucracy. Under colonial rule, the teacher had a prescribed job to do that was based on what the authorities wanted the children to learn. Textbooks were mandatory so that Gandhi found that 'the living word of the teacher has very little value. A teacher who teaches from textbooks does not impart originality to his pupils'. Gandhi's plan, on the other hand, implied the end of the teacher's subservience to the prescribed textbook and the curriculum. It presented a concept of learning that simply could not be fully implemented with the help of textbooks.

Of equal, if not more importance, was the freedom it gave the teacher in matters of curriculum. It denied the state the power to decide what teachers taught and what they did in the classroom. It gave autonomy to the teacher but it was, above all, a libertarian approach to schooling that transferred power from the state to the village. Gandhi's basic education was, therefore, an embodiment of his perception of an ideal society consisting of small, self-reliant communities with his ideal citizen being an industrious, self-respecting and generous individual living in a small co-operative community.

For informal educators, we can draw out a number of useful pointers. First, Gandhi's insistence on autonomy and self-regulation is reflected in the ethos of informal education. Gandhi's conception of basic education was concerned with learning that was generated within everyday life which is the basis on which informal educators work. It was also an education focused on the individual but reliant on co-operation between individuals. There is also a familar picture of the relationships between educators and students/learners:

> A teacher who establishes rapport with the taught, becomes one with them, learns more from them than he teaches them. He who learns nothing from his disciples is, in my opinion, worthless. Whenever I talk with someone I learn

> from him. I take from him more than I give him. In this way, a true teacher regards himself as a student of his students. If you will teach your pupils with this attitude, you will benefit much from them.

Lastly, it was an education that aimed at educating the whole person, rather than concentrating on one aspect. It was a highly moral activity.

RABINDRANATH TAGORE

Rabindranath Tagore (1861-1941), Asia's first Nobel Laureate, was born into a prominent Calcutta family known for its socio-religious and cultural innovations during the 19th Bengal Renaissance. The profound social and cultural involvement of his family would later play a strong role in the formulation of Rabindranath's educational priorities. His grandfather Dwarkanath was involved in supporting medical facilities, educational institutions and the arts, and he fought for religious and social reform and the establishment of a free press. His father was also a leader in social and religious reform, who encouraged a multi-cultural exchange in the family mansion Jorasanko. Within the joint family, Rabindranath's thirteen brothers and sisters were mathematicians, journalists, novelists, musicians, artists. His cousins, who shared the family mansion, were leaders in theatre, science and a new art movement.

The tremendous excitement and cultural richness of his extended family permitted young Rabindranath to absorb and learn subconsciously at his own pace, giving him a dynamic open model of education, which he later tried to recreate in his school at Santiniketan. Not surprisingly, he found his outside formal schooling to be inferior and boring and, after a brief exposure to several schools, he refused to attend school. The only degrees he ever received were honorary ones bestowed late in life.

His experiences at Jorasanko provided him with a lifelong conviction concerning the importance of freedom in education.

He also realized in a profound manner the importance of the arts for developing empathy and sensitivity, and the necessity for an intimate relationship with one's cultural and natural environment. In participating in the cosmopolitan activities of the family, he came to reject narrowness in general, and in particular, any form of narrowness that separated human being from human being. He saw education as a vehicle for appreciating the richest aspects of other cultures, while maintaining one's own cultural specificity. As he wrote:

> I was brought up in an atmosphere of aspiration, aspiration for the expansion of the human spirit. We in our home sought freedom of power in our language, freedom of imagination in our literature, freedom of soul in our religious creeds and that of mind in our social environment. Such an opportunity has given me confidence in the power of education which is one with life and only which can give us real freedom, the highest that is claimed for man, his freedom of moral communion in the human world.... I try to assert in my words and works that education has its only meaning and object in freedom–freedom from ignorance about the laws of the universe, and freedom from passion and prejudice in our communication with the human world. In my institution I have attempted to create an atmosphere of naturalness in our relationship with strangers, and the spirit of hospitality which is the first virtue in men that made civilization possible.
>
> I invited thinkers and scholars from foreign lands to let our boys know how easy it is to realise our common fellowship, when we deal with those who are great, and that it is the puny who with their petty vanities set up barriers between man and man.

As well as growing up in a household that was the meeting place for leading artists and intellectuals from India and the West, Rabindranath had a further experience which was unusual for someone of his upbringing. In the 1890s, he was put in charge of the family's rural properties in East Bengal. His first experiments in adult education were carried out there as he gradually became aware of the acute material and cultural poverty that permeated the villages, as well as the great divide between the uneducated rural areas and the city elites. His experiences made him determined to do something about rural uplift, and later at Santiniketan, students and teachers were involved with literacy training and social work and the promotion of cooperative schemes. As an alternative to the existing forms of education, he started a small school at Santiniketan in 1901 that developed into a university and rural reconstruction centre, where he tried to develop an alternative model of education that stemmed from his own learning experiences.

Rabindranath composed his first poem at age eight, and by the end of his life, had written over twenty-five volumes of poetry, fifteen plays, ninety short stories, eleven novels, thirteen volumes of essays, initiated and edited various journals, prepared Bengali textbooks, kept up a correspondence involving thousands of letters, composed over two thousand songs; and - after the age of seventy - created more than two thousand pictures and sketches. He dedicated forty years of his life to his educational institution at Santiniketan, West Bengal. Rabindranath's school contained a children's school as well as a university known as Visva-Bharati and a rural education Centre known as Sriniketan.

Rabindranath did not write a central educational treatise, and his ideas must be gleaned through his various writings and educational experiments at Santiniketan In general, he envisioned an education that was deeply rooted in one's immediate surroundings but connected to the cultures of the wider world, predicated upon pleasurable learning and individualized to the personality of the child. He felt that a curriculum should revolve organically around nature with classes held in the open air under the trees to provide for a spontaneous appreciation of the fluidity of the plant and animal kingdoms, and seasonal changes.

Children sat on hand-woven mats beneath the trees, which they were allowed to climb and run beneath between classes.

Nature walks and excursions were a part of the curriculum and students were encouraged to follow the life cycles of insects, birds and plants. Class schedules were made flexible to allow for shifts in the weather or special attention to natural phenomena, and seasonal festivals were created for the children by Tagore. In an essay entitled "A Poet's School," he emphasizes the importance of an empathetic sense of interconnectedness with the surrounding world:

> We have come to this world to accept it, not merely to know it. We may become powerful by knowledge, but we attain fullness by sympathy. The highest education is that which does not merely give us information but makes our life in harmony with all existence. But we find that this education of sympathy is not only systematically ignored in schools, but it is severely repressed. From our very childhood habits are formed and knowledge is imparted in such a manner that our life is weaned away from nature and our mind and the world are set in opposition from the beginning of our days. Thus the greatest of educations for which we came prepared is neglected, and we are made to lose our world to find a bagful of information instead. We rob the child of his earth to teach him geography, of language to teach him grammar. His hunger is for the Epic, but he is supplied with chronicles of facts and dates...Child-nature protests against such calamity with all its power of suffering, subdued at last into silence by punishment.

In Tagore's philosophy of education, the aesthetic development of the senses was as important as the intellectual—if not more so—and music, literature, art, dance and drama were given great prominence in the daily life of the school. This was particularly so after the first decade of the school. Drawing on his home life at Jorasanko, Rabindranath tried to create an atmosphere in which the arts would become instinctive. One of the first areas to be emphasized was music. Rabindranath writes that in his adolescence, a 'cascade of musical emotion' gushed forth day after day at Jorasanko. 'We felt we would try to test everything,' he writes, 'and no achievement seemed impossible...We wrote, we sang, we acted, we poured ourselves out on every side.'

In keeping with his theory of subconscious learning, Rabindranath never talked or wrote down to the students, but rather involved them with whatever he was writing or composing. The students were allowed access to the room where he read his new writings to teachers and critics, and they were encouraged to read out their own writings in special literary evenings. In teaching also he believed in presenting difficult levels of literature, which the students might not fully grasp, but which would stimulate them. The writing and publishing of periodicals had always been an important aspect of Jorasanko life, and students at Santiniketan were encouraged to create their own publications and put out several illustrated magazines. The children were encouraged to follow their ideas in painting and drawing and to draw inspiration from the many visiting artists and writers.

Most of Rabindranath's dramas were written at Santiniketan and the students took part in both the performing and production sides. He writes how well the students were able to enter into the spirit of the dramas and perform their roles, which required subtle understanding and sympathy without special training.

As Rabindranath began conceiving of Visva-Bharati as a national centre for the arts, he encouraged artists such as Nandalal Bose to take up residence at Santiniketan and to devote themselves full-time to promoting a national form of art. Without music and the fine arts, he wrote, a nation lacks its highest means of national self-expression and the people remain inarticulate. Tagore was one of the first to support and bring together different forms of Indian dance. He helped revive folk dances and introduced dance forms from other parts of India, such as Manipuri, Kathak and Kathakali. He also supported modern dance and was one of the first to recognize the talents of Uday Sankar, who was invited to perform at Santiniketan.

The meeting-ground of cultures, as Rabindranath envisioned it at Visva-Bharati, should be a learning centre where conflicting interests are minimized , where individuals work together in a common pursuit of truth and realise 'that artists in all parts of the world have created forms of beauty, scientists discovered secrets of the universe, philosophers solved the problems of existence, saints made the truth of the spiritual world organic in their own lives, not merely for some particular race to which they belonged, but for all mankind.'

To encourage mutuality, Rabindranath invited artists and scholars from other parts of India and the world to live together at Santiniketan on a daily basis to share their cultures with Visva-Bharati. The Constitution designated Visva-Bharati as an Indian, Eastern and Global cultural centre whose goals were:

— To study the mind of Man in its realisation of different aspects of truth from diverse points of view.

— To bring into more intimate relation with one another through patient study and research, the different cultures of the East on the basis of their underlying unity.

— To approach the West from the standpoint of such a unity of the life and thought of Asia.

— To seek to realise in a common fellowship of study the meeting of East and West and thus ultimately to strengthen the fundamental conditions of world peace through the free communication of ideas between the two hemispheres.

— And with such Ideals in view to provide at Santiniketan a centre of culture where research into the study of the religion, literature, history, science and art of Hindu, Buddhist, Jain, Zoroastrian, Islamic, Sikh, Christian and other civilizations may be pursued along with the culture of the West, with that simplicity of externals which is necessary for true spiritual realisation, in amity, good-fellowship and co-operation between the thinkers and scholars of both Eastern and Western countries, free from all antagonisms of race, nationality, creed or caste and in the name of the One Supreme Being who is Shantam, Shivam, Advaitam.

In terms of curriculum, he advocated a different emphasis in teaching. Rather than studying national cultures for the wars won and cultural dominance imposed, he advocated a teaching system that analysed history and culture for the progress that had been made in breaking down social and religious barriers. Such an approach emphasized the innovations that had been made in integrating individuals of diverse backgrounds into a larger framework, and in devising the economic policies which emphasized social justice and narrowed the gap between rich and poor.

Art would be studied for its role in furthering the aesthetic imagination and expressing universal themes. It should be noted that Rabindranath in his own person was a living icon of the type of mutuality and creative exchange that he advocated. His vision of culture was not a static one, but one that advocated new cultural fusions, and he fought for a world where multiple voices were encouraged to interact with one another and to reconcile differences within an overriding commitment to peace and mutual interconnectedness. His generous personality and his striving to break down barriers of all sorts gives us a model for the way multiculturalism can exist within a single human personality, and the type of individual which the educational process should be aspiring towards.

Tagore's educational efforts were ground-breaking in many areas. He was one of the first in India to argue for a humane educational system that was in touch with the environment and aimed at overall development of the personality. Santiniketan became a model for vernacular instruction and the development of Bengali textbooks; as well, it offered one of the earliest coeducational programs in South Asia. The establishment of Visva-Bharati and Sriniketan led to pioneering efforts in many directions, including models for distinctively Indian higher education and mass education, as well as pan-Asian and global cultural exchange.

One characteristic that sets Rabindranath's educational theory apart is his approach to education as a poet. At

Santiniketan, he stated, his goal was to create a poem 'in a medium other than words.' It was this poetic vision that enabled him to fashion a scheme of education which was all inclusive, and to devise a unique program for education in nature and creative self-expression in a learning climate congenial to global cultural exchange.

SWAMI VIVEKANANDA

Swami Vivekananda (1863 – 1902), a great thinker and reformer of India, embraces education, which for him signifies 'man-making', as the very mission of his life. In this section, which purports to expound and analyze Vivekananda's views on education, an endeavor has been made to focus on the basic theme of his philosophy, viz. the spiritual unity of the universe. Whether it concerns the goal or aim of education, or its method of approach or its component parts, all his thoughts, we shall observe, stem from this dormant theme of his philosophy which has its moorings in Vedanta.

Vivekananda realizes that mankind is passing through a crisis. The tremendous emphasis on the scientific and mechanical ways of life is fast reducing man to the status of a machine. Moral and religious values are being undermined. The fundamental principles of civilization are being ignored. Conflicts of ideals, manners and habits are pervading the atmosphere. Disregard for everything old is the fashion of the day. Vivekananda seeks the solutions of all these social and global evils through education. With this end in view, he feels the dire need of awakening man to his spiritual self wherein, he thinks, lies the very purpose of education.

The Goal or Objective of Education

Vivekananda points out that the defect of the present-day education is that it has no definite goal to pursue. A sculptor has a clear idea about what he wants to shape out of the marble block; similarly, a painter knows what he is going to paint. But a teacher, he says, has no clear idea about the goal of his teaching. Swamiji attempts to establish, through his words and deeds, that the end of all education is man making. He prepares the scheme of this man-making education in the light of his over-all philosophy of Vedanta.

According to Vedanta, the essence of man lies in his soul, which he possesses in addition to his body and mind. In true with this philosophy, Swamiji defines education as 'the manifestation of the perfection already in man.' The aim of education is to manifest in our lives the perfection, which is the very nature of our inner self. This perfection is the realization of the infinite power which resides in everything and every-where-existence, consciousness and bliss (satchidananda). After understanding the essential nature of this perfection, we should identify it with our inner self. For achieving this, one will have to eliminate one's ego, ignorance and all other false identification, which stand in the way.

Meditation, fortified by moral purity and passion for truth, helps man to leave behind the body, the senses, the ego and all other non-self elements, which are perishable. He thus realizes his immortal divine self, which is of the nature of infinite existence. infinite knowledge and infinite bliss. At this stage, man becomes aware of his self as identical with all other selves of the universe, i.e. different selves as manifestations of the same self. Hence education, in Vivekananda's sense, enables one to comprehend one's self within as the self everywhere. The essential unity of the entire universe is realized through education.

Accordingly, man making for Swamiji stands for rousing mans to the awareness of his true self. However, education thus signified does not point towards the development of the soul in isolation from body and mind. We have to remember that basis of Swamiji's philosophy is Advaita which preaches unity in diversity. Therefor, man making for him means a harmonious development of the body. mind and soul.

In his scheme of education, Swamiji lays great stress on physical health because a sound mind resides in a sound body. He often quotes the Upanishadic dictum 'nayamatma balahinena labhyah'; i.e. the self cannot be realized by the physically weak. However, along with physical culture, he harps on the need of paying special attention to the culture of the mind. According to Swamiji, the mind of the students has to be controlled and trained through meditation, concentration and practice of ethical purity. All success in any line of work, he emphasizes, is the result of the power of concentration.

By way of illustration, he mentions that the chemist in the laboratory concentrates all the powers of his mind and brings them into one focus-the elements to be analyzed-and finds out their secrets. Concentration, which necessarily implies detachment from other things, constitutes a part of Brahmacharya, which is one of the guiding mottos of his scheme of education. Brahmacharya, in a nutshell, stands for the practice of self-control for securing harmony of the impulses. By his philosophy of education, Swamiji thus brings it home that education is not a mere accumulation of information but a comprehensive training for life. To quote him: 'Education is not the amount of information that is put into your brain and runs riot there undigested, all your life.' Education for him means that process by which character is formed, strength of mind is increased, and intellect is sharpened, as a result of which one can stand on one's own feet.

Method or Procedure

Having analyzed the goal or objective of education, the next question that naturally arises is about the method of imparting education. Here again, we note the Vedantic foundation of Swamiji's theory. According to him, knowledge is inherent in every man's soul. What we mean when we say that a man 'knows' is only what he 'discovers' by taking the cover off his own soul. Consequently, he draws our attention to the fact that the task of the teacher is only to help the child to manifest its knowledge by removing the obstacles in its way. In his words: 'Thus Vedanta says that within man is all knowledge even in a boy it is so and it requires only an awakening and that much is the work of a teacher.'

To drive his point home, he refers to the growth of a plant. Just as in the case of a plant, one cannot do anything more than supplying it with water, air and manure while it grows from within its own nature, so is the case with a human child. Vivekananda's method of education resembles the heuristic method of the modern educationists. In this system, the teacher invokes the spirit of inquiry in the pupil who is supposed to find out things for himself under the bias-free guidance of the teacher.

Swamiji lays a lot of emphasis on the environment at home and school for the proper growth of the child. The parents as well as the teachers should inspire the child by the way they live their lives. Swamiji recommends the old institution of gurukula (living with the preceptor) and similar systems for the purpose. In such systems, the students can have the ideal character of the teacher constantly before them, which serves as the role model to follow.

Although Swamiji is of the opinion that mother tongue is the right medium for social or mass education, he prescribes the learning of English and Sanskrit also. While English is necessary for mastering Western science and technology, Sanskrit leads one into the depths of our vast store of classics. The implication is that if language does not remain the privilege of a small class of people, social unity will march forward unhampered.

Fields of Study

Vivekananda, in his scheme of education, meticulously includes all those studies, which are necessary for the all-around development of the body, mind and soul of the individual.

These studies can be brought under the broad heads of physical culture, aesthetics, classics, language, religion, science and technology. According to Swamiji, the culture values of the country should form an integral part of the curriculum of education. The culture of India has its roots in her spiritual values. The time-tested values are to be imbibed in the thoughts and lives of the students through the study of the classics like Ramayana, Mahabharata, Gita, Vedas and Upanishads. This will keep the perennial flow of our spiritual values into the world culture.

Education, according to Swamiji, remains incomplete without the teaching of aesthetics or fine arts. He cites Japan as an example of how the combination of art and utility can make a nation great.

Swamiji reiterates that religion is the innermost core of education. However, by religion, he does not mean any particular kind of it but its essential character, which is the realization of the divinity already in man. He reminds us time and again that religion does not consist in dogmas or creeds or any set of rituals. To be religious for him means leading life in such a way that we manifest our higher nature, truth, goodness and beauty, in our thoughts, words and deeds. All impulses, thoughts and actions which lead one towards this goal are naturally ennobling and harmonizing, and are ethical and moral in the truest sense. It is in this context that Swamiji's idea of religion, as the basis of education should be understood. We note that in his interpretation, religion and education share the identity of purpose.

Why religion forms the very foundation of education becomes clear in his following words: 'In building up character, in making for everything that is good and great, in bringing peace to others, and peace to one's own self, religion is the highest motive power, and, therefore, ought to be studied from that standpoint. Swamiji believes that if education with its religious core can invigorate man's faith in his divine nature and the infinite potentialities of the human soul, it is sure to help man become strong, yet tolerant and sympathetic. It will also help man to extend his love and good will beyond the communal, national and racial barriers.

It is a misinterpretation of Vivekananda's philosophy of education to think that he has overemphasized the role of spiritual development to the utter neglect of the material side. Vivekananda, in his plan for the regeneration of India, repeatedly presses the need for the eradication of poverty, unemployment and ignorance. He says, We need technical education and all else which may develop industries, so that men, instead of seeking for service, may earn enough to provide for them-selves, and save something against a rainy day. He feels it necessary that India should take from the Western nations all that is good in their civilization.

However, just like a person, every nation has its individuality, which should not be destroyed. The individuality of India lies in her spiritual culture. Hence in Swamiji's view, for the development of a balanced nation, we have to combine the dynamism and scientific attitude of the West with the spirituality of our country. The entire educational program should be so planned that it equips the youth to contribute to the material progress of the country as well as to maintaining the supreme worth of India's spiritual heritage.

Another important aspect of Swamiji's scheme of education is women's education. He realizes that it if the women of our country get the right type of education, then they will be able to solve their own problems in their own way. The main objective of his scheme of female education is to make them strong, fear-less, and conscious of their chastity and dignity. He observes that although men and women are equally competent in academic matters, yet women have a special aptitude and competence for studies relating to home and family. Hence he recommends the introduction of subjects like sewing, nursing, domestic science, culinary art, etc wnich were not part of education at his time.

AUROBINDO (1872–1950)

An explorer and adventurer in consciousness, a visionary of evolution, Sri Aurobindo, had disclosed 'No one can write about my life because it has not been on the surface for man to see' finds echo in Rabindranath Tagore, the fellow Bengali poet-artist and a Nobel laureate with whom Aurobindo felt a deep mutuality, who too had warned that one should not look for the poet in his biography.

In fact, McDermott felt that 'interpreting the life of a great spiritual personality is always a treacherous enterprise, and the life of Sri Aurobindo is peculiarly inscrutable'. Born in Calcutta, then the capital of British India on 15 August 1872, Aurobindo Ackroyd Ghose—the Western middle name was given to by his father at birth—was the third son of his parents—Dr. Krishnadhan Ghose and Swarnalata Devi. The honorific 'Sri' was traditionally used as a mark of respect or worship forming an integral part of his name.

In Sanskrit, the word Aurobindo means lotus. Aurobindo's father chose this name for him, thinking that it was unique, but he little suspected that, in the language of occultism, the lotusis the symbol of divine consciousness. Aurobindo received his early education in a convent school intended for European children and in 1879 was taken by his father to England for schooling in Manchester and later at St. Paul's School, London. A scholarship from St. Paul's enabled Aurobindo to go to King's College, Cambridge, in 1889. He practically won all the prizes in Greek and Latin. He passed the first part of the classical Tripos in the first class in 1892. The same year he successfully passed his Indian Civil Service Examination. But he did not report for the riding test and thereby was disqualified for the civil service.

Sri Aurobindo, who had started writing at an early age, even during his study at Manchester, had continued with his creativity through all the turbulent phases of his life, even during his incarceration. His first book, a collection of poems, entitled

Songs to Myrtilla, was published in 1895. Between that and the last work to be published during his lifetime, Savitri, he had written extensively on Yoga, culture, sociology, in addition to his poetry and plays—contributions of far-reaching and multifaceted importance to humanthought and in action. He has given a new cosmology and a new metaphysics in his Life divine 'considered as the philosophical masterpiece of the century' which has revolutionized our very conception of psychology and gave it a new basis in Life divine and in his letters. He formulated a profoundly new approach to sociology in his The human cycle and showed through a searching analysis of past and current systems of social and political thought how a truly spiritual attitude is essential as a foundation of a new and lasting social order. He extended the application of this very approach to the sphere of international politics in his The ideal of human unity.

In his writings on education, he formulated a theory that could, with some variations, be adapted to all the nations of the 22 world, fostering the growth of the integral consciousness in every pupil and bringing back to legitimate authority of the Sprit over a matter fully developed and utilised. He showed in his The synthesis of Yoga how all the systems of Yoga combine and converge on the path to Supermind. In his The secret of the Vedas, The essays on the Gita and writings on Upanishads, he opened up new and epoch-making ways of studying the ancient Indian texts, throwing new light on philosophy and reducing both anthropology and anthropomorphology to their proper place in a balanced scheme of knowledge. He offered an illuminating interpretation of Indian culture down the centuries in his The foundations of Indian culture.

Sri Aurobindo's elaborated epic, Savitri reveals the consummation of the many poetic styles that he attempted in all his works. Written in nearly 24, 000 lines in blank verse, Sri Aurobindo's Savitri has been estimated to be the largest poem in the English language. In The future poetry, Sri Aurobindo worked out a literary iheory considered as an original contribution to aesthetics in its concept of poetry. All this and his translations, letters and minor works were compiled and published in a systematic manner after his passing away on the 5 December 1950.

A new edition of them, in thirty volumes, was brought out on the occasion of the centenary of his birth in 1972. The Swedish Academy considered him for the nomination for the Nobel Prize of 1950, the last year of Sri Aurobindo's life. There are many ways of approaching Sri Aurobindo, but the light that one can gain from him, as Joshi noted, will depend upon the height and breadth of one's own quest. It is in raising most comprehensive questions in their profundity relating to the worldand its future possibilities and the role that we are required to play as also how we should prepare ourselves to fulfil that role that we shall find the real relevance of Sri Aurobindo and find ourselves truly equipped to study him and the supramental consciousness that he has discovered and brought down on the earth.

Three fundamental problems which gave direction to the spiritual quest and philosophical thinking and helped to fashion Sri Aurobindo's major theories, relate to the paradox of the national life of India, the supposed conflict between spirituality and action, and the evolution of man. The search for solutions to these problems relates to the unique and creative tension in his own experience between spirituality and politics, both during his years of political activity and during his four decades of sadhana at Pondicherry.

Aurobindo's writings provide the needed force for action, realization and transformation which is reflected in his philosophy arrived at through inner experience. He wrote 'in fact I was never satisfied till experience came and it was on this experience that later on I founded my philosophy'. His integral philosophy grew out of his Yoga—not the other way round. Two phrases that surge out of Sri Aurobindo's writings that sum up his message are: 'Integral perfection' and 'Spiritual religion of humanity'. His call for integrality and synthesis is most distinctively reflected in his statements: 'We of the coming day stand at the head of anew age of development which must lead to such a new and larger synthesis. [. . .] We do not belong to the past dawns, but to the noons of the future'.

To attainintegral perfection, Sri Aurobindo has found education to be critical. Integral education for the growth of the soul Originally a poet and a politician, not a philosopher, Sri Aurobindo engaged himself for forty-five years out of his seventy-eight years in the practice of Yoga, and developed aphilosophy of complete affirmation, affirming the reality of the world from the ultimatest and point and the meaningfulness of socio-political action from the spiritual standpoint. He was sovereignly aware of the significance of variations in the concept of man, his life and destiny, of the nation and of humanity and the life of human race, which get reflected in the respective philosophies of education, and developed his scheme of integral education rooted in 'the developing soul of India, to her future need, to the greatness of her coming self creation, to her eternal spirit'.

India, according to Sri Aurobindo, has seen always in man the individual a soul, aportion of the Divinity enwrapped in mind and body, a conscious manifestation in Nature of the universal self and spirit. In his educational philosophy, Sri Aurobindo upheld the basic but commonly forgotten principle that 'it is the spirit, the living and vital issue that we have to do with, and there the question is not between modernism and antiquity, but between an imported civilisation and the greater possibilities of the Indian mind and nature, not between the present and the past, but between the present and the future'.

In devising a true and living education, three things according to Sri Aurobindo—the man, the individual in his commonness and his uniqueness, the nation or people and universal humanity—should be taken into account. Accordingly, Aurobindo conceived of education as an instrument for the real working of the spirit in the mind and body of the individual and the nation. He thought of education that for the individual will make its one central object the growth of the soul and its powers and possibilities, for the nation will keep first in view the preservation, strengthening and enrichment of the nation—soul and its Dharma (virtue) and raise both into powers of the life and ascending mind and soul of humanity. And at no time will it lose sight of man's highest object, the awakening and development of his spiritual being.

A concept underlying the true and living integral education. Integrality of education is conceived as a process of organic growth, and the way in which various faculties could be developed and integrated is dependent upon each child's inclination, rhythm of progression and law of development, Swabhava (inherent disposition) and Swadharma (inner nature). Integral education is not conceived as a juxtaposition of a number of subjects and even juxtaposition of varieties of faculties. The idea is to provide facilities for varieties of faculties, varieties of subjects and various combinations of pursuits of Knowledge, Power, Harmony and Skill in works. These faculties are so provided that they could be made use of by each student and the teacher so that a natural process of harmonious development could be encouraged.

Antahkarna (mind): the instrument of the educationist According to Sri Aurobindo, mind or antahkarana which consists of four layers is the instrument of the educationist. 'The reservoir of past mental impressions, the citta or store house of memory, which must be distinguished from the specific act of memory, is the foundation on which all the other layers stand. The passive memory or citta needs no training, it is automatic and naturally sufficient to its task; there is not the slightest object of knowledge coming within its field which is not secured, placed and faultlessly preserved in that admirable receptacle. It is the active memory, a higher but less perfectly developed function, which is in need of improvement'. Manas or mind proper, the sixth sense of Indian psychology, is the second layer. Its function is to receive the images of things translated into sight, sound, smell, taste and touch, the five senses and translate these again into thought—sensations. Therefore right use of the six senses is vital to see that they are not stunted or injured by disuse, but trained by the child himself under the teacher's direction to that perfect accuracy and keen subtle sensitiveness of which they are capable.

In addition, whatever assistance can be gained by the organs of action, should be thoroughly employed. The hand, for instance, should be trained to reproduce what the eye sees and the mind senses. The speech should be trained to a perfect expression of the knowledge which the whole antahkarna possesses. The real instrument of thought which forms the third layer is the intellect or buddhi. It orders and disposes of the knowledge acquired by the other parts of the machine. In finitely the most important of the three thus far named for education, Sri Aurobindo considers intellect as an organ composed of several groups of functions, divisible into two important classes, the functions and faculties of the right hand, the functions and faculties of the left hand.

'The faculties of the right-hand are comprehensive, creative and synthetic; the faculties of the left-hand critical and analytic. To the right-hand belong judgement, imagination, memory, observation; to the left-hand comparison and reasoning. The critical faculties distinguish, compare, classify, generalise, deduce, infer, conclude; they are the component parts of the logical reason. The right-hand faculties comprehend, command, judge in their own right, grasp, hold and manipulate. The right-hand mind is the master of the knowledge, the left-hand its servant. The left-hand touches only the body of knowledge, the right-hand penetrates its soul.

The left-hand limits itself to ascertained truth, the right-hand grasps that which is still elusive or unascertained. Both are essential to the completeness of the human reason. These important functions of the machine have all to be raised to their highest and finest working-power, if the education of the child is not to be imperfect and one-sided'. Sri Aurobindo adds that there is another layer of faculty which, not as yet entirely developed in man, is attaining gradually to a wider development and more perfect evolution. 'The powers peculiar to this highest stratum of knowledge are chiefly known to us from the phenomena of genius, — sovereign discernment, intuitive perception of truth, plenary inspiration of speech, direct vision of knowledge to an extent often amounting to revelation, making a man a prophet of truth.

These powers are rare in their higher development, though many possess them imperfectly or by flashes. They are still greatly distrusted by the critical reason of mankind because of the admixture of error, caprice and a biased imagination which obstructs and distorts their perfect workings. Yet it is clear that humanity could not have advanced to its present stage if it had not been for the help of these faculties, and it is a question with which educationists have not yet grappled, what is to be done with this mighty and baffling element, the element of genius in the pupil. The mere instructor does his best to discourage and stifle genius, the more liberal teacher welcomes it'.

The significance of physical and moral education Seeking to effect a synthesis of the values of the East and the West in the contemporary philosophy of education, Sri Aurobindo insisted that a healthy body is a necessary condition for intellectual or spiritual attainment. For him physical education means not only the proper functioning of the various organs of the body but also the development of strength, balance, and a sense of beauty. According to him, beauty is the ideal which physical life has to realise. ' If our seeking is for a total perfection of the being', says Aurobindo, 'the physical part of it cannot be left aside; for the body is the material basis, the body is the instrument which we have to use. [. . .] The perfection of the body, as great a perfection as we can bring about by means at our disposal' must be the ultimate aim of physical culture'.

Therefore, 'a development of the physical consciousness must always be a considerable part of our aim, but for that the right development of the body itself is an essential element; health, strength, fitness are the first needs, but the physical frame itself must be the best possible'. The education of the intellect, says Aurobindo, divorced from the perfection of the moral and emotional nature, is injurious to human progress. He admits the difficulties involved in providing a suitable moral training for the school and college. He distinguishes the heart from the mind, and says, that to instruct the mind is not to instruct the heart. He senses the danger of moral textbooks being used for the purpose, in that they make the thinking of high things mechanical and artificial, and whatever is mechanical and artificial is inoperative for good.

Further, he points out pertinently that 'the attempt to make boys moral and religious by the teaching of moral and religious text-books is a vanity and a delusion, precisely because the heart is not the mind and to instruct the mind does not necessarily improve the heart . The best kind of moral training for a man, that Sri Aurobindo conceives of is, 'to habituate himself to the right emotions, the noblest associations, the best mental, emotional and physical habits and the following out in right action of the fundamental impulses of his essential nature'.

By way of moral and religious education, any attempt at imposition of a certain discipline on children, dressing them into a certain mould, lashingthem into a desired path is essentially hypocritical and heartless. Only what the man admires and accepts, becomes part of himself; the rest is a mask. On the other hand, to neglect moral and religious education is to corrupt the race. In moral training, Sri Aurobindo stresses the value of suggestion and deprecates imposition. 'The first rule of moral training', he says, 'is to suggest and invite, not command or impose. The best method of suggestion is by personal example daily converse and the books read from day to day'. 'Every boy should', says Aurobindo, 'therefore be given practical opportunity as well as intellectual encouragement to develop all that is best in the nature.

If he has bad qualities, bad habits, bad samaskar as (behaviour patterns), whether of mind or body, he should not be treated harshly as a delinquent, but encouraged to get rid of them by the Rajayogic (a type of yoga) method of samyama (self-control), rejection and substitution'. Instead of discouraging such people, Aurobindo would like them to be rather encouraged to think such bad traits, 'not as sins or offences, but as symptoms of a curable disease, alterable by a steady and sustained effort of the will—falsehood being rejected [...] and replaced by truth, fear by courage, selfishness by sacrifice and renunciation, malice by love'.

Unformed virtues may not be rejected as faults. No religious teaching, according to Aurobindo is of any value 'unless it is lived, and the use of various kinds of sadhana, (spiritual self-training and exercise) is the only effective preparation for religious living. The ritual of prayer, homage, ceremony is carved for by many minds as an essential preparation and, if not made an end itself, is a great help tospiritual progress; if it is withheld, some other forms of meditation, devotion or religious duty must be put in its place. Otherwise, religious teaching is of little use and would almost be better ungiven'.

The principles of teaching and the training of the senses

In a series of articles that Sri Aurobindo wrote in 1909–10, he enunciated three fundamental principles of teaching. 'The first principle of true teaching is that nothing can be taught. The teacher is not an insiructor or task master; he is a helper and a guide. His business is to suggest and not to impose'. The second principle according to Sri Aurobindo, is that 'the mind has to be consulted in its growth'. He pointed out that the idea of hammering the child into the shape desired by the parents or teacher is a barbarous and ignorant superstition. He warned that to force the nature to abandon its own dharma is to do it permanent harm, mutilate its growth and deform its perfection, and that there can be no greater error than for the parents or the teachers to arrange beforehand that the given student shall develop particular qualities, capacities, ideas, virtues or be prepared for a prearranged career. And the third principle of education that Sri Aurobindo laid down is to work from near to the far, from that which is to that which shall be.

In other words, Sri Aurobindo underlined that education must proceed from direct experience and that even that which is abstract and remote from experience should be brought to the ken of experience. Knowledge has to be a growth from personal experience to larger and intenser and higher experience. There are several other guidelines that we find in Sri Aurobindo. While explaining the instruments of the work of the teacher, he writes 'Teaching, example, influence—these are the three instruments of the guru (teacher or guide). But the wise teacher will not seek to impose himself or his opinions on the passive acceptance of the receptive mind; he will throw in only what is productive and sure as a seed that will grow under the divine fostering within. He will seek to awaken much more than to instruct; he will aim at the growth of faculties and the experiences by a natural process and free expansion. He will give a method as an aid, as autilisable device, not as an imperative formula or a fixed routine.

And he will be on his guard against any turning of the means into a limitation, against the mechanising of process'. 'What is his method and his system?' asks Sri Aurobindo and answers, 'He has no method and every method. His system is a natural organization of the highest processes and movements of which the nature is capable. Applying themselves even to the pettiest details and to actions the most insignificant in their appearance with as much care and thoroughness as to the greatest, they in the end lift all into the Light and transform all'. 'This imperfect nature of ours, ' 'explains Sri Aurobindo, 'contains the materials of our perfection, but inchoate, distorted, misplaced, thrown together in disorder or a poor imperfect order. All this material has to be patiently perfected, purified, reorganised, new—moulded and transformed, not hacked and hewn and slain or mutilated, not obliterated by simple coercion and denial'.

These principles, it will be observed, are subtle and complex, and no rigid formula of practice can be derived from them. They impose a great responsibility on the teacher and demand from him extraordinary qualities of a profound psychologist. In the matter of the training of the senses, Aurobindo aims at nothing less than perfection. This, he says, must be one of the first cares of the teacher. The two important things that are needed of the senses, he points out are "accuracy and sensitiveness". The senses depend for their accuracy and sensitiveness on the unobstructed activity of the nerves which are the channels of their information and the passive acceptance of the mind, the recipient.

In case of any obstruction, the remedy lies in the purification of the nerve system. 'This process inevitably restores the perfect and unobstructed activity of the channels and, if well and thoroughly done, leads to a high activity of the senses. The process is called in yogic discipline nadi-suddhi or nerve – purification'. Six senses which minister to knowledge, sight, learning, smell, touch and taste, mindor manas (the sixth sense of the Indian psychology) can be developed through the physical nerves and their end—organs, but manas could be developed through yogic discipline suksmadristi or subtle reception of images.

Aurobindo wrote: Telepathy, clairvoyance, clair audience, presentiment, thought-reading, character-reading and many other modern discoveries are very ancient powers of the mind which have been left undeveloped, and they all belong to the manas. The development of the sixth sense has never formed part of human training. In a future age it will undoubtedly take a place in the necessary preliminary training of the human instrument. Meanwhile there is no reason why the mind should not be trained to give a correct report to the intellect so that our thought may start with absolutely correct if not with full impressions.

Sri Aurobindo while analysing the causes of inefficiency of the senses, as gatherers of knowledge, attributes it to 'insufficient use'. Students, he suggests, should over cornetamasic (optuseness of the mind and the senses) inertia and ought to be accustomed to catch the sights, sounds, etc. , around. them, distinguish them, mark their nature, properties and sources and fix them in the citta so that they may be always ready to respond when called for by the memory. 'Attention' according to him, is the chief factor in knowledge and considersit the first condition of right memory and accuracy.

Besides attention 'concentration on several things at a time' says Aurobindo is often indispensable. He holds the view that it is quite possible to develop the power of double concentration, triple concentration, multiple concentration, which is a matter of abhy as a or steady natural practice. Along with faculties of memory, judgement, observation, comparing and contrasting and analogy which are indispensable aids in the acquisition of knowledge, Aurobindo emphasizes Imagination as the most important and indispensable instrument.

It has be endivided into three functions,. the forming of mental images, the power of creating thoughts, images and imitations or new combinations of existing thoughts and images, the appreciation of the soul in things, beauty, charm, greatness, hidden suggestiveness, the emotion and spiritual life that pervades the world. 'This is in every way as important as the training of the faculties which observe and compare outward things'. These mental faculties, as Aurobindo suggests, should first be exercised on things, afterwards on words and ideas. . . . All this should be done informally, drawing on the curiosity and interest, avoiding set teaching and memorising of rules. Sri Aurobindo is critical of the practice of teaching by snippets which is in practice in the existing system of education.

Teaching by snippets, says Aurobindo, must be relegated to the lumber—room of dead sorrows. He is critical since: A subject is taught a little at a time, in conjunction with a host of others, with the result that what might be well learnt in a single year is badly learned in seven and the boy goes out ill—equipped, served with imperfect parcels of knowledges, master of none of the great departments of human knowledge. He characterizes such a system of education as one attempting to 'heighten this practice of teaching by snippets at the bottom and the middle and suddenly change it to a grandiosespecialism at the top. This is to base the triangle on its apex and hope that it will stand'.

Aurobindo has, therefore, found some meaning in the old system which was more rational than the modern: 'If it did not impart so much varied information, it built up a deeper, nobler and much more real culture. Much of the shallowness, discursive lightness and fickle mutability of the average modern mind is due to the vicious principle of teaching by snippets'.

However, Aurobindo is clear that in the future education we need not bind ourselves either by the ancient or the modern system but select only the most perfect and rapid means of mastering knowlege. For him, every child is an inquirer, an investigator, analyser, amerciless anatomist. Appeal to these qualities in him and let him acquire without knowing it the right temper and the necessary fundamental knowledge of the scientist. Every child has an insatiable intellectual curiosity and turn for metaphysical enquiring. Use it to draw him on slowly to an understanding of the world and himself. Every child has the gift of imitation and a touch of imaginative power. Use it to give him the ground work of the faculty of the artist.

It is by allowing Nature to work that we get the benefit of the gifts she has bestowed on us Aurobindo is particular that the first attention of the teacher must be given to the medium and the instruments and, until these are perfected, to multiply subjects of regular instruction is to waste time and energy. 'The mother tongue', he says 'is the proper medium of education and therefore the first energies of the child should be directed to the thorough mastering of the medium'.

In connection with language teaching he advocates that when the mental instruments are sufficiently developed to acquire a language easily and swiftly, that is the time to introduce him to many languages, not when he can partially understand what he is taught and masters it laboriously and imperfectly. He believes in the disciplinary value of learning one language, especially one's own language, which he says, prepares one for mastering another. He maintains that with the facility developed in one's own language, to master others in easier.

The psychic and spiritual education

Aurobindo also speaks of mental and psychic education, but his real interest is in a still higher stage, which according to him is spiritual or supramental education. This does notimply the annihilation of the individual but his enrichment through contact with the Absolute. The spiritual stage transcends the mental and the psychic stage. The justification for psychic and spiritual education rests upon three important considerations: a) education should provide to the individual a steady exploration of something that is inmost in the psychological complexity of human consciousness; (b) the most important question of human life is to consider the aim of human life and the aim of one's own life and one's own position and the role in the society; and this question can best be answered only when the psychic and spiritual domains are explored and when one is enabled to develop psychic and spiritual faculties of knowledge; and (c) the contemporary crisis of humanity has arisen because of the disbalancement between the material advancement on the one hand and inadequate spiritual progression.

If, therefore, this crisis has to be met, development of psychic and spiritual consciousness should be fostered.

Aurobindo tries to draw a distinction between psychic and spiritual in the following terms. At the life of psychic life, the individual feels an unbroken continuity in the world of forms and sees level as an immortal function in endless time and limitless space. The spiritual consciousness goes beyond time and space and is an identification with the infinite and the eternal. Aurobindo is expressing the same idea when he says that in psychic life selfishness must be discarded, but in the spiritual life there is nosense of the separate self.

Aurobindo insists that it is not annihilation of the individual but its transformation which is the end of integral education. When man attains such education there is total transformation of matter. He calls it supramental education as it will work, not only upon the consciousness of individual beings, but upon the very substance of which they are built and even upon the physical environment in which they live. An unprecedented kind of experiment in education was launched by Sri Aurobindo and the Mother, when in 1943, a school came to be established at Sri Aurobindo Ashram at Pondicherry with merely 20 students on its rolls, soon it began to grow, and in 1951, when the number of students had increased, and studies in Higher Education had to be organized, it was expanded into Sri Aurobindo International University Centre.

The Centre was conceived as one of the best means of preparing humanity for future that would be marked by the manifestation of a new light and power—the supramental light and power. It was launched so that the elite of the humanity may be made ready who would be able to work for the progressive unification of the race and who at the same time would be prepared to embody the new force descending upon the earth to transform it. The Centre conducted a programme of experimental research under the direct guidance of the Mother, and it became a laboratory of education for tomorrow.

The educational doctrine of Sri Aurobindo is closely linked with his futuristic vision of human destiny which is reflected in his statement:

> They should be children of the past, possessors of the present, creators of the future. The past is our foundation, the present our material, the future our aim and summit. Aurobindo's visionary mystic mind articulated a concept of life which was unique since he conceived of it as a lavish and manifold opportunity given us to discover, realize, express the Divine and accordingly, visualized a system of education which would help expression of unrealized potentialities, in line with his concept of life.

This called for a creative vision and an extraordinary adventure. For him human destiny is an ascent towards the supermind, towards realization of the Godhead and his philosophy of education provides a forceful and resilient framework to attain this goal.

5

EDUCATION ACCORDING TO WESTERN THINKERS

OUTDOOR EDUCATION PHILOSOPHY

Brookes proposed that the meaning of outdoor education is relative to time and place. To help convey the diversity of what is meant by "outdoor education", many definitions are provided below. But be warned — such definitions can and should evolve and transform.

There are at least five major "schools" of philosophy used within outdoor education:

— *Wilderness experience* - especially wilderness, nature, and indigenous philosophies

— *Experiential learning* - particularly John Dewey's work on the nature of experience and education

— *Psychological growth* - especially humanistic and personal growth psychology

— *Outdoor education* - philosophical approaches generated from within outdoor education, usually by outdoor educators and/or those studying outdoor education, including personal philosophies of outdoor education

— *Postmodernism* - deconstructions of education, society, culture, and outdoor education

"Several researchers state that the elements of a philosophical basis for outdoor education can be found in the doctrines of Comenius, Rousseau, and Pestalozzi.

ROUSSEAU

Popular song lyrics often have a way of reflecting what many people think, but rarely articulate. Recently, a song with a catchy tune and lots of airtime verbalized a way of thinking about God that is quite popular. The song, *What God Said* by a group called the Uninvited begins with the lyrics, "I talked to God and God said 'Hey! I've got a lot of things to say; write it down this very day and spread the word in every way.'" This is a remarkably evangelistic idea in this day of absolute tolerance for other people's beliefs. However, this god who has revealed himself to the songwriter doesn't expect much from the listener. According to the first verse we are to floss between each meal, drive with both hands on the wheel, and not be too sexually aggressive on the first date. In the second verse god wants us to ride bikes more, feed the birds, and clean up after our pets.

The third verse gets a little more interesting. God supposedly reveals that humans killed his only son and that his creation is undone, but that he can't help everyone. These obvious references to the incarnation of Christ and the Fall of Adam set up the listener for the solution to mankind's situation which, according to the song, is to "start with the basics—just be nice and see if that makes things all right." The chorus drives home this theology by repeating often that "I talked to God and God said nothing special, I talked to God and God said nothing that we shouldn't already know, shouldn't already know."

This idea, namely that any revelation from God would consist primarily of common sense notions, is a product of the

Enlightenment and found an extraordinary voice in the philosopher Jean-Jacques Rousseau. Rousseau argued that all one needs to know about God has been revealed in nature or in one's own conscience. Rousseau is often called the father of the French revolution, a movement that exalted the worship of reason and attempted to purge the clergy and Christianity from French culture. Although Rousseau wasn't around for the bloodshed of the revolution itself, his idea of a natural theology helped to provide a framework for rejecting special revelation and the organized church.

Few people in history have caused such a wide spectrum of responses to their ideas. At his death, Rousseau's burial site became a place of pilgrimage. George Sand referred to him as "Saint Rousseau," Shelly called him a "sublime genius," and Schiller, a "Christ-like soul for whom only Heaven's angels are fit company." However, others had a different perspective. His one and only true love, Sophie d'Houdetot, referred to him as an "interesting madman." Diderot, a long time acquaintance, summed him up as "deceitful, vain as Satan, ungrateful, cruel, hypocritical and full of malice." In addition to anything else that might be said about Rousseau, he was at least an expert at being a celebrity. He was a masterful self-promoter who knew how to violate public norms just enough to stay in the public eye.

Interestingly enough, Rousseau's ideas have actually had greater and longer impact outside of France. Two centuries later, his natural theology plays a significant role in determining our society's view of human nature as well as how we educate our children. Thus it is important to consider the thoughts of Rousseau and see how they impact our culture today, especially in the realm of education.

Rousseau's Natural Theology

Rousseau often claims in his writings that all he seeks is the truth, and he is very confident that he knows it when he sees it. Being a child of the Enlightenment, Rousseau begins with the Cartesian assumption that he exists and that the universe is real. He then decides that the first cause of all activity is a will, rather than matter itself. He states, "I believe therefore that a will moves the universe and animates nature. This is my first dogma, or my first article of faith." He then argues that this "will" that moves matter is also intelligent.

Finally, Rousseau writes that "This 'being' which wills and is powerful, this being active in itself, this being, whatever it may be, which moves the universe and orders all things, I call *God*.". So far, so good, but according to Rousseau, to guess the purpose of this being or to ask questions beyond immediate necessity would be foolish and harmful. Rousseau writes "But as soon as I want to contemplate Him in Himself, as soon as I want to find out where He is, what He is, what His substance is, He escapes me, and my clouded mind no longer perceives anything."

The problem with Rousseau's view of God is that we can know so little of Him. Rousseau rejects special revelation and argues that it is only by observing nature and looking inward that we can perceive anything at all about the Creator. Rousseau perceives from nature that the earth was made for humans and that humanity is to have dominion over it. He also argues that humanity will naturally worship the Creator, stating, "I do not need to be taught this worship; it is dictated to me by nature itself.". In Rousseau's opinion, to seek any other source than nature for how to worship God would be to seek man's opinion and authority, both of which are rejected as destructive.

Rousseau believes that humans are autonomous creatures, and that humanity is free to do evil, but that doing evil detracts from satisfaction with oneself. Rousseau thanks God for making him in His image so that he can be free, good, and happy like God. Death is merely the remedy of the evils that we do. As he puts it, "nature did not want you to suffer forever."

Rousseau is clear about the source of evil. He writes, "Man, seek the author of evil no longer. It is yourself. No evil exists other than that which you do or suffer, and both come to you from yourself. . . .Take away the work of man, and everything is good." It is reason that will lead us to the "good." A divine instinct has been placed in our conscience that allows us to judge what is good and bad. The question remains that if each person possesses this divine instinct to know the good, why do so many not follow it? Rousseau's answer is that our conscience speaks to us in "nature's voice" and that our education in civil man's prejudices causes us to forget how to hear it. So the battle against evil is not a spiritual one, but one of educational methods and content.

Although Rousseau thought he was saving God from the rationalists, mankind is left to discern good and evil with only nature as its measuring rod, and education as its savior.

A Philosophy of Education

Whether you agree with his ideas or not, Rousseau was an intellectual force of such magnitude that his ideas still impact our thinking about human nature and the educational process two centuries later. His work *Emile* compares to Plato's *Republic* in its remarkable breadth. Not only does the book describe a pedagogical method for training children to become practically perfect adults, but he also builds in it an impressive philosophical foundation for his educational goals. *Emile* is a very detailed account of how Rousseau would raise a young lad (Emile) to adulthood, as well as a description of the perfect wife for his charge. Along the way, Rousseau proposes his natural theology which finds ardent followers all over the world today.

Although *Emile* was written in the suburbs of Paris, Rousseau's greatest impact on educational practice has actually been outside of France. French educators have been decidedly non-Romantic when it comes to early childhood education. Rousseau had a great deal of influence on the inventor of the

Kindergarten, Friedrich Froebel, as well as the educational Romantics Johann Pestalozzi and Johann Herbart. These three educators' names are engraved on the Horace Mann building on the campus of Teachers College, Columbia University. Columbia has been, and continues to be, at the center of educational reform in America, and happens to have been the home of John Dewey, America's premier progressive thinker and educational philosopher. Dewey and William Heard Kilpatrick further secularized and applied the thinking of Froebel, Pestalozzi, and Herbart, and thus Rousseau.

The common bond that connects these educators is a Romantic view of human nature. Besides a general faith in the goodness of all humanity, there are two other Romantic fallacies that are particularly dangerous when carried to extremes. The first is what is called the doctrine of developmentalism, or natural tempo, which states that bookish knowledge should not be introduced at an early age. Second is the notion of holistic learning, which holds that natural or lifelike, thematic methods of instruction are always superior. Both ideas tend to be anti-fact oriented and regard the systematic instruction of any material at an early age harmful. This has had a profound effect on how we teach reading in this country. The ongoing battle between whole- language methods and the use of systematic phonics centers on this issue. When the Romantic view prevails, which it often does in our elementary schools, systematic phonics disappears.

Rousseau's theology and educational methods are tightly bound together. He argues against the biblical view that humanity is fallen and needs a redeemer. He believes that our reason and intellect are fully capable of discerning what is right and wrong without the need of special revelation or the indwelling of the Holy Spirit. As a result, Rousseau argues that a proper education is man's only hope for knowing what limited truth is available.

Rousseau and Childhood Education

An interesting aspect of Rousseau's child-raising techniques is his reliance on *things* to constrain and train a child rather than people. Rousseau rightfully asserts that education begins at birth, a very modern concept. However, in his mind early education should consist mainly of allowing as much freedom as possible for the child. Rebellion against people is to be avoided at all costs because it could cause an early end to a student's education and result in a wicked child. He puts it this way: "As long as children find resistance only in things and never in wills, they will become neither rebellious nor irascible and will preserve their health better."

Rousseau believed that a teacher or parent should never lecture or sermonize. Experience, interaction with things, is a far more effective teacher. This dependence on experience is at the core of modern progressive education as well. As a result, Rousseau was remarkably hostile towards books and traditional education's dependency on them. From the very beginning of *Emile*, he is adamant that books should play little or no part in the young man's education. He claims that, "I take away the instruments of their greatest misery—that is books. Reading is the plague of childhood and almost the only occupation we know how to give it. At twelve, Emile will hardly know what a book is." At one point Rousseau simply says, "I hate books. They only teach one to talk about what one does not know."

A corollary aspect of this negative view of books is Rousseau's belief that children should never be forced to memorize anything. He even suggests that an effort be made to keep their vocabulary simple prior to their ability to read. This antagonism towards books and facts fits well with Rousseau's notion that people "always try to teach children what they would learn much better by themselves." He also believed that children should never memorize what they can not put to immediate use. Rousseau acknowledged that children memorize easily, but felt that they are incapable of judgment and do not have what he calls true memory. He argued that children are unable to learn two languages prior to the age of twelve, a belief that has been refuted by recent research.

Prior to that age, Emile is allowed to read only one book, *Robinson Crusoe*. Why *Crusoe*? Because Rousseau wants Emile to see himself as Crusoe, totally dependent upon himself for all of his needs. Emile is to imitate Crusoe's experience, allowing necessity to determine what needs to be learned and accomplished. Rousseau's hostility towards books and facts continues to impact educational theory today. There is a strong and growing sentiment in our elementary schools to remove the shackles of book knowledge and memorization and to replace them with something called the "tool" model of learning.

Rousseau's Philosophy and Modern "Tools"

Rousseau argued against too much bookish knowledge and for natural experiences to inform young minds. Today, something called the "tool" model carries on this tradition. It is argued that knowledge is increasing so rapidly that spending time to stockpile it or to study it in books results in information that is soon outdated. We need to give our students the "tools" of learning, and then they can find the requisite facts, as they become necessary to their experience.

Two important assumptions are foundational to this argument. First, that the "tools" of learning can be acquired in a content neutral environment without referring to specific information or facts. And secondly, that an extremely child-centered, experience driven curriculum is always superior to a direct instruction, content oriented approach. The "tool" model argues that "love of learning" and "critical thinking skills" are more important to understanding, let's say chemistry, than are the facts about chemistry itself. Some argue that facts would only slow them down.

Unfortunately, research in the real world does not support this view of learning. Citing numerous studies, E.D. Hirsch contends that learning new ideas is built upon previously acquired knowledge. He calls this database of information "intellectual capital" and just as it takes money to make money, a knowledge framework is necessary to incorporate new knowledge. To stress "critical thinking" prior to the acquisition of knowledge actually reduces a child's capacity to think critically.

Students who lack intellectual capital must go through a strenuous process just to catch up with what well-educated children already know. If children attempt to do algebra without knowing their multiplication tables, they spend a large amount of time and energy doing simple calculations. This distracts and frustrates children and makes learning higher math much more difficult. The same could be said for history students who never learn names and dates.

The second idea is that students should learn via natural experience within a distinctly passive curriculum. While there is wisdom in letting nature set as many of the limits as possible for a child—experience is probably the most powerful teaching method—Rousseau and progressive educational theory go too far in asserting that a teacher should never preach or sermonize to a child. At an early age, children can learn from verbal instruction, especially if it occurs along with significant learning experiences. In fact, certain kinds of learning often contradict one's experience.

The teaching of morality and democratic behavior involves teaching principles that cannot be experienced immediately, and virtually everything that parents or teachers tell children about sexual behavior has religious foundations based on assumptions about human nature. The bottom line seems to be that if higher math, morality, and civilized behavior could be learned from simply interacting with nature, Rousseau's system would be more appealing. However, his version of the naturalistic fallacy—assuming that everything that is natural is right—would not serve our students well.

Rousseau's observations about the student-teacher relationship fall short first because of his overly optimistic view of human nature and because we believe that there is truth to convey to the next generation that cannot be experienced within nature alone.

JOHANN HEINRICH PESTALOZZI

Johann Heinrich Pestalozzi (1746 - 1827). Born in Zurich, Pestalozzi took up Rousseau's ideas and explored how they might be developed and implemented. His early experiments in education (at Neuhof) ran into difficulties but he persisted and what became known as the 'Pestalozzi Method' came to fruition in his school at Yverdon (established in 1805). Instead of dealing with words, he argued, children should learn through activity and through things. They should be free to pursue their own interests and draw their own conclusions.

Pestalozzi quoted:

> I wish to wrest education from the outworn order of doddering old teaching hacks as well as from the new-fangled order of cheap, artificial teaching tricks, and entrust it to the eternal powers of nature herself, to the light which God has kindled and kept alive in the hearts of fathers and mothers, to the interests of parents who desire their children grow up in favour with God and with men.

Pestalozzi goes beyond Rousseau in that he sets out some concrete ways forward - based on research. He tried to reconcile the tension, recognized by Rousseau, between the education of the individual (for freedom) and that of the citizen (for responsibility and use). He looks to 'the achievement of freedom in autonomy for one and all' Soëtard 1994: 308).

His initial influence on the development of thinking about pedagogy owes much a book he published in 1801: *How Gertrude Teaches Her Children* - and the fact that he had carried his proposals through into practice. He wanted to establish a 'psychological method of instruction' that was in line with the 'laws of human nature. As a result he placed a special emphasis on spontaneity and self-activity. Children should not be given ready-made answers but should arrive at answers themselves. To do this their own powers of seeing, judging and reasoning should be cultivated, their self-activity encouraged. The aim is to educate the whole child - intellectual education is only part of a wider plan. He looked to balance, or keep in equilibrium, three elements - hands, heart and head.

William H. Kilpatrick has summarized six principles that run through Pestalozzi's efforts around schooling.

1. Personality is sacred. This constitutes the 'inner dignity of each individual for the young as truly as for the adult.
2. As 'a little seed... contains the design of the tree', so in each child is the promise of his potentiality. 'The educator only takes care that no untoward influence shall disturb nature's march of developments'.
3. Love of those we would educate is 'the sole and everlasting foundation' in which to work. 'Without love, neither the physical not the intellectual powers will develop naturally'. So kindness ruled in Pestalozzi's schools: he abolished flogging - much to the amazement of outsiders.
4. To get rid of the 'verbosity' of meaningless words Pestalozzi developed his doctrine of *Anschauung* - direct concrete observation, often inadequately called 'sense perception' or 'object lessons'. No word was to be used for any purpose until adequate *Anschauung* had preceded. The thing or distinction must be felt or observed in the concrete. Pestalozzi's followers developed various sayings from this: from the known to the unknown, from the simple to the complex, from the concrete to the abstract.
5. To perfect the perception got by the *Anschauung* the thing that must be named, an appropriate *action* must follow. 'A man learns by action... have done with [mere] words!' 'Life shapes us and the life that shapes us is not a matter of words but action'.

6. Out of this demand for action came an emphasis on repetition - not blind repetition, but repetition of action following the *Anschauung*.

And what is his significance to informal educators today? First, there is his concern with social justice and his commitment to work with those who have suffered within society. He saw education as central to the improvement of social conditions

Second, he used his sympathy for peasant life and his remembrance of his mother's care as paradigms - as ways of thinking about the form education should take. In a famous phrase he declared: ' There can be no doubt that within the living room of every household are united the basic elements of all true human education in its whole range'. This underlines the potential of everyday life for educators. That said though, Pestalozzi made a significant contribution to the establishment of the school as a central educational force (in contrast to Rousseau's emphasis on the tutor).

Third, there is Pestalozzi's concern with equilibrium between elements - head, hands and heart - and the dangers of attending to just one.

Fourth, Pestalozzi is a classic example of the 'reflective practitioner'. He is concerned with action, with experimentation and yet, at the same time, he is committed to observation and reflection, and to trying to make sense of experiences and situations.

Fifth, in his failed experiment at Neuhof he attempted to a form of schooling that has subsequently appealed to Gandhi and others concerned with combating colonialism and its legacy. He wanted the school to combine education with work. The school was to be a production unit so that children could finance their own learning - and in so doing they would be under no obligation to anyone. Furthermore, the school could be free from state interference.

Last, and not least, he strove to combat the tyranny of method and 'correctness' It is ironical that his approach should become known as a method; and that observers attempted to systematize his thought. It was his commitment to people and their well-being that animated his life's work - and in Aristotle's terms he would put that which is 'right' or good before that which is 'correct'.

JOHN DEWEY

Theory of Value

What knowledge and skills are worthwhile learning? What are the goals of education?

The term "value" has two quite different meanings. On the one hand, it denotes the attitude of prizing a thing, finding it worth while, for its own sake, or intrinsically This is a name for a full or complete experience. To value in this sense is to appreciate. But to value also means a distinctly intellectual act-an operation of comparing and judging to evaluate. This occurs when direct full experience is lacking, and the question arises which of the various possibilities of a situation is to be preferred in order to reach a full realization, or vital experience.

Values that are "extrinsic" or instrumental may be rationally estimated. For they are only means; are not ends in any genuine sense. As means their efficacy may be determined by methods that will stand scientific inspection. But the "ends" they serve (ends which are truly ends) are just matters of what groups, classes, sects, races, or whatever, happen irrationally to like or dislike.

Of the many consequences that result, the state of education is perhaps the most significant. As the means of the general institution of intelligent action, it holds the key to orderly social reconstruction.

We cannot establish a hierarchy of values among studies. In so far as any study has a unique or irreplaceable function in experience, in so far as it marks a characteristic enrichment of life, its worth is intrinsic or incomparable. Since education is not a means to living, but is identical with the operation of living a life which is fruitful and inherently significant, the only ultimate value which can be set up is just the process of living itself. And this is not an end to which studies and activities are subordinate means; it is the whole of which they are ingredients the absence of a social environment in connection with which learning is a need and a reward is the chief reason for the isolation of the school; and this isolation renders school knowledge inapplicable to life and so infertile in character

Theory of Knowledge

What is knowledge? How is it different from belief? What is a mistake? A lie?

Knowledge is the tool for managing experience-no such thing as genuine knowledge and fruitful understanding except as the offspring of doing.

Knowledge is power and knowledge is achieved by sending the mind to school of nature to learn her processes of change.

On the side of knowledge, the division carried with it a difference between knowledge, in its full sense, and belief. The former is demonstrative, necessary-that is sure. Belief on the contrary is only opinion; in its uncertainty and mere probability, it relates to the world of change as knowledge corresponds to the realm of true reality.

But in popular usage, belief also means a personal matter; something that some human being entertains or holds; a position,. which under the influence of psychology, is converted into the notion that belief is merely a mental or psychical state.

There is not belief so settled as not to be exposed to further inquiry.

The great thing is not to avoid mistakes but to have them take place under conditions such that they can be utilized to increase intelligence in the future.

Knowledge is a perception of those connections of an object which determine its applicability in a given situation. our beliefs are only hypotheses, theories, suggestions, guesses, and are to be entertained tentatively and to be utilized as 'indications of experiments to be tried making mistakes is an incidental requirement. appliances which forbid a chance for mistakes to occur, restricts initiative, reduces judgment to a minimum, and compels the use of methods which are so remote from the complex situations of life that the power gained is of little availability. Intellectual integrity, honesty, and sincerity are at bottom not matters of conscious purpose by of quality of active response

Theory of Human Nature

What is a human being? How does it differ from other species? What are the limits of human potential?

Human nature being what it is, however, it tends to seek its motivation in the agreeable rather than in the disagreeable, in direct pleasure rather than in alternative pain.

Everything which is distinctively human is learned, not native, even though it could not be learned without native structures which mark man off from other animals.

The interaction of human beings, namely, association, is not different in origin from other modes of interaction .... Everything that exists in as far as it is known and knowable is in interaction with other things .... The significant consideration is that assemblage of organic human beings transforms sequence and coexistence into participation.

Even dogs and horses have their actions modified by association with human beings; they form different habits because human beings are concerned with what they do. There was no complete discussion related to the distinctions between animal and man in this resource. Limitation of capacity is one of the things which has to be learned; like other things, it is learned through the experience of consequences.

Theory of Learning

What is learning? How are skills and knowledge acquired?

Learning is active. It involves reaching out of the mind. It involves organic assimilation starting from within. Literally, we must take our stand with the child and our departure from him. It is he and not the subject-matter which determines both quality and quantity of learning.

> ... learning means something which the individual does when he studies. He learns in consequence of his direct activities. Thinking is the method of intelligent learning, of learning that employs and rewards the mind.

There are two senses of the word "learning"; (1) the sum total of what is known, as that is handed down by books and learned men, and (2) something which the individual does when he studies; an active, personally conducted affair. This transmission occurs by means of communication of habits of doing, thinking, and feeling from the older to the younger

Theory of Society

What is society? What institutions are involved in the educational process?

Society is one word, but infinitely many things. It covers all the ways in which by associating together men share their experiences, and build up common interests and aims.

Any education given by a group tends to socialize its members, but the quality and value of the socialization depends upon the habits and aims of the group.

As societies become more complex in structure and resources, the need of formal or intentional teaching and learning increases.

All institutions are educational in the sense that they operate to form the attitudes, dispositions, abilities and disabilities that constitute a concrete personality.

The social environment consists of all the activities of fellow beings that are bound up in the carrying on of the activities of any one of its members.

Theory of Opportunity

Who is to be educated? Who is to be schooled?

The dominant vocation of all human beings at all times is living-intellectual and moral growth.

Since growth is the characteristic of life, education is all one with growing; it has no end beyond itself. The criterion of the value of school education is the extent in which it creates a desire for continued growth and supplies means for making the desire effective in fact.

The inclination to learn from life itself and to make the conditions of life such that all will learn in the process of living is the finest product of schooling.

John Dewey wrote:

> I believe that education is the fundamental method of social progress and reform .... By law and punishment, by social agitation and discussion, society can regulate and form itself in a more or less haphazard and chance way. But through education society can formulate its own purpose, can organize its own means and resources, and thus shape itself with definiteness and economy in the direction in which it wishes to move .... Education thus conceived marks the most perfect and intimate union of science and art conceivable in human experience

There is the necessity that these immature members (of society) be not merely physically preserved in adequate numbers, but that they be initiated into interests, purposes, information, skill, and practices of the mature members: otherwise the group will cease its characteristic life. The inclination to learn from life itself and to make the conditions of life such that all will learn in the process of living is the finest product of schooling.

Theory of Consensus

Why do people disagree? How is consensus achieved? Whose opinion takes precedence?

Solutions of problems comes only by getting away from the meaning of terms that is already fixed upon and coming to see the conditions from another point of view, and hence in a fresh light.

Opinions should be treated as a factor in a problem needing adjustment.

Consensus demands communication The experience has to be formulated in order to be communicated. To formulate requires getting outside of it, seeing it as another would see it,

Considering what points of contact it has with the life of another so that it may be got into such form that he can appreciate its meaning. Except in dealing with commonplaces and catch phrases one has to assimilate imaginatively, something of another's experience in order to tell him intelligently of one's own experience.

Consensus demands communication. To be a recipient of a communication is to have an enlarged and changed experience. The experience has to be formulated in order to be communicated.

FROEBEL

One of the traditions of the Elementary School of the University of Chicago is of a visitor who, in its early days, called to see the kindergarten. On being told that the school had not as yet established one, she asked if there were not singing, drawing, manual training, plays and dramatizations, and attention to the children's social relations. When her questions were answered in the affirmative, she remarked, both triumphantly and indignantly, that was what she understood by a kindergarten, and that she did not know what was meant by saying that the school had no kindergarten. The remark was perhaps justified in spirit, if not in letter. At all events, it suggests that in a certain sense the school endeavours throughout its whole course — now including children between four and thirteen —to carry into effect certain principles which Froebel was perhaps the first consciously to set forth. Speaking still in general, these principles are:

1. That the primary business of school is to train children in co-operative and mutually helpful living; to foster in them the consciousness of mutual interdependence; and to help them practically in making the adjustments that will carry this spirit into overt deeds.

2. That the primary root of all educative activity is in the instinctive, impulsive attitudes and activities of the child, and not in the presentation and application of external material, whether through the ideas of others or through the senses; and that, accordingly, numberless spontaneous activities of children, plays, games, mimic efforts, even the apparently meaningless motions of infants —exhibitions previously ignored as trivial, futile, or even condemned as positively evil— are capable of educational use; nay, are the foundation-stones of educational method.

3. That these individual tendencies and activities are organized and directed through the uses made of them in keeping up the co-operative living already spoken of; taking advantage of them to reproduce on the child's plane the typical doings and occupations of the larger, maturer society into which he is finally to go forth; and that it is through production and creative use that valuable knowledge is secured and clinched.

So far as these statements correctly represent Froebel's educational philosophy, the School should be regarded as its exponent. An attempt is making to act upon them with as much faith and sincerity in their application to children of twelve as to children of four. This attempt, however, to assume what might be called the kindergarten attitude throughout the whole school makes necessary certain modifications of the work done in what is more technically known as the kindergarten period—that is, with the children between the ages of four and six. It is necessary only to state reasons for believing that in spite of the apparently radical character of some of them they are true to the spirit of Froebel.

As regards play and games

Play is not to be identified with anything which the child externally does. It rather designates his mental attitude in its entirety and in its unity. It is the free play, the interplay, of all the child's powers, thoughts, and physical movements, in embodying, in a satisfying form, his own images and interests. Negatively, it is freedom from economic pressure—the necessities of getting a living and supporting others—and from the fixed responsibilities attaching to the special callings of the adult. Positively, it means that the supreme end of the child is fulness of growth—fulness of realization of his budding powers, a realization which continually carries him on from one plane to another.

This is a very general statement, and taken in its generality, is so vague as to be innocent of practical bearing. Its significance in detail, in application, however, means the possibility, and in many respects the necessity, of quite a radical change of kindergarten procedure. To state it baldly, the fact that "play" denotes the psychological attitude of the child, not his outward performances, means complete emancipation from the necessity of following any given or prescribed system, or sequence of gifts, plays, or occupations.

The judicious teacher will certainly look for suggestions to the activities mentioned by Froebei (in his Mother-Play and elsewhere), and to those set forth in such minute detail by his disciples; but she will also remember that the principle of play requires her carefully to investigate and criticize these things, and decide whether they are really activities for her own children, or just things which may have been vital in the past to children living in different social conditions. So far as occupations, games, etc., simply perpetuate those of Froebel and his earlier disciples, it may fairly be said that in many respects the presumption is against them—the presumption is that in the worship of the external doings discussed by Froebel we have ceased to be loyal to his principle.

The teacher must be absolutely free to get suggestions from any and from every source, asking herself but these two questions: Will the proposed inside of play appeal to the child as his own ? Is it something of which he has the instinctive roots in himself, and which will mature the capacities that are struggling for manifestation in him ? And again: Will the proposed activity give that sort of expression to these impulses that will carry the child on to a higher plane of consciousness and action, instead of merely exciting him and then leaving him just where he was before, plus a certain amount of nervous exhaustion and appetite for more excitation in the future?

There is every evidence that Froebel studied carefully—inductively we might now say—the children's plays of his own time, and the games which mothers played with their infants. He also took great pains —as in his Mother-Play— to point out that certain principles of large import were involved. He had to bring his generation to consciousness of the fact that these things were not merely trivial and childish because done by children, but were essential factors in their growth.

Moreover, it is hardly likely that Froebel himself would contend that in his interpretation of these games he did more than take advantage of the best psychological and philosophical insight available to him at the time; and we may suppose that he would have been the first to welcome the growth of a better and more extensive psychology (whether general, experimental, or as child study), and would avail himself of its results to reinterpret the activities, to discuss them more critically, going from the new standpoint into the reasons that make them educationally valuable.

Symbolism

It must be remembered that much of Froebel's symbolism is the product of two peculiar conditions of his own life and work. In the first place, on account of inadequate knowledge at that time of the physiological and psychological facts and principles of child growth, he was often forced to resort to strained and artificial explanations of the value attaching to the plays, etc. To the impartial observer it is obvious that many of his statements are cumbrous and far-fetched, giving abstract philosophical reasons for matters that may now receive a simple, everyday formulation.

In the second place, the general political and social conditions of Germany were such that it was impossible to conceive continuity between the free, cooperative social life of the kindergarten and that of the world outside. Accordingly, he could not regard the "occupations" of the schoolroom as literal reproductions of the ethical principles involved in community life —the latter were often too restricted and authoritative to serve as worthy models.

Accordingly he was compelled to think of them as symbolic of abstract ethical and philosophical principles. There certainly is change enough and progress enough in the social conditions of the United States of today, as compared with those of the Germany of his day, to justify making kindergarten activities more natural, more direct, and more real representations of current life than Froebel's disciples have done. Even as it is, the disparity of Froebel's philosophy with German political ideals has made the authorities in Germany suspicious of the kindergarten, and has been undoubtedly one force operating in transforming its social simplicity into an involved intellectual technique.

Imagination and play

An excessive emphasis on symbolism is sure to influence the

treatment of imagination. It is of course true that a little child lives in a world of imagination. In one sense, he can only "make believe." His activities represent or stand for the life that he sees going on around him. Because they are thus representative they may be termed symbolic, but it should be remembered that this make-believe or symbolism has reference to the activities suggested. Unless they are, to the child, as real and definite as the adult's activities are to him, the inevitable result is artificiality, nervous strain, and either physical and emotional excitement or else deadening of powers.

There has been a curious, almost unaccountable, tendency in the kindergarten to assume that because the value of the activity lies in what it stands for to the child, therefore the materials used must be as artificial as possible, and that one must keep carefully away from real things and real acts on the part of the child. Thus one hears of gardening activities which are carried on by sprinkling grains of sand for seeds; the child sweeps and dusts a make-believe room with make-believe brooms and cloths; he sets a table using only paper cut in the flat (and even then cut with reference to geometric design, rather then to dishes), instead of toy tea things with which the child outside of the kindergarten plays. Dolls, toy locomotives, and trains of cars, etc., are tabooed as altogether too grossly real —and hence not cultivating the child's imagination.

All this is surely mere superstition. The imaginative play of the child's mind comes through the cluster of suggestions, reminiscences, and anticipations that gather about the things he uses. The more natural and straightforward these are, the more definite basis there is for calling up and holding together all the allied suggestions which make his imaginative play really representative. The simple cooking, dishwashing, dusting, etc., which children do are no more prosaic or utilitarian to them than would be, say, the game of the Five Knights. To the children these occupations are surcharged with a sense of the mysterious values that attach to whatever their elders are concerned with. The materials, then, must be as "real," as direct and straightforward, as opportunity permits.

But the principle does not end here— the reality symbolized must also lie within the capacities of the child's own appreciation. It is sometimes thought the use of the imagination is profitable in the degree it stands for very remote metaphysical and spiritual principles. In the great majority of such cases it is safe to say that the adult deceives himself. He is conscious of both the reality and the symbol, and hence of the relation between them. But since the truth or reality represented is far beyond the reach of the child, the supposed symbol is not a symbol to him at all. It is simply a positive thing on its own account.

Practically about all he gets out of it is its own physical and sensational meaning, plus, very often, a glib facility in phrases and attitudes that he learns are expected of him by the teacher —without, however, any mental counterpart. We often teach insincerity, and instil sentimentalism, and foster sensationalism when we think we are teaching spiritual truths by means of symbols. The realities reproduced, therefore, by the child should be of as familiar, direct, and real a character as possible. It is largely for this reason that in the kindergarten of our School the work centres so much about the reproduction of home and neighbourhood life This brings us to the topic of

Subject matter

The home life in its setting of house, furniture, utensils, etc., together with the occupations carried on in the home, offers, accordingly, material which is in a direct and real relationship to the child, and which he naturally tends to reproduce in imaginative form. It is also sufficiently full of ethical relations and suggestive of moral duties to afford plenty of food for the child on his moral side. The program is comparatively unambitious compared with that of many kindergartens, but it may be questioned whether there are not certain positive advantages in this limitation of the subject-matter. When much ground is covered (the work going over, say, industrial society, army, church, state, etc.), there is a tendency for the work to become over symbolic.

So much of this material lies beyond the experience and capacities of the child of four and five that practically all he gets out of it is the physical and emotional reflex—he does not get any real penetration into the material itself. Moreover, there is danger, in these ambitious programs, of an unfavourable reaction upon the child's own intellectual attitude. Having covered pretty much the whole universe in a purely make-believe fashion, he becomes blase, loses his natural hunger for the simple things of direct experience, and approaches the material of the first grades of the primary school with a feeling that he has had all that already. The later years of a child's life have their own rights, and a superficial, merely emotional anticipation is likely to do the child serious injury.

Moreover, there is danger that a mental habit of jumping rapidly from one topic to another be induced. The little child has a good deal of patience and endurance of a certain type. It is true that he has a liking for novelty and variety; that he soon wearies of an activity that does not lead out into new fields and open up new paths for exploration. My plea, however, is not for monotony. There is sufficient variety in the activities, furnishings, and instrumentalities of the homes from which the children come to give continual diversity! It touches the civic and the industrial life at this and that point; these concerns can be brought in, when desirable, without going beyond the unity of the main topic. Thus there is an opportunity to foster that sense which is at the basis of attention and of all intellectual growth—a sense of continuity.

This continuity is often interfered with by the very methods that aim at securing it. From the child's standpoint unity lies in the subject-matter—the present case, in the fact that he is always dealing with one thing: home life. Emphasis is continually passing from one phase of this life to another; one occupation after another, one piece of furniture after another, one relation after another, etc., receive attention; but they all fall into building up one and the same mode of living, although bringing now this feature, now that, into prominence. The child is working all the time within a unity, giving different phases of its clearness and definiteness, and bringing them into coherent connection with each other. When there is a great diversity of subject-matter, continuity is apt to be sought simply on the formal side; that is, in schemes of sequence, "schools of work," a rigid program of development followed with every topic, a "thought for the day" from which the work is not supposed to stray.

As a rule such sequence is purely intellectual, hence is grasped only by the teacher, quite passing over the head of the child. Hence the program for the year, term, month, week, etc., should be made out on the basis of estimating how much of the common subject-matter can be covered in that time, not on the basis of intellectual or ethical principles. This will give both definiteness and elasticity.

Method

The peculiar problem of the early grades is, of course, to get hold of the child's natural impulses and instincts, and to utilize them so that the child is carried on to a higher plane of perception and judgment, and equipped with more efficient habits; so that he has an enlarged and deepened consciousness and increased control of powers of action. Wherever this result is not reached, play results in mere amusement and not in educative growth.

Upon the whole, constructive or "built up" work (with, of course. the proper alternation of story, song, and game which may be connected, so far as is desirable, with the ideas involved in the construction) seems better fitted than anything else to secure these two factors-initiation in the child's own impulse and termination upon a higher plane. It brings the child in contact with a great variety of material: wood, tin, leather, yarn, etc.; it supplies a motive for using these materials in real ways instead of going through exercises having no meaning except a remote symbolic one; it calls into play alertness of the senses and acuteness of observation; it demands clear-cut imagery of the ends to be accomplished, and requires ingenuity and invention in planning; it makes necessary concentrated attention and personal responsibility in execution, while the results are in such tangible form that the child may be led to judge his own work and improve his standards.

A word should be said regarding the psychology of imitation and suggestion in relation to kindergarten work. There is no doubt that the little child is highly imitative and open to suggestions; there is no doubt that his crude powers and immature consciousness need to be continually enriched and directed through these channels. But on this account it is imperative to discriminate between a use of imitation and suggestion which is so external as to be thoroughly non-psychological, and a use which is justified through its organic relation to the child's own activities.

As a general principle no activity should be originated by imitation. The start must come from the child; the model or copy may then be supplied in order to assist the child in imaging more definitely what it is that he really wants —in bringing him to consciousness. Its value is not as model to copy in action, but as guide to clearness and adequacy of conception. Unless the child can get away from it to his own imagery when it comes to execution, he is rendered servile sand dependent, not developed. Imitation comes in to reinforce and help out, not to initiate.

There is no ground for holding that the teacher should not suggest anything to the child until he has consciously expressed a want in that direction. A sympathetic teacher is quite likely to know more clearly than the child himself what his own instincts are and mean. But the suggestion must fit in with the dominant mode of growth in the child; it must serve simply as stimulus to bring forth more adequately what the child is already blindly striving to do. Only by watching the child and seeing the attitude that he assumes toward suggestions can we tell whether they are operating as factors in furthering the child's growth, or whether they are external, arbitrary impositions interfering with normal growth.

The same principle applies even more strongly to so-called dictation work. Nothing is more absurd than to suppose that there is no middle term between leaving a child to his own unguided fancies and likes or controlling his activities by a formal succession of dictated directions. As just intimated, it is the teacher's business to know what powers are striving for utterance at a given period in the child's development, and what sorts of activity will bring these to helpful expression, in order then to supply the requisite stimuli and needed materials.

The suggestion, for instance, of a playhouse, the suggestion that comes from seeing objects that have already been made to furnish it, from seeing other children at work, is quite sufficient definitely to direct the activities of a normal child of five. Imitation and suggestion come in naturally and inevitably, but only as instruments to help him carry out his own wishes and ideas. They serve to make him realize, to bring to consciousness, what he already is striving for in a vague, confused, and therefore ineffective way. From the psychological standpoint it may safely be said that when a teacher has to rely upon a series of dictated directions, it is just because the child has no image of his own of what is to be done or why it is to be done. Instead, therefore, of gaining power of control by conforming to directions, he is really losing it —made dependent upon an external source.

MERLEAU-PONTY

The Primacy of Perception

Merleau-Ponty constitutes his philosophical project on the polemical boundary between the empirical tradition of psychological behaviorism and the Kantian-Husserlian intellectualism of the transcendental ego. The former reflects the empirical mechanism of cause-effect that is independent of the conscious subject; the latter, a conscious subject constitutive of the real that is independent of corporeal implications. Within the parameters of this polemical problematic, Merleau-Ponty constructs a dialectical phenomenological ontology of the human subject.

Merleau-Ponty begins with Descartes's provocative depiction of the soul as being "not merely in the body as a pilot in his ship," but "wholly intermingled". His constructive mediation of the relation of the subject to his/her body centers upon the primacy of perception. Perception, for Merleau-Ponty, is opposed to empirical sensation as simply a reflexive response to a physical or chemical action of a stimulus on an organ as an objective event in the natural world without the complications of a conscious subject who perceives. He succinctly states the substance of his position that perception is an original modality of consciousness:

> we cannot apply the classical distinction of form and matter to perception, nor can we conceive the perceiving subject as a consciousness which "interprets," "deciphers," or "orders" a sensible matter according to an ideai law which it possesses. Matter is "pregnant" with its form, which is to say that in the final analysis every perception takes place within a certain horizon and ultimately in the "world." We experience a perception and its horizon "in action" [pratiquement] ràther than "posing" them or explicitly "knowing" them. Finally the quasi-organic relation of the perceiving subject and the world involves, in principle, the contradiction of immanence and transcendence.

The human subject as being in the world is first a lived body. Prior to the split between subject and object, the act of perceiving displays a phenomenal mode of preexistence. Neither passive as in empirical sensation nor active as in idealist construction, perception discloses one's own body as not simply an object , a thing in itself, but a way of being present to, and perceiving in, a world. Although body and soul are irreducibly distinct from, and ambiguously incongruent to, one another, nonetheless, they constitute a primordial dialectical unity. Unlike Sartre, for Merleau-Ponty the human subject is a strange mixture of being-in-itself and being-for-itself.

The lived body, conscious of itself, is reciprocally subject and object: The enigma is that my body simultaneously sees and is seen. That which looks at all things can also look at itself and recognize, in what it sees, the "other side" of its power of looking. It sees itself seeing; it touches itself touching; it is visible and sensitive for itself. It is not a self through transparence, like thought, which only thinks its object by assimilating it, by constituting it, by transforming it into thought. It is a self through confusion, narcissism, through inherence of the one who sees in that which he sees, and through inherence of sensing in the sensed - a self, therefore, that is caught up in things, that has a front and a back, a past and a future.

Touching one hand with another, a sensing subject becomes a sensed object. Touching and being touched, subject and object, in a reversible circularity, is an incendiary chiasm:

> The body's animation is not the assemblage or juxtaposition of its parts. Nor is it a question of a mind or spirit coming down from somewhere else into an automaton; this would still suppose that the body itself is without an inside and without a "self." There is a human body when, between the seeing and the seen, between touching and the touched, between one eye and the other, between hand and hand, a blending of some sort takes place - when the spark is lit between sensing and the sensible, lighting the fire that will not stop burning until some accident of the body will undo what no accident would have sufficed to do.

In the act of perception, furthermore, the perceiving subject is already intentionally related to a perceived world:

> "Our own body is in the world as a heart is in the organism." The body is my conscious insertion in the world, the presence of the world within me. The world, discovered through conscious reflection and its objectification, is always

> already the world I inhabit through my body with which I experience a profound communication and natural transaction.
>
> Perception reveals my primordial coexistence of being in the world through my body to things. Knowledge as connaisance is a co-nascence, a co-birthing. The foundation of knowing is an original being begotten together. The body is the medium of things. My body as my presence to the world makes it be that there are things. The perceived world is a projection of the perceiving subject as correlative to it.

The supreme perception is perception of the other, the mutual presence of embodied subjects to one another. One's own body and that of the other, not being objects, open out dialectically to one another. Each, not being pure subjective interiority, but being embodied and borne beyond oneself, relates to the embodied other, like unto oneself, in reciprocal corporeal encounter.

Mutual perception is not of two autonomous Cogitos who infer one another, but two incarnate minds that dialectically couple and diametrically feel one another. As each incarnate subject is reflective of its own bodiliness, each reflects the bodiliness of the other as semblables, as one's own likeness . There is fullness of life in the resonant reflection of mutual beholding and saluting, two gazes which light and mirror each other, and which coexist, one in the other. There are no longer two independent consciousnesses, with their own different teleologies and distinctive destinies, but two mutually enfolding glances. One's own body can assume segments derived from the body of another, just as the substance of one's own being passes into the other.

This communion of body-subjects is not, however, an anonymous interaction, a total undifferentiation between self and other. Each embodied self is open to the other as not simply itself and experiences the other, albeit like one's self, as other than itself. The self and the other are grounded in a primordial unity in which each Cogito is not an assertive self-positing, but given to itself and to one another in an original bestowal of being:

> The central phenomenon, at the root of both my subjectivity and my transcendence toward others, consists in my being given to myself. I am given, that is, I find myself already situated and involved in a physical and social world - I am given to myself, which means that this situation is never hidden from me, is never round about me as an alien necessity, and I am never in effect enclosed in it like an object in a box. My freedom, the fundamental power which I enjoy in being the subject of all my experiences, is not distinct from my insertion into the world.

The Ego discovers the One as essential to its being, and as always already having been there. Being in the world as body-subject essentially entails being with others as with oneself. As the parts of my body together comprise an organic system, so my body and the body of the other are one whole, two sides of one and the same phenomenon, mutually implicated in an organic unity, "collaborators for each other in consummate reciprocity". Integral to Merleau-Ponty's project is the foundation of the Cogito:

> The perceiving mind is an incarnated mind. I have tried, first of all, to re-establish the roots of the mind in its body and in its world, going against doctrines which treat perception as a simple result of the action of external things on our body as well as against those which insist on the autonomy of consciousness. These philosophies commonly forget - in favor of a pure exteriority or of a pure interiority - the insertion of the mind in corporeality, the ambiguous relation which we entertain with our body and, correlatively, with perceived things.

The body-subject as inserted in the world with others among things and is radicalized in obscure depths, an abyss into which bodily being recedes and out of which bodily being arises. It is, as it were, an umbilical cord that connects it with the bowels of the earth. This visceral rootedness of the incarnate self, the dark, dense well-springs of its being, is the organic link with nature that binds the thinking subject and its body, and that bonds the conscious self to others and the world.

One's own lived body is a natural subject. Meaning for the subject does not exist in nature as an object in itself, but as perceived. Nor does meaning come to be as an act of signification by the subject, but is bestowed, as it were, from below, founded upon its original collusion, hidden yet revealed, with the earth and from a bodily cohabitation with the world that plunges into chthonic depths.

The body is the condition of the possibility of all expression of, and perspective on, the world. There is an intractable rootedness of one's being in the body-world, in which prior mystery, a silent Logos dwells in emergent expectation. The corporeal estate in which the Cogito inheres is pregnant with the possibility of a luminous birth.

Being present as a lived body-subject to the world in perception, one experiences, simultaneously, the world as wholly within oneself and oneself as being wholly with-out of the world, as being ex-stasis. The dialectical interaction of lived body and perceived world is an internal relation constitutive of transcendent possibilities. From the perspective of the embodied subject as cohabitative with the world, it is a relation of expressivity, in which an internal dialogue of body and world articulate and delineate themselves. The "natal pact" between one's body and the world, between one's self and the body, emerges in the light of reason.

This culminates in language, the act of human speech, the vocalization of an otherwise hitherto fore mute world. The poet Rilke most eloquently celebrates this event:

> Perhaps we are here in order to say: house,
>
> bridge, fountain, gate, pitcher, fruit-tree, window -
>
> at most: column, tower....But to say them, you must understand,

> oh to say them more intensely than the Things themselves
>
> ever dreamed of existing. Isn't the secret intent
>
> of this taciturn earth, when it forces lovers together,
>
> that inside their boundless emotion all things may shudder with joy?.

For Merleau-Ponty, speech is the power of the lived body, reflecting and experiencing itself.

> I celebrate myself, and sing myself. I sing the body electric. This primordial process of signification, the primal poetic, is grounded in the expressive function of the body and its extension. Existence is an act of human self-transcendence.

Speech, by revealing the world in its truth as indicative of an infinite Telos, is founded upon a surplus of Being at the core of human existence: "Being is nothing; it is nothing but explosion, radiance, and opening - never fully is". It is an opening in which the invisible world becomes visible for "every visual something...gives itself as a result of a dehiscence of Being," of a "deflagration of Being".

For Merleau-Ponty, being human is ultimately a movement of transcendence. Human being is a transcendental being in whom a universal natural light appears through the movement of history. The Logos bestows upon human being the task of articulating a preexistent mute universe. From within the deep of being, in the opaque reservoir of the unconscious and involuntary, emerges a presentiment of light, an intimation of Logos, as human being creatively expresses itself, a miracle without cause and a marvel without explanation - a primal act and the primitive fact. That there is something - ilya - is reflected in the incarnate existence of the subject by coming to expression in him/her. Human being is in the world as an internal transcendence of the subject toward it and simultaneously as the very transcendence of the world into him/her.

For Merleau-Ponty human being is both rooted and transcendent. The dialectic of archeology and teleology, of the chthonic realms below and the starry heavens above, distend the narrative drama of human existence. The archeological exploration of the abysmal chiaroscuro of origins and the teleological projection of anticipated destinies reciprocally implicate one another in the constitutive ambiguity of life.

The being of the world is in correlation to the subject; the being of the subject, in projection of the world. The project of the subject and the logic of the world are dialectically interrelated, not in perfect integration, but in an ever on-going, always unfinished determination. In the phenomenon of experience, human being in the dialectic of the lived body and the perceived world is at once rooted and transcendent, simultaneously a natura naturata and natura naturans, always at the same time given and invented, an inheritor and a creator.

Implications for Education

The implications of these fundamental themes of Merleau-Ponty's phenomenological ontology for education would be many. I shall focus on three: aesthetics, communication and ecology.

The ultimate justification of life is neither in the scientific nor in the ethical but in the aesthetic vision. For Merleau-Ponty, art is revelatory of the truth of being. Being conceals itself in its disclosure: "The proper essence of the visible is to have a lining (doublure) of invisibility in the strict sense, which it makes present as a certain absence". There is an inner dialectic within the work of art between the hidden and revealed, the unseen in what is seen, the unfinished in what is done. "Being is nothing; it is nothing but explosion, radiance and opening - that which it never fully is".

Creative expressiveness is not, furthermore, prose, an exact reproduction of a world already sufficient to itself, but poetry, the evocation and sublation of a world in the process of being born. Art does not merely re-produce the visible; it makes visible. The "oneiric universe of carnal essences, of effective likenesses, mute meanings" comes to presence and appearance in art.

Being displays itself in the work of art, whose primary and privileged form for Merleau-Ponty is painting. Painting celebrates no other enigma but that of visibility. Painting is the genesis of the visible, the coming to itself of the Invisible. It hails and hearkens to the always renewed fact that there is something - il y a - wondrous to behold. Painting as "a Logos of lines, of lighting, of colors, of reliefs, of masses" is "a conceptless presentation of universal Being...mute Being which itself comes to show forth its own meaning". As the mind is in the eye of the painter, so the mind is in the eye of the beholder. Vision is not a certain mode of thought or presence to oneself. It is the means given to one for being absent from oneself, for being present at the fusion of being from inside. For every visual something gives itself, as a result of a dehiscence of Being, of a deflagration of Being.

In concurrence with Merleau-Ponty, it seems to me, first, that the aesthetic, so often deemed of peripheral import to the core of disciplines and relegated in the curriculum to the margins of significance, should constitute its refulgent center.

It seems to me, secondly, that painting need not be privileged as primary among the arts. Merleau-Ponty enables me to appreciate the difficult value of modern painting, especially Cezanne, van Gogh and Klee. The significance of modern art in its depiction of the beauty of form seems to be in its arrangement of color, unlike to classical, in its arrangement of lines; the former, more explosive in its uneven containment, the latter, more pacific in its geometric proportion. The modern, moreover, seems to intimate the sublime in the play of colors; the classical renaissance, as in Rembrandt and Vermeer, in the play of light, shadow and darkness. With respect to the romantic, the modern seems more expressively transgressive in its extending limits to the breaking point, less finesse and more aggressive.

Unlike Merleau-Ponty, however, "I do not understand poetry, sculpture, music, or dancing as being less revelatory of Being than painting. Painting may communicate to us the appearance of Being and convey to us its mute meanings, but Speech is Being coming to expressive self-possession, the disclosure of the truth as Being reflective of itself". Language speaks Being, but the voices of painting are the voices of its silence. Is there any greater depiction of the poignant, yet radiant, revelation of Being than Rilke's Duino Elegies? Is the pursuit of likeness in sculpture, as in the craft of a Giacometti, any less an intimate intensity of seeing than painting in making visible the invisible in structuring figures across distance and space, at once receding and engulfing?

The aural manifests deeper possibilities of Being resonant in sympathetic accord. The visual communicates by an exterior "objectivity," in which understanding is in looking, thinking as seeing; the aural, by an interior "subjectivity," in which understanding is in feeling, intimating the ever elusive presence of Being in the vibration of the music. And the dance, is it not the consummate revelatory magic of bodily vitality in which Being comes to glorious presence?

For Merleau-Ponty, perception discloses a solidarity of enveloping beings in Being in and through their bodily being. There is a profound desire to share perception, not simply subsequently as mediated through language, a third thing, as it were, between individual subjects, but by the object perceived in its demand upon the respective subjects to be perceived. This bodily communication, moreover, grounds the possibility of a shared understanding as the goal of universal communication. This primordial communication constitutes one's relationship with others "open to the same truths as I am".

Given this corporeal context of Merleau-Ponty for all communication, he would offer three comments. First, this original intercorporeal solidarity of persons, often neglected but nonetheless important, resonates in and reinforces the undeniable significance of non-verbal communication, preeminently in sexual interaction, dance, and mime. The nascent logic inherent in bodily interaction, albeit ambiguous in its density and intensity, is nevertheless luminous in its import, perhaps because it is fuller, richer, deeper, darker in its dense texture.

Second, there us an inextricable bodily reference in all conceptualizations contributive to a fundamental corporeal metaphoricity in all utterance. The body is the natural symbol of society, the ontological reference of all human organization and our unconscious transference of it. In Toni Morrison's Sula, an anal economics and an excremental vision characterizes the social world of the Afro-American community: "A joke. A nigger joke...Not the town, of course, but that part of town where the negroes lived, that part they called the Bottom in spite of the fact that it was up in the hills. Just a nigger joke."

Language itself, moreover, is indicative of being physical gesture in words: "Did you grasp the idea?" "Your words touched me." "You are rubbing me the wrong way!" Abstraction ultimately manifests an inerradicable material foundation. An etymological analysis of language discloses a profound corporeal ground.

Third, although communication is universal in its intentional projection of comprehensibility, it is particular in its concrete, practical realization. Although communication presupposes an horizon of universal intelligibility in the corporeal transcendence of the Logos, actually, the radical bodiliness of its expression constitutes the zero point of one's individual origination of discourse, conditions all knowing as perspectival, and delimits all communicative competencies by an incurable wound of ambiguity.

All communication is from a body somewhere - and ultimately opaque in its elusive significations. Communication is grounded ultimately in a radical incommunicability, not only because we have - and are - our own bodies, bodies that are gendered, bodies of different races, but also each one's own unique complex comportment of flesh, forever permeates an evasive ideal of perfect communication. Although "the thing imposes itself not as true for every intellect, but as real for every subject who is standing where I am," "I will never know how you see red, and you will never know how I see it".

One is confronted by Merleau-Ponty with the indefferable demand for communication as an inner Telos of Being, that what I see be seen by the other and shared with one another, and the impossibility of its consummate realization, that it cannot, despite all innate yearning to the contrary, become a fait accompli.

A respect for the unspeakable in the pregnant silence of our bodily being bespeaks a reverence for the incarnate mystery of life: the Invisible. The eye and ear of the heart has its reasons that the mind can never know.

The ecological crisis is evident: the spoliation of pristine wilderness, the wanton violation of animal habitats, the profligate depletion of natural resources, and the abject pollution of the earth's environment. The cause of the environmental ravagement is ultimately charged to the Cartesian metaphysics of split reality, res cogitans and res extensa, from which modern science, in its objectification of nature, and technology, in its manipulation of nature, came to dominate Western consciousness and practice.

Merleau-Ponty's critique of the Cartesian metaphysics projects the possibility of a new ontology that reflects the inextricable intertwining of the human body-subject with the world it inhabits. Mind is not impervious to a plenum of dead matter, but rooted in the body and the world, constituting, as it were, a universal sensorium. The primordial commonality, prior to the subject-object and fact-value dichotomy, is in being Flesh, that is, the concrete emblem of a general manner of being. In a manner reminiscent of the chora of Plato's Timaeus, Merleau-Ponty states: "The flesh of the lived body and the world is not inert matter, but perpetual pregnancy, perpetual parturition, generativity and generality, brute essence and brute existence." Flesh is already symbol and metamorphosis of life. The Flesh entails an ontology of the lived body as the visibility of the Invisible.

The constitutive reversibility in being, itself perceiving and itself perceived, the chiasm, grounds intuition and reflection in an original wonder of the subject before the face of Being to which it intrinsically belongs: "In a forest I have felt many times over that it was not I who looked at the forest. Some days I felt the trees were looking at me". The implication here is not, I believe, the elusive notion of trees as having conscious vision, but of human being as coming to itself vis-a-vis the tree. The "gaze of the tree" is one's own recognition as self-possession from the depth of Being.

Merleau-Ponty constructs his philosophical project by re-rooting his thinking in the Flesh of Being, by returning to the "there is"(il y a)..."to the soil of the sensible and opened world such as it is in our life and for our body". What ultimately is implied in Merleau-Ponty's corporeal ontology, in its significance for a philosophy of education, is a post-Cartesian reconstruction of an integral anthropology of the embodied person in a final exorcism of the ghost of Descartes that has haunted the history of modern thought.

Questions for further reflection

First, Merleau-Ponty constitutes the ground of communication and communion with the other as oneself, the recognition of the similarity of the other, an identity in/despite difference. Ipseity in relation to alterity is grounded in a dialectical identity that reflects symmetry, reciprocity and substitutability. The question arises as to what extent Merleau-Ponty recognizes the other in its inalienable and incommunicable otherness, an asymmetrical relation that honors the other in its absolute otherness, in its non-reciprocal difference, and in the non-substitutability of one for another as depicted by Levinas. Is it possible to construct a dialectical reversibility with difference in Merleau-Ponty's play of mirrors?

Second, Merleau-Ponty's metaphysics of the Flesh in its implications for an ontological ecotology depicts a natural mysticism or mystical naturalism. Could one not engage Merleau-Ponty's corporeal ontology with Luce. Irigaray's ontological retrieve of a pre-discursive Empedoclean elemental vision of the universe in its constitutive primordiality of earth, air, water, and fire?

Third, Merleau-Ponty and Martin Heidegger move/turn from a philosophy centered on the human subject to a philosophy centered on Being, that is, from Dasein to Sein in Heidegger, and from the lived-body to the Invisible in Merleau-Ponty. How may one compare Merleau-Ponty with Heidegger's indirect ontology via an aesthetic whose privileged access for Merleau-Ponty is painting and for Heidegger, poetry?

Fourth, although Merleau-Ponty did not develop a formal ethic, does not his corporeal grounding of philosophical reflection support a Marxist project responsive to the material conditions of life and human needs? Does not his bodily sense of communication sustain a compassionate tenderness resonant with a feminist ethic of original relation and responsible caring? Would not the starting point, furthermore, of an ethic in the light of Merleau-Ponty's thinking be Being in its disclosure and demand as World upon human being, rather than as in Kant with an autonomous human subject constituting and constructing an ethic?

Fifth, can Merleau-Ponty's construction of an ontology that is profoundly physical and in which perception is primary, be critically and creatively related, despite the apparently radically different language worlds, to Whitehead's metaphysics whose dialectical polarity of the physical and the mental deploys the significant distinction between causal efficacy and presentational immediacy?

Finally, Merleau-Ponty's basic insights entail the anticipatory articulation of postmodern themes: the relinquishment of metanarratives, the rejection of a purely objective realm and the decentering of the master subject. His phenomenological philosophy may be depicted as a celebration of radical contingency, the recognition of irreducible ambiguity and the givenness of the subject to itself rather than its self-positing self-assertion. To what extent may one regard Merleau-Ponty as an actual, if not simply a precursory, postmodern thinker?

In other words, to what extent is Merleau-Ponty's sense of Being in its dehiscence and deflagration more indicative of Jacques Derrida's difference and dissemination than Plotinus' fragmentation of and reintegration into, the One?

Merleau-Ponty does philosophy as interrogation. Unlike Deconstruction he does not, it seems to me, aver the death of man nor the end of philosophy, but affirms human being and the world in all its questionableness, and philosophy as its intelligible reflection, a quest which is as inescapable and irreducible as it is inexhaustible.

6

Role of Education in the Development of Wisdom

When contemplating what philosophical contribution can be made to education, one way to begin is to look at the origin of the word "philosophy," which derives from Greek, and means literally "the love of wisdom." In Plato's Phaedrus, Socrates says that those whose ideas are based on the knowledge of the truth and who can defend or prove them, when they are put to the test by spoken arguments, are to be called not merely poets, orators, or legislators, but are worthy of a higher name, befitting the serious pursuit of their life. However, we cannot give them the name of "wise," since only God is worthy to be called wise. Therefore we call these lovers of wisdom "philosophers."

Let us pursue this idea of wisdom to see what it might be and whether it would be worthy of our attention. Then we can consider the role of education in the development of wisdom. Wisdom is described in The Encyclopedia of Philosophy as being a practical knowledge based on reflection and judgment concerned with the art of living. However, if the art of living is based on value judgments which involve intuitions, feelings, and desires, then we must take these into consideration if we are to truly discover what wisdom is and how it works psychologically. Also "wisdom" is a positive connotation word implying more than being concerned with the art of living but also being successful at this art.

Living creatures are characterized by the ability to move and grow, whereas dead or non-living matter can only be moved by something else outside of itself. Even in plants, the simplest forms of life, we see the abilities of self-organization and adaptability through mobility to be much more developed and complex. However, although higher animals have the advantage of the five senses common to man, still their activities are guided by instinct rather than deliberate reasoning. In discussing the hemispheres of the human brain as the seat of memory, William James indicates how other animals are lacking in prudence, which is a similar concept to the "practical wisdom" (phronesis) of the Greeks.

> First, no animal without it can deliberate, pause, postpone, nicely weigh one motive against another, or compare. Prudence, in a word, is for such a creature an impossible virtue. Accordingly we see that nature removes those functions in the exercise of which prudence is a virtue from the lower centers and hands them over to the cerebrum. Whenever a creature has to deal with complex features of the environment, prudence is a virtue. The higher animals have so to deal; and the more complex thc features, the higher we call the animals.

For example, the animal's inability to transcend the instincts for food or sex make it incapable of making a decision based on a higher value than immediate nourishment and reproduction or pleasure. James also describes how humans may vary in the use of their intelligence in relation to time.

> In all ages the man whose determinations are swayed by reference to the most distant ends has been held to possess the highest intelligence. The tramp who lives from hour to hour; the bohemian whose engagements are from day to day: the bachelor who builds but for a single life; the father who acts for another generation; the patriot who thinks of a whole community and many generations; and finally, the philosopher and saint whose cares are for humanity and for eternity, -these range themselves in an unbroken hierarchy, wherein each successive grade results from an increased manifestation of the special form of action by

which the cerebral centers are distinguished from all below them.

Animals which depend on instinct do not require a long period of development, and in fact cannot be educated beyond the level of training. However, humans require a longer period of care and development in the early period of life, being uniquely educable. Recent man is in fact the only species named "wise" -homosapiens. Having looked at wisdom in a broad way as being in some way a process of life as movement and adaptability, and that beyond the instinctual level it may be particularly important for man, let us now turn to examine wisdom in human experience.

Wisdom has been valued in virtually every age and society. Why is it valued? To perceive what something non-material is, we may use our spiritual intuition. Then we can employ reasoning to ascertain whether our intuitive understanding is correct or will work. Let us then begin with an intuitive description of wisdom, and then analyze it rationally. Wisdom is the awareness used by the self to relate successfully to the environment; to be practical in acting upon the environment it must include both knowledge and action. We have described awareness as the consciousness of life. By "self" is meant our subjective identity as an individual, and we might describe "environment" as the field of experience for the self.

Now we must explore what constitutes "success." Since wisdom is defined as including both knowledge and action, then we must discover what is the success of each. The goal of knowledge is to understand the truth, and the purpose of action is to do what is good. Understanding of the truth can be described as awareness of reality, of what is actual, which usually can be objectified by inter-subjective agreement with others. However, to universalize "good action," we must develop a theory of values.

Let us begin by analyzing how people experience what is valued as good. Everyone desires or loves what he considers to be good. Or we might say, relative good is what a person loves as indicated by what he pursues. The difficulty here is that not everyone agrees as to what is good due to various situations and sets of consciousness. Yet in each case, love in this sense is one's movement toward what he believes is good, whether it be love of security, love of excitement, love of money, love of power, love of affection, love of truth, etc. By analyzing these expressions we may find that some of these goods are more temporary or selfish than others, seeming at first better than they actually are in the long run.

In fact, in-depth study and the results of experience may reveal that some temporary pleasures valued as good may have painful consequences not recognized by the consciousness which is seeking them, yet be eventually experienced nonetheless. It is adaptation to these types of experiences which tends to develop greater wisdom through the life-process of trial and error. To the extent that the end good which is sought is found to be a limited or lesser good, the love moving toward it must be less pure and limited by the goal it is seeking.

The greater the good is, the greater will be the love experienced moving toward it, and the more fulfilling will be the results. This is so, because the nature of the love is conditioned by the good it is pursuing. Wisdom is what enables the consciousness to perceive what is truly good in the widest context through the love of greater and more universal values. The wisest person will know and act for the highest good, that is, for the highest good of all who are concerned in the action. A person is wise, then, to the extent that he knows what is for the highest good of all concerned and acts accordingly.

What are these universal human values? A universal value is one which is good in every situation, unless another higher universal value for some reason takes precedence over it in a certain situation. A primary value is life from which we derive the value of health. Perhaps the most essential value is happiness, from which some philosophers have derived calmness and imperturbability as the most stable forms of happiness. All other human values may be related to happiness, since happiness generally means the achieving or experiencing of what is good.

Certainly liberty is recognized as a fundamental value by many, because it allows people to seek the good in their own way, and thus develop their own wisdom. An overview of human relations has made justice a value of society as a protection for each individual, and the consequences of injustice have shown that justice is for the highest good of all concerned. When a human consciousness is able to interact with others and the natural environment so as to attain universal values such as these, then we usually call it wisdom.

Now, how can we achieve this wisdom? Whereas everyone desires happiness just as we love what we believe is good, again we find that we are not always happy, which indicates that we do not always know the true path to happiness. Or shall we say, there are degrees of happiness, and most of us have plenty of room for improvement, considering the varying levels of happiness among humans. Yet by means of everyday trial-and-error experience we tend to grow wiser throughout most of life; but obviously some are wiser than others, and some increase in wisdom more rapidly than others.

Wisdom is in fact learned or developed, even if it is not taught by a person. How is it learned? If wisdom involves an inter- action between the self and the environment, then a greater knowledge of the environment makes wiser action possible. Yet wisdom is not merely objective knowledge or science, but also involves the subjective factor and personal values, due to each person's unique situation and choices. People must act for themselves and are responsible for their decisions even if they are influenced by others, if for no other reason than it is they themselves who do their own actions.

To know one's own consciousness in terms of desires, feelings, intuitions, reasoning, and one's various predilections and tendencies psychologically is to be able to make better decisions. Therefore self-knowledge and self-improvement along with a comprehension of universal values are helpful in making wiser decisions which link knowledge and action, and the subjective and objective. The learning of wisdom, then, may be accelerated by self-examination and the directing of one's love or motivation toward greater values.

Although these things may or may not be taught per se, we may be able to investigate how another human being may assist, stimulate, awaken, and encourage a person in this striving for wisdom by looking at his or her actions and words in helping others to become wiser themselves. There is also the spiritual and religious perspective which holds that the good itself, an all-wise being, or God, can communicate with and guide the individual who directs his or her consciousness towards these things. Wisdom then becomes an attribute of a higher reality which can be our teacher and guide.

Is wisdom needed today? From the above discussion it is not difficult to see that wisdom could be helpful in any human situation. In fact it appears that wisdom is needed now more than any other time in history. In the ancient times wisdom was proverbially sought after, but in the modern age science and technology have dominated. With these advances the decisions we must make are even more critical and consequential. Joseph Wood Krutch discusses the dilemma:

> Perhaps we are wiser, less selfish and more far-seeing than we were two hundred years ago. But we are still imperfectly all these good things, and since the turn of the century it has been remarked that neither wisdom nor virtue have increased as rapidly as the need for both.

In an article on "Humanism" he explains the difference between science and wisdom. "Science can tell us how to do many different things but not whether any specific thing which can be done, ought to be done." He then gives the example of the hydrogen bomb. Alice Bailey describes the difference between wisdom and science as relating to the spiritual and material respectively. "Wisdom is the science of the spirit, just as knowledge is the science of matter. Knowledge is separative and objective, whilst wisdom is synthetic and subjective. Knowledge divides; wisdom unites. Knowledge differentiates whilst wisdom blends.... Wisdom concerns the one Self, knowledge deals with the not-self." She also points out the importance of wisdom in the world today:

> Wisdom, actuated and motivated by love, and intelligently applied to world problems, is much needed today, and is not yet to be found, except among the few illumined souls in every nation---in every nation I say, without exception. Many more must love with wisdom, and appreciate the group aspiration, before we shall see the next reality to be known and to emerge out of the darkness which we are now in the process of dispelling.

The world crises of the twentieth century are demanding the development of greater wisdom. In his book Small is Beautiful, E. F. Shumacher sees the need for wisdom to solve our economic dilemmas.

The neglect, indeed the rejection of wisdom has gone so far that most of our intellectuals have not even the faintest idea what the term could mean. As a result, they always tend to try and cure a disease by intensifying its causes. The disease having been caused by allowing cleverness to displace wisdom, no amount of clever research is likely to produce a cure. But what is wisdom? Where can it be found? Here we come to crux of the matter: it can be read about in numerous publications but it can be found only inside oneself. To be able to find it, one has first to liberate oneself from such masters as greed and envy. The stillness following liberation---even if only momentary--- produces the insights of wisdom which are obtainable in no other way.

They enable us to see the hollowness and fundamental .satisfactoriness of a life devoted primarily to the pursuit of material ends, to the neglect of the spiritual. Such a life necessarily sets man against man and nation against nation, because man's needs are infinite and infinitude can be achieved only in the spiritual realm, never in the material. Man assuredly needs to rise above this humdrum "world"; wisdom shows him the way to do it; without wisdom, he is driven to build up a monster economy, which destroys the world, and to seek fantastic satisfactions, like landing a man on the moon. Instead of overcoming the "world" by moving towards saintliness, he tries to overcome it by gaining preeminence in wealth, power, science, or indeed any imaginable "sport."

These are the real causes of war, and it is chimerical to try to lay the foundations of peace without removing them first. It is doubly chimerical to build peace on economic foundations which, in turn, rest on the systematic cultivation of greed and envy, the very forces which drive men into conflict.

Yet how many courses in our traditional education deal with self-knowledge, self-improvement, or human values? Our schools and universities are so objectively oriented that most educators would not even understand what is meant by subjective knowledge or self-awareness. Although some individuals and a few groups are beginning to pursue this awareness, we certainly have a long way to go. It is not necessary to cite statistics on crime or to discuss the problems of human interaction, which have become so familiar that they are a part of the way of life in modern times.

Before we compare our description of wisdom to that of various philosophers, let us summarize our preliminary definition. Wisdom is the knowledge of and action for the highest good of all concerned. There are two necessary conditions, neither of which is sufficient by itself: 1) knowledge of the highest good, and 2) action for the highest good. To know what is right to do and not to do it certainly is not wisdom, though it is a kind of knowledge. Also to do what is right without knowing it is right is not usually considered wisdom, but rather good fortune.

However, it is difficult to judge this since the person may know what is right unconsciously, a process which we might call innate wisdom. Both of these conditions together might be considered sufficient, if indeed any verbal definition could be sufficient unto wisdom which is infinite. At least we have a definition,. even if it does not explain the dynamics of how wisdom works. There are certain enabling conditions which can make wisdom possible, namely the virtues of courage and temperance or propriety. Courage is the power which enables one to do what he knows is right, while temperance and propriety restrain and moderate one's desires and instincts into expressions which are appropriate.

Now let us briefly look at some of the descriptions of wisdom throughout history to compare them with our preliminary discussion. Wisdom was often mentioned in the ancient religious books, particularly those of Judaism. In the book of Job we find confirmation for the idea that it is not the material but the spiritual awareness which deals with wisdom. "Let days speak, and many years teach wisdom. But it is the spirit in a man, the breath of the Almighty, that makes him understand."

Plato summarizes the idea of correct knowledge and action leading to happiness in the Euthydemus.

> Seeing that all men desire happiness, and happiness, as has been shown, is gained by a use, and a right use, of the things of life, and the right use of them, and good fortune in the use of them, is given by knowledge,---the inference is that every- body ought by all means to try and make himself as wise as he can.

Aristotle supports the point that he who has knowledge of what he does is better off and wiser than the man who merely acts, such as the manual worker. Knowledge is also necessary for teaching.

> But yet we think that knowledge and understanding belong to art rather than to experience, and we suppose artists to be wiser than men of experience (which implies that Wisdom depends in all cases rather on knowledge); and this because the former know the cause, but the latter do

> not.... And in general it is a sign of the man who knows and of the man who does not know, that the former can teach, and therefore we think art more truly knowledge than experience is; for artists can teach, and men of mere experience cannot.

In the Nicomachean Ethics, Aristotle's definitions of practical wisdom are very close to ours.

> Now it is thought to be the mark of a man of practical wisdom to be able to deli- berate well about what is good and expedient for himself, not in some particular respect, e.g. about what sorts of things conduce to health or to strength, but about what sorts of things conduce to the good life in general.... Practical wisdom, then, must be a reasoned and true state of capacity to act with regard to human goods.

Aristotle also correlates happiness with virtue an d wisdom.

> If happiness is activity in accordance with virtue, it is reasonable that it should be in accordance with the highest virtue; and this will be that of the best thing in us. Whether it be reason or something else that is this element which is thought to be our natural ruler and guide and to take thought of things noble and divine, whether it be itself also divine or only the most divine element in us, the activity of this in accordance with its proper virtue will be perfect happiness.

Likewise he distinguishes the happiness based on wisdom from good fortune which does not derive from any virtue.

> Let us acknowledge then that each one has just so much of happiness as he has of virtue and wisdom, and of virtuous and wise action. God is a witness to us of this truth, for he is happy and blessed, not by reason of any external good, but in himself and by reason of his own nature. And herein of necessity lies the difference between good fortune and happiness; for external goods come of themselves, and chance is the author of them, but no one is just or temperate by or through chance.

Epictetus give us an analysis of the relationship between the good, love, and wisdom in his discourse "On Friendship." His common-sense psychology comes to the same conclusion.

> What a man applies himself to earnestly, that he naturally loves. Do men then apply themselves earnestly to the things which are bad? By no means. Well, do they apply themselves to things which in no way concern themselves? Not to these either. It remains, then, that they employ themselves earnestly only about things which are good; and if they are earnestly employed about things, they love such things also. Whoever, then, understands what is good, can also know how to love; but he who cannot distinguish good from bad, how can he possess the power of loving? To love, then, is only in the power of the wise."

Another Stoic philosopher, Marcus Aurelius, found that several essential human values depended on wisdom. He asks why temporary pleasures tend to deceive us, and then writes,

> And consider if magnanimity, freedom, simplicity, equanimity, piety, are not more agreeable. For what is more agreeable than wisdom itself, when you think of the security and the happy course of all things which depend on the faculty of understanding and knowledge.

Plotinus in a passage on "Dialectic" focuses on the decision-making process which unites knowledge and action, and which according to wisdom must consider universals.

> And while the other virtues bring the reason to bear upon particular experiences and acts, the virtue of Wisdom is a certain super-reasoning much closer to the Universal; for it deals with correspondence and sequence, the choice of time for action and inaction, the adoption of this course, the rejection of that other: Wisdom and Dialectic have the task of presenting all things as Universals and stripped of matter for treatment by the Understanding.

Another Neo-Platonist, Boethius, who synthesized much wisdom in his Consolation of Philosophy, described the highest good.

> The trouble of the many and various aims of mortal men bring them much care, and herein they go forward by

> different paths but strive to reach one end, which is happiness. And that good is that, to which if any man attain, he can desire nothing further. It is that highest of all good things, and it embraces in itself all good things: if any good is lacking, it cannot be the highest good, since then there is left outside it something which can be desired. Wherefore happiness is a state which is made perfect by the union of all good things. This end all men seek to reach, as I said, though by different paths. For there is implanted by nature in the minds of men a desire for the true good; but error leads them astray towards false goods by wrong paths.

Thus we see the need for greater wisdom to discern the true good. Immanuel Kant in examining virtue also describes practical wisdom as the cause of various human values.

> It is also called the true wisdom, namely, the practical, because it makes the ultimate end of the existence of man on earth its own end. Its possession alone make men free, healthy, rich, a king, etc., nor can either chance or fate deprive him of this, since he possesses himself, and the virtuous cannot lose his virtue.

In the modern context we find a description of wisdom related to the inner self given by a Mason to Pierre in Tolstoy's War and Peace.

> The highest wisdom is not founded on reason alone, not on those worldly sciences of physics, history, chemistry, and the like, into which intellectual knowledge is divided. The highest wisdom has but one science---the science of the whole---the science explaining the whole creation and man's place in it. To receive that science it is necessary to purify and renew one's inner self, and so before one can know, it is necessary to believe and to perfect one's self. And to attain this end, we have the light called conscience that God has implanted in our souls.

This leads us into the esoteric and mystical views of wisdom such as those of Emerson and Maurice Maeterlinck, who wrote in his book Wisdom and Destiny about depths of wisdom beyond conscious-reasoning.

> He who knows himself is wise; yet have we no sooner acquired real consciousness of our being than we learn that true wisdom is a thing that lies far deeper than consciousness. The chief gain of increased consciousness is that it unveils an ever-loftier unconsciousness, on whose heights do the sources lie of the purest wisdom. The heritage of unconsciousness is for all men the same; but it is situate partly within and partly without the confines of normal consciousness....
>
> We shall not become wise through worshipping reason alone; and wisdom means more than perpetual triumph of reason over inferior instincts. Such triumphs can help us but little if our reason be not taught thereby to offer profoundest submission to another and different instinct - that of the soul. These triumphs are precious, because they reveal the presence of diviner instinct, that grows ever diviner still. And their aim is not in themselves; they serve but to clear the way for the destiny of the soul, which is a destiny, always, of purification and light.

Alice Bailey also sees a wisdom which is greater than reasoning and which continually develops over many lifetimes.

> (Wisdom) has to do with the development of the life within the form, with the progress of the spirit through those ever-changing vehicles, and with the expansions of consciousness that succeed each other from life to life. It deals with the life side of evolution. Since it deals with the essence of things and not with the things themselves, it is the intuitive apprehension of the truth apart from reasoning faculty, and the innate perception that can distinguish between the false and the true, between the real and the unreal. It is more than that, for it is also the growing capacity of the Thinker to enter increasingly into the mind of the Logos, to realize the true inwardness of the great pageant of the universe, to vision the objective and to harmonize more and more with the higher measure.

Thus the development of wisdom may have importance beyond the physical existence of one lifetime, but may actually promote the spiritual evolution of the soul.

In returning to earth, we turn to the ideas of a hard-headed scientist, Jonas Salk, who in his book The Survival of the Wisest discusses the necessity of learning from outer nature also a greater wisdom. He writes,

> Importance is attached to the notion that wisdom is of 'practical value' for human survival and for the maintenance and enhancement of the quality of life. The hypothesis proposed and elaborated in this book is that Man can learn wisdom from Nature.

In his conclusion, he expresses the need to overcome the recent purposelessness and pathological behavior.

> By suggesting the idea of survival of the wisest I mean not only that the more discerning will survive but also that the survival of Man. with a life of high quality, depends upon the prevalence of respect for wisdom and for those possessing a sense of the being of Man and of the laws of Nature.

So we return once more to our own century, where the poet T. S. Eliot asks, "Where is the wisdom we have lost in knowledge? Where is the knowledge we have lost in information?" How can we become wiser? Salk proposes learning from Nature, which has been the way of modern science and through which we certainly have made great gains. Yet as we noted earlier, the great need today appears to be in the subjective areas of self-knowledge and human values. How can we stimulate the present generations to take up these studies? One way is to examine the wisest of men throughout history, especially those who helped to educate others in wisdom. Kant discusses the awesome characteristics of such an individual.

> For a teacher of wisdom would mean something more than a scholar who has not come so far as to guide himself, much less to guide others, with certain expectation of attaining so high an end: it would mean a master in the knowledge of wisdom, which implies more than a modest man would claim for himself.... and no one would be

> justified in professing to be in possession of it so as to assume the name of philosopher who could not also show its infallible effects in his own person as an example (in his self-mastery and the unquestioned interest that he takes pre-eminently in the general good), and this the ancients also required as a condition of deserving that honorable title.

If, then, we are to learn about wisdom by studying another individual, the first requirement is that he be wise. Then we may proceed to examine what he did to help others to become wiser. Kant also indicated that this process of guiding others toward wisdom is an important aspect of philosophy. He ends his Critique of Practical Reason with these statements.

> In one word, science (critically undertaken and methodically directed) is the narrow gate that leads to the true doctrine of practical wisdom, if we understand by this not merely what one ought to do, but what ought to serve teachers as a guide to construct well and clearly the road to wisdom which everyone should travel, and to secure others from going astray. Philosophy must always continue to be the guardian of this science; and although the public does not take any interest in its subtle investigations, it must take an interest in the resulting doctrines, which such an examination first puts in a clear light.

Now if we are concerned not merely with the practice of wisdom but also the teaching of it to others, then we must also select someone about whom we have adequate information as to their methods, style, and results in educating. Investigating how the wisest of men taught or assisted others may give us insights and guidelines for the education of wisdom today.

In the history of civilization there are four men who created and demonstrated a way of life which caught on in their own time and has been followed by countless numbers of people for centuries since. Karl Jaspers calls them the "four paradigmatic individuals;" they are Buddha, Confucius, Socrates, and Jesus. Each is unique, and they sprang from four quite different cultures - India, China, Greece, and Israel. Each of the exerted a profound influence on his culture in terms of fundamental beliefs, philosophies, and the methods of carrying them out in daily living.

In the Orient Buddhism and Confucianism eventually became complementary to each other as in the West Christianity and philosophical inquiry have for the most part been able to co-exist. This is probably because Buddha and Jesus were spiritual teachers and founders of religions employing meditation and prayer, while Confucius and Socrates were primarily educators emphasizing learning. Consequently instead of being mutually exclusive and conflicting with each other as two religions tend to be, the religious and educational approaches were able to complement and supplement each other. Due to this similarity of emphasis, comparisons between Buddha and Jesus or between Confucius and Socrates would be most likely to show parallel methods.

There are no writings by any of these four men today. However, in each case their disciples wrote about their lives and teachings in remarkable detail. Consequently we have more information on their actions, manners, and teaching styles than on those of the great philosophers who wrote down their own ideas such as Lao Tzu, Mencius, Chuang Tzu, Plato, Aristotle, Chu Hsi, Aquinas, Kant, etc. Confucius and Socrates have been chosen here for a humanistic study of learning and teaching. By "humanistic" is meant an attitude of concern for human values such as freedom, individual dignity, justice in relationships, self-knowledge, the improvement of character, and a love for one's fellow humans.

That both Confucius and Socrates pre-eminently represent rationality and a concentration on educational pursuits was recognized by Carl G. Jung when he wrote, "Confucius and Socrates compete for first place as far as reasonableness and a pedagogic attitude to life are concerned." Both of them appeared at key transitional periods in the evolution of culture when their fellow humans were ready for educational methods of self-improvement and discussions on ethical questions. Confucius is credited with being the first professional teacher of higher education in, China, and their first and greatest ethical philosopher.

In Greece the professional sophists sprang up during Socrates' lifetime, but though he remained an "amateur" or informal teacher, it was Socrates who was recognized by Aristotle for introducing the study of ethics in addition to the use of inductive logic and universal definitions. It is hard to imagine the history of Oriental culture without Confucius, and it would be difficult to conceive of Plato without Socrates, Aristotle without Plato, and Western philosophy without any of them.

Confucius and Socrates are outstanding examples in humanistic education, and by studying their lives and pedagogy in detail, we may gain a greater understanding of what good humanistic pedagogy is. Since there was no known influence between Chinese and Hellenic culture before 400 BC, these can be treated as independent case studies. Both of these men spent their lives learning and seeking wisdom and the good life. What was wisdom and goodness for Confucius and Socrates, and how did they attempt to realize them themselves and help others to achieve them also? By examining the actions, manner, methods, and subjects of discussion for each of them, it will then be possible to compare them to each other and to formulate key principles and techniques which were successful for them. It is hoped that many of these will be applicable today by formal teachers and informal seekers of greater wisdom and a better life. An underlying assumption is that human nature has not changed too much in the last 2500 years.

In spite of the accumulation of culture and the advance of technology, the fundamental ethical problems of right and wrong, justice, goodness, self-knowledge, and the improvement of character still persist. Both Confucius and Socrates used a conversational style, and with the recent increase of leisure time and the advent of radio and television interviews which for many people are beginning to replace some of the burden of reading, dialogues are as important today as ever.

Confucius and Socrates have inspired countless men and women over two dozen centuries; a description of what they were doing may not only be able to inspire readers today to pursue a better life, but may give some perceptive readers tools they can use to stimulate and assist others to greater wisdom. The original model for this is Plutarch's Lives of the Noble Grecians and Romans, though he only selected politicians and generals. At the beginning of his life of Alexander, Plutarch emphasizes that he is not writing histories, but lives.

> Therefore, as portrait-painters are more exact in the lines and features of the face, in which the character is seen, than in the other parts of the body, so I must be allowed to give my more particular attention to the marks and indications of the souls of men.

Nonetheless due to the antiquity of Confucius and Socrates, the historical difficulties are immense. It is necessary to rely on the written documents of other ancient writers, and the historical accuracy of those available is questionable and highly controversial.

In the case of Confucius, the primary source used is The Analects which was compiled by disciples within a generation or two of Confucius' death. These anecdotes and conversations between Confucius and his disciples (students) are simply and realistically portrayed, as no attempt is made to write a long, philosophical treatise. Other ancient documents from later periods such as Mencius and Ssu-ma Ch'ien's biography are used sparingly for background and are specifically mentioned when so used. Two Confucian classics, usually translated as The Great Learning and The Doctrine of the Mean, were probably written about a century or more after the time of Confucius. They have not been used to describe Confucius as a teacher, but the texts without their commentaries have been presented in the Wisdom Classics as Higher Education and The

Center of Harmony, because they express the spirit of Confucius' teachings.

With Socrates the situation is much more complex. How the sources for Socrates are used are explained in an introduction to the Socrates chapters called "The Socratic Problem."

CONFUCIUS

Confucius considered himself a teacher and worked as diligently as he could to instruct his students. How did he relate to them? The main requirement to study with Confucius was a desire to learn, although he did accept pay or gifts. "From the very poorest upwards--- beginning even with the man who could bring no better present than a bundle of dried meat---none has ever come to me without receiving instruction." Confucius did not set himself up as a man of wisdom, and no matter how humble the student may have been, he was ready and willing to discuss the issue on its own terms; thus anyone in the world could become a fellow learner with him due to his openness. "Do I regard myself as a possessor of wisdom? Far from it? But if even a simple peasant comes in all sincerity and asks me a question, I am ready to thrash the matter out, with all its pros and cons, to the very end."

Although he was willing to instruct anyone, he did not necessarily agree to take on responsibility for all of the person's future actions. Once while in a village where the people were not very receptive to his teachings, an "uncapped boy" asked to be admitted. The disciples were in doubt whether to bring him in before the master, but Confucius clarified the point: "In sanctioning his entry here I am sanctioning nothing he may do when he retires. We must not be too particular. If anyone purifies himself in order to come to us, let us accept this purification. We are not responsible for what he does when he goes away."

There is no definite indication of what age his students were, but this does appear to be an exceptional case due to the lack of interest among the adults of the community. It is generally assumed that most of Confucius' students and disciples were adults, some of them even in his own age group. Two other incidents concern boys or young men. When he found Yuan Jang waiting for him in a sprawling position, Confucius said, "Those who when young show no respect to their elders achieve nothing worth mentioning when they grow up. And merely to live on, getting older and older, is to be a useless pest." With this he struck him across the shins with his staff.

This is the only known case where Confucius used anything like physical punishment. Perhaps it was used because what needed correction had to do with physical posture and respect. Another time someone asked him about the progress of a youth who gained entrance to Confucius' house as a messenger. With insightful observation Confucius said, "Judging by the way he sits in grown-up people's places and walks alongside of people older than himself, I should say he was bent upon growing up quickly rather than upon improving himself." After all, learning was the important thing, not mere association.

Effort in Learning

The most important characteristic which Confucius asked from his students, then, was that they make the effort to learn. He encouraged them to make this effort by allowing them room to think for themselves. "I do not enlighten those who are not eager to learn, nor arouse those who are not anxious to give an explanation themselves. If I have presented one corner of the square and they cannot come back to me with the other three, I should not go over the points again." Naturally it is helpful if the student is intelligent and can grasp things easily.

Yet he emphasizes that as long as the student is making the effort he will continue to help him. "The case is like that of someone raising a mound. If he stops working, the fact that it perhaps needed only one more basketful makes no difference; I stay where I am. Whereas even if he has not got beyond leveling the ground, but is still at work, the fact that he has only tilted one basketful of earth makes no difference. I go to help him." Here Confucius also indicates that how far a person has advanced in his studies does not determine how much help he will receive from his teacher, but again whether he is working to continue to improve himself.

When it came to the essential self-improvement of one's character, Confucius did not even allow his own limitations to hold back the student, but encouraged them even through friendly rivalry. "When it comes to goodness, one need not avoid competing with one's teacher." However, he could not find too many who were willing to apply themselves to learning strictly for self-improvement rather than for extrinsic rewards such as career gain. "One who will study for three years without thought of reward would be hard indeed to find." Jan Ch'iu was one of those who only stayed with Confucius until he was able to receive a good position in the government.

Jan Ch'iu made this excuse: "It is not that your Way does not commend itself to me, but that it demands powers I do not possess." Whereupon Confucius rebuked him for quitting: "He whose strength gives out collapses during the course of the way, but you deliberately draw the line." A keen student of human nature, Confucius was able to see that people tended to be lazy rather than work too hard. So he naturally pointed this out: "Those who err on the side of strictness are few indeed!" When he did find a student whose diligence exceeded what was expected, he showed his approval by a warm response. When Ch'i-tiao K'ai was encouraged by the master to take office, he replied, "I have not yet sufficiently perfected myself in the virtue of good faith." Confucius was delighted.

Not only did Confucius encourage his students to make effort in learning, but most important was that they put what they heard into practice through actual deeds. Can there be any wisdom without action? Self-improvement to this teacher meant actually changing oneself for the better. "The words of the Model Sayings cannot fail to commend themselves to us; but what matters is that we should carry them out. For those who approve but do not carry out, who are stirred, but do not change. I can do nothing at all."

Perhaps we need to revise the common notion that wisdom consists of proverbs and moral homilies or even appreciation of same. To Confucius, of ultimate importance was the improvement of character, and when he saw someone working to better himself, he did all he could to assist him. In these ways, then, he encouraged his students to put forth positive effort.

How Confucius perceived that he himself learned naturally influenced greatly how he taught others. Although he does not rule out the possibility of acting correctly without having to think, Confucius' own experience was that he had to learn by observation and study what was best to do. "There are those who act without knowing why, but I am not one of them. To hear much and select what is good and follow it, to see much and take note of it, is the second type of knowledge." His feeling that he did not act best spontaneously and automatically was probably a major reason why he emphasized learning so much.

Consequently this is the method he used in teaching. He had experimented one time with meditation, but he did not consider the results to be as good as from study. "I once spent a whole day without food and a whole night without sleep, in order to meditate. It was no use. It is better to learn." Confucius was not one to reject something without trying it. As a teacher he recommended to his students what he found to be most successful in his own experience.

What really did impress Confucius was the teaching of the ancients. In humility and perhaps also with the awareness that the valuable wisdoms are eternal and not original with any one individual, he claimed he was only a transmitter not a creator of new ideas. "I have transmitted what was taught me without making up anything of my own. I believe in and love the ancients." Like a good transmitter he allowed the information to continually flow through without trying to hold anything back. His openness and honesty allowed his disciples to learn all that he knew, if they could. "My friends, I know you think that there is something I am keeping from you. There is nothing at all that I keep from you. I take no steps about which I do not consult you, my friends." This does not necessarily mean that he told everyone everything, but the close disciples he was addressing here he has taken into his fullest confidence. Yet at the same time he did not waste his time by trying to teach advanced ideas to those who were not capable of understanding them. "To those who have risen above the middling sort, one may talk of the higher things. But to those who are below the middling sort it is useless to talk of things that are above them."

To be a good teacher Confucius believed he had to continually be a good student. Thus one of his most important methods of teaching was to be an attentive listener in order to learn from his students how to teach them. "To listen silently, to learn untiringly, and to teach others without being wearied---that is just natural with me." Patience and perseverance were qualities which apparently enabled Confucius to stay with his students until they finally saw the light. This continual striving to better himself and others must have given the master an enduring energy.

If he was so vigilant and disciplined with himself, he must have been an ever-present model for his students even if he did not expect as much from them as he required from himself. "The thought that I have not properly cultivated virtue, that what is learned has not been thoroughly discussed, that knowing what is right I have not moved toward it, that what is wrong I have not been able to change ---these are the things which bother me." By examining himself so conscientiously he was inviting his listeners to work on improving their characters also, but he was doing it authentically without preaching or inflicting upon their freedom. By thinking out loud in this way he was showing them how to begin the work on oneself.

Although most of Confucius' teaching was through the conversational style, he once expressed the wish not to speak. One of his disciples immediately objected; they expected their teacher always to be talking with them so they could pass on his teachings. Confucius used the situation to call their attention to the silent teachings of Nature. "Does Heaven speak? Yet the four seasons run their course and all creatures are born according to it. Does Heaven speak?" Perhaps he was pointing out that there is a greater teacher which would remain even after he had gone.

Individualized Instruction

Confucius recognized that people learn in different ways with varying abilities, and the highest class was even beyond him. "Highest are those who are born wise. Next are those who become wise by learning. After them come those who have to work hard in order to acquire learning. Finally, to the lowest class of the common people belong those who work hard without ever managing to learn." The master carefully observed each of his students to study the strengths and weaknesses of their character. When Tzu-kung asked Confucius who was better between Shih and Shang, he readily replied, "Shih goes too far and Shang does not go far enough." Tzu-kung assumed that this meant that Shih excelled, but the master corrected him, "To go too far is as bad as not to go far enough."

Once he understood the character of his students he was then able to individualize his teaching for the good of each person. Tzu-lu and Jan Ch'iu both became important in government, yet Confucius knew that he had to handle them in opposite ways if each was to improve. Tzu-lu once asked Confucius whether one should put a maxim into practice as soon as he heard it. Confucius pointed out that Tzu-lu's father and elder brother were still alive, and asked him how could he apply it immediately, probably hoping that he would take counsel before rushing off into action.

Yet when Jan Ch'iu asked exactly the same question, Confucius told him that one should immediately put it into practice. A third student who had heard both conversations became confused, and asked Confucius for an explanation. The master said, "Ch'iu is retiring and slow, so I urged him on. Yu tends to be fanatical, so I held him back."

Tzu-lu was well-known for his boldness and daring, and Confucius was aware of this. Another time when he was in a humorous mood, probably to overcome his discouragement, Confucius said, "The Way makes no progress. I shall get upon a raft and float out to sea. I am sure Yu (Tzu-lu's nickname) would come with me." Hearing this, Tzu-lu became enthusiastic, so that Confucius said, "That is Yu indeed! He sets far too much store by feats of physical daring, but he does not exercise his judgment." Thus Confucius labored to encourage him to do so.

When asked whether Tzu-lu was good, Confucius said he did not know. When the question was repeated, he responded, "In a country of a thousand war-chariots Yu could be trusted to carry out the recruiting. But whether he is good I do not know." Then he was asked about Jan Ch'iu. The master believed that he could govern a clan of a hundred chariots, but he did not know whether he was good. A third student he said could take a place at court and converse but again he did not know whether he was good. Although Confucius knew the practical abilities of his students, he still did not claim to know if they were truly virtuous, so high a value did he place on goodness itself.

Tzu-kung, another important disciple, asked the master's opinion of him. Confucius called him a vessel. Tzu-kung asked, "What sort of vessel?" Confucius replied, "A sacrificial vase of jade!" This implies again that the master would not call him good, although he was capable of being used on high occasions. On another occasion Tzu-kung expressed Confucius' version of the golden rule: "What I do not want others to do to me, I do not want to do to them." Confucius was quick to point out that he had not lived up to that yet. "Ah Tz'u! You have not quite got to that point yet." Apparently Tzu-kung was often criticizing other people. Confucius must have considered this a negative activity, because he said, "It is fortunate for Tz'u that he is so perfect himself as to have time to spare for this. I myself have none." By giving his own positive example with a little irony, Confucius subtly attempts to move Tzu-kung away from the fault-finding of others to the positive improvement of himself.

Confucius had a way of correcting a person without telling him directly that he was wrong. Chi Wen Tzu thought three times before acting. Confucius heard of it and said that twice is quite enough. Continually we see the master focusing on and emphasizing what is right and proper; he did not say that three times is wrong, but merely that twice is sufficient. He does not want his students to be influenced by a poor example, so he has to correct it in a positive way.

Confucius was not afraid of correcting men in power if they asked for his advice. When Chi K'ang-tzu was upset about all the thieves, he asked Confucius what he should do. Confucius replied, "If only you were free from desire, they would not steal even if you paid them to." This was hardly the answer the ruler would have been expecting! Most people want to try and change others' behavior by external means, but here the master suggests changing one's internal state so that others will also adapt their internal condition; then conduct will improve in a natural way. If the ruler does not horde and covet all the luxurious items, then others will more likely be content with what they have, and stealing will be a dangerous and superfluous task.

Confucius was asked about the treatment of parents by four different men, and he gave four differing answers stressing obedience according to propriety, behavior which would not make parents anxious, sincere feeling of respect, and proper demeanor. Not only was each answer probably suited to the questioner, but also Confucius was able to examine the issue from several perspectives for the sake of the other listeners also.

Questions and Answers

In using the conversational style, Confucius would often answer questions put to him by his students. However, he did not attempt to answer if it concerned something which someone else might know better than he. When he was asked about farming and gardening, he recommended that the inquirer go to an experienced husbandman and to an experienced vegetable gardener. He also did not claim to know about such auspicious matters as the Ancestral Sacrifice, but in this case he did not know of anyone to recommend. "Anyone who knew the explanation could deal with everything under Heaven as easily as I lay this here." He laid his finger upon the palm of his hand.

When a ruler asked him a question, Confucius was able to give an answer which could probably work if applied. Duke Ting asked him for a precept on how a ruler should use his ministers and how the ministers should serve the ruler. Confucius had a ready response: "A ruler should employ his ministers according to the rules of propriety; ministers should serve their ruler with fithfulness." Such an answer was simple to understand and easy to remember.

Many of the questions Confucius answered had to do with virtue, character and correct conduct. These questions he was eager to answer if he could help to clarify the understanding of students. Fan Ch'ih asked first about wisdom and then about goodness. Confucius said, "Devote yourself earnestly to the duties due to men, and respect spiritual beings but keep them at a distance; this may be called wisdom.... The good man first considers what is difficult and only then thinks of success. Such a man may be called good." He extends his descriptions by using natural metaphors showing the quality and result of these virtues. "The wise man delights in water; the good man delights in mountains. For the wise are active, and the good are tranquil. The wise enjoy happiness, and the good enjoy long life."

On another occasion Fan Ch'ih asked again about the good and the wise. Confucius said that the good man loves men and the wise man knows men. Fan Ch'ih did not understand the second part, so Confucius told him, "By raising the straight and putting them on top of the crooked, he can make the crooked straight." Apparently Fan Ch'ih still did not understand, because he asked a disciple to explain what Confucius had said; Tzu-hsia gave an example from history to clarify the principle. In this way Confucius encouraged his students to think about his own enigmatic responses.

Confucius was always anxious to correct ideas and beliefs which could be improved. Here he uses a rhetorical question to make his point. Someone had asked him about the principle of repaying injury with virtue. He responded, "In that case how will you repay virtue? Rather, repay injury with justice, and repay virtue with virtue." Confucius was practical and discriminating in his ethics so that his precepts could be easily followed and would prove successful. The following incident shows how seriously some of the students took the master's precepts. Tzu-chang asked how to get along with people, the fundamental humanistic question.

Confucius said, "Be sincere and true to your word, serious and careful in your actions; and you will get along even among barbarians. But if you are not sincere and untrustworthy in your speech, frivolous and careless in your actions, how will you get along even among your own neighbours? When standing, see these principles in front of you; in your carriage see them on the yoke. Then you may be sure to get along." So Tzu-chang inscribed these words upon his sash. Apparently the students often memorized the master's precepts, and Confucius appears to have encouraged this practice. This is probably how these conversations were passed down until they were recorded in The Analects.

Often an enterprising student would ask follow-up questions in order to draw forth more information from his teacher. Tzu-lu asked about the true gentleman, and Confucius said, "He cultivates himself carefully." Tzu-lu asked if that was all. and Confucius said, "He cultivates himself so as to help other people." Tzu-lu asked again if that was all and Confucius said, "He cultivates himself so as to help all the people. Even Yao and Shun found that difficult." Confucius began with the primary step - improve yourself. If a person could do that, then he could help others. If he could help some, then he could strive to help all humanity. Thus he showed the successive stages. On another occasion Tzu-lu asked about government, and Confucius said, "Lead by example; work hard for them." Again Tzu-lu asked for further instruction, and Confucius said, "Untiringly."

Tzu-kung asked about the true knight and received an answer related to an officer in the court. When he asked the next rank, Confucius answered concerning one who acts well in his community. Then Tzu-kung asked for the next rank, and Confucius referred to the individual level in regard to truthful words and successful accomplishment of one's tasks; these can be attained even by one in humble circumstances. Finally Tzu-kung asked about those in the present government, whereupon Confucius grimaced and said they were not worth taking into account. Again we see how the questions enable him to discuss the various levels of a situation.

Sometimes Confucius would ask his students questions. Often these were very open-ended and personal, so that there was no single right answer. Rather, each person was allowed to express his personal preference, and they could learn from and about each other. When Confucius asked Tzu-lu and Yen Hui their life's ambition, he was likely to receive opposite responses. Perhaps by the interplay of opposite temperaments, each man's character might be broadened. Tzu-lu, as we have seen, was active and oriented toward the physical. Yen Hui, on the other hand, was quiet and sensitive.

In fact Confucius said he was not very helpful in discussions, because he agreed with everything the master said. Maybe he could draw Yen Hui out a little this way. Tzu-lu said, "I wish to have horses, carriages, and fur clothes, to share them with my friends, and I should not be upset if they wore them all out." Yen Hui said, "I wish never to boast of my good qualities and never to mention the trouble I have taken for others." In the midst of the camaraderie of the group, Tzu-lu said he wished to hear the master's ambition. Confucius said, "It is my ambition to comfort the old, to be faithful to friends, and to cherish the young."

In another similar exercise, Confucius asked Tzu-lu, Tseng Hsi, Jan Ch'iu and Kung-hsi Hua to forget for a moment that they usually consider him as older than themselves, and to say what office they would like to have. Tzu-lu was the first to reply, and he did so characteristically as he said, "Give me a country of a thousand war-chariots, hemmed in by powerful enemies, or even invaded by hostile armies, with drought and famine in addition; within three years I could make the people courageous and teach them in what direction right conduct lies." Confucius smiled at him, and asked Ch'iu, who said, "Give me a domain of sixty or seventy li, or say fifty or sixty, and within three years I could make plenty abound among the common people.

As to the principles of propriety and music, I shall have to wait for a real gentleman." Ch'ih then wished to be a junior assistant at the ceremonies of the Ancestral Temple. When Tseng Hsi was asked, he stopped the music he was softly playing and said his wishes were not as select as the others. Confucius said that that did not matter, but only that he should speak his desire. Tseng Hsi said, "At the end of spring when the clothes of the season are all complete, I would like to go with five or six newly-capped youths and six or seven uncapped boys, and wash in the River I, enjoy the breeze at rain altars, and return home singing." Confucius sighed and said he agreed with him. Then the other three men went away, and Confucius answered Tseng Hsi's questions as to why the other three's wishes were not proper.

Here we see Confucius only agreeing with the one whose ambition was practical and humble. If the other three left because offended, then they missed the special attention which Tseng Hsi received. Often Confucius encouraged his students to think and discuss the ideas on their own which he only tersely mentioned. For example, he said his Way had an all-pervading unity. After he left they discussed the issue, and Tseng Tzu said that it was sincerity and benevolence. In this way Confucius did not always hand-feed them, but stimulated his students to think for themselves.

Correct Use of Language

Sincerity and trustworthiness were important to Confucius, because words were often worthless if not backed up by equivalent deeds. Language has the peculiar attribute of being able to be true or false to actual situations, past or future actions. In good human relations Confucius believed that honesty was essential. "I do not know how a man without truthfulness is to get along. How can a wagon be made to go if it has no yoke-bar, or a carriage if it has collarbar?" Confucius tells us that he learned that some men do not do what they say; therefore wisdom demands that he not only listen to people's words but watch their actions as well.

Tsai Yu used to sleep during the day. Not able to reform him, the master decided to make it an object lesson, saying, "Rotten wood cannot be carved, nor a wall of dried dung be trowelled. What use is there in my scolding him anymore? There was a time when I merely listened attentively to what people said, and took for granted that they would carry out their words. Now I am obliged not only to give ear to what they say, but also to keep an eye on what they do. It was my dealings with Tsai Yu that brought about the change."

If the students were to learn to be true to their word, then one way that Confucius could help them was to caution them on their speech. "Do not be too ready to speak of it, lest the doing of it should prove to be beyond your powers." The "it" could refer to anything, but it could have strongly implied goodness (jen) itself. Confucius demonstrated that he was especially careful about discussing this great ideal since its perfection was so difficult to attain. When Ssu-ma Niu asked about goodness, he used an appropriate pun. "The good (jen) man is careful (jen) in speech." Ssu-ma Niu wanted to know if this was the definition of goodness -"careful in speech." Confucius replied, "Seeing that the doing of it is so difficult, how can one be otherwise than careful in talking about it." Perhaps he is implying that no verbal definition would be sufficient, because goodness can only be expressed through action.

Confucius hated the misuse of language, because it could destroy communication and intellectual discussion. When Tzu-lu got an uneducated man appointed governor of Pi, Confucius felt that he was injuring someone; for if he was not capable of the position he could only come to harm. Tzu-lu defends his judgment by saying that he will only be in charge of peasants and the ritual of the grain. Then he quotes a proverb which may have been from Confucius himself; "Learning consists of other things besides reading books." Since the maxim has been misappropriated and does not apply to this man who has not learned how to govern at all, Confucius severely criticizes Tzu-lu's sophistry. "It is remarks of that kind that make me hate glib people."

A necessary part of communication through language is that both parties agree on the meaning of the words which they are using; otherwise confusion results. If Confucius thought that the word another man was using did not mean the same thing to him as to the other, he would ask him his definition of it. Tzu-chang asked about the knight who is to be called "influential." Confucius replied, "That depends on what you mean by 'influential'?" It turns out that Tzu-chang's idea of the word is really much closer to the common meaning of the word "famous." Whereupon Confucius proceeds to describe how the Chinese word for "influential" implies the effective use of virtue (moral power) while anyone with a cocky manner and a reputation, without necessarily any good conduct, may became famous.

Confucius spent considerable time with his students describing what he meant by various key terms so that they could understand them and apply them in practice. This clarification of language was later to become a key Confucian doctrine known as the "rectification of names." Confucius was adamant that the mental communication correspond to the actual reality, even in small matters such as the name of a container. "A cornered vessel without any corners! Should it be called a cornered vessel? Should it?

Metaphors and Poetry

Confucius used commonplace things as metaphors to describe deeper truth. The following implies that pulling on the negative trait too much can ruin the wholeness of the character. "He who acts to work upon a loose strand destroys the whole fabric." In fact, some translate it metaphorically: "The study of strange doctrines is injurious indeed!"

Much like Heracleitus, Confucius recognized the continuity of change as being like a river. Once when standing by a stream, he pondered, "It passes on like this, never ceasing day or night!" He liked to express philosophical ideas the way the Book of Changes does, through natural imagery. Here is a metaphor of the type of people who can endure hard times due to their lasting virtue: "Only when the year grows cold do we see that the pine and cypress are the last to fade." By relating his ideas to natural events, the students could see in actual experience what was to remind them of the higher ideals.

Confucius loved to discuss poetry and songs with his students and drew many lessons from them. This incident shows an enlightening discussion, as Confucius improves on Tzu-kung's ideas and then is pleased by a suitable reference to poetry.

Tzu-kung said, "What do you think of a man who is poor and yet does not flatter, and the rich man who is not proud?" Confucius replied, "They will do, but they are not as good as the poor man who is happy with the Way, and the rich man who loves the rules of propriety."

Tzu-kung said, "It is said in the Book of Poetry:

As a thing is cut and filed,

As a thing is carved and polished ...

Does that not mean what you have just said?"

Confucius said, "Ah Tz'u! Now I can begin to talk about the odes with you. When I have told you what has gone before, you know what is to follow."

For Confucius, to be able to properly interpret poetry was an advanced study, since he felt that very few of his disciples were ready to do so. Tzu-hsia (nicknamed Shang) was another disciple who could discuss poetry with the master. He asked Confucius the meaning of these lines:

Oh the sweet smile dimpling,

The lovely eyes so black and white!

Plain silk that would take the colours.

Confucius said, "The painting comes after the plain groundwork." Tzu-hsia correctly apprehends the symbolism that the ceremonies come after virtue. The master is pleased: "It is Shang who can bring out my meaning. Now I can begin to talk about the odes with him." A student must be prepared and demonstrate it before Confucius would consider going into an advance study with him.

Confucius apparently gave his own son no particular treatment. The son told one of the disciples that his father recommended to him that he study the Odes, or he will not do well in conversation. On another occasion Confucius asked him if he had studied the rules of propriety; again the son replied he had not. This was necessary in order to become established. Confucius here did not command even his son to study certain things, but merely said what the results would be if he did or did not. The disciple was able to get this information by questioning the son. Apparently Confucius made no requirements, but students could not enter into the advanced studies until they knew the preliminary subjects such as poetry and propriety. Even so, these were secondary to virtue and character development.

Lines from poetry could be used as references to personal character. Confucius felt that he and Yen Hui fulfilled the maxim:

> When in office, do your duty;
>
> When not in office, stay out of sight.

Then Tzu-lu impetuously asked him whom he would take to help him if he had command of the whole army. To soften the rejection, Confucius quotes a line from a poem. "Not the man who was ready to 'attack a tiger barehanded or swim across a river' not caring whether he lived or died, but I should take someone who approaches difficulties with due caution, who likes to plan precisely and carry it out." By using poetic imagery as a mirror, the students of Confucius could see themselves more clearly.

Poetry and ceremonies were often formal activities, and it was in these cases that Confucius used the more universally correct pronunciation rather than his native dialect. Confucius as much as anyone knew the impressiveness and majesty of the ancient heritage. This is why he criticized the Three Families' use of the Yung Ode which was only appropriate for the Emperor's Court.

Confucius did not revere the poems to the point that he could not correct their ideas, if it would help his students' understanding. In the following lines he shows the shallowness of the feeling, inspiring the listener to a deeper and more actualized love.

> The flowery branch of the wild cherry,
>
> How swiftly it flies back!
>
> It is not that I do not love you;
>
> But your house is far away.

Confucius said, "He did not really love her. Had he done so, he would not have worried about the distance." Another poem which begins with the cry of the ospreys tells of a lover grieved by separation from his lady, but concludes with their happy union. In this poem Confucius elucidates the proper handling of the two emotional extremes. "The ospreys! Pleasures not carried to the point of debauch; grief not carried to the point self-injury." Thus by interpreting poetry well-known to his students, Confucius could help them to refine their feelings.

Human Examples

Confucius used many human examples to illustrate various lessons. He was especially fond of referring to the legendary emperors of the ancient golden age (before 2000 BC). Because of their great antiquity he could use them as models of perfection, and no one could deny it. Yet if they were the greatest men over a period of thousands of years, then maybe they were great indeed! Confucius said, "Greatest as sovereign was Yao. How majestic was he. 'There is no greatness like the greatness of Heaven,' yet Yao could emulate it. So boundless was it that the people could find no name for it; yet how majestic were his achievements, how brilliant the expression of his culture!" Here he points out how the best ruler follows the Way of Heaven.

Nearly as great were the other two emperors of early antiquity whom Confucius loved to mention. "How majestic was the manner of Shun and Yu! Everything under Heaven was theirs, yet they remained aloof from it." These were the two who did not begin to rule until the people came to them and they were assured that they had the mandate of Heaven. In this way Confucius uses them as models of perfect detachment. Yu was known as a great engineer who drained the land so that it could be used for farming, before he was chosen as emperor because of his ability. Nan-kung Kuo once pointed out to Confucius that, "Yi was a mighty archer and Ao overturned a boat; yet both of them came to a bad end.

Whereas Yu and Chi, who devoted themselves to agriculture, came into possession of everything under Heaven." Confucius did not respond until Nan-kung had left; then he praised him as a true gentleman who knew how to value the power of virtue. This way the master could make clear the lesson to the students without making Nan-kung egotistical by praising him to his face.

Humility could accompany detachment as in the case of T'ai Po, a legendary ancestor of the Chou sovereigns. "Of T'ai Po it may indeed be said that he attained to the very highest pitch of virtue. No less than three times he renounced the sovereignty of everything under Heaven, without letting the people praise his actions." When the last Shang ruler's actions became too corrupt, the Chou clan attacked him. Two brothers were famous for renouncing violence despite their sufferings. Confucius cites them as worthy examples, "Po I and Ch'i never bore old wrongs in mind and had but the faintest feelings of resentment."

Confucius used historical examples to contrast two kinds of behavior, each insufficient. "Duke Wen of Chin could rise to an emergency, but failed to carry out the rules of propriety. Duke Huan of Ch'i carried out the rules of propriety, but failed when it came to an emergency." The history lesson goes on. Tzu-lu said, "When Duke Huan put to death Prince Chiu (his brother). Shao Hu gave his life in an attempt to save the prince; but Kuan Chung did not. Must one not say that he fell short of goodness?"

However, Confucius suggests they look at other considerations even though he may not exemplify perfect goodness, saying, "That Duke Huan was able to convene the rulers of all the states without resorting to the use of his war-chariots was due to Kuan Chung. But as to his goodness, as to his goodness!?" Tzu-kung felt that he was not good, so Confucius makes even more clear the benefits he gave to their culture. "Through having Kuan Chung as his minister, Duke Huan became leader of the feudal princes, uniting and bringing order to everything under Heaven; so that even today the people are benefiting by what he then did for them. Were it not for Kuan Chung we might now be wearing our hair loose and folding our clothes to the left (as the barbarians). We must not expect from him what ordinary men and women regard as fidelity---to go off and strangle oneself in some ditch or drain, and no one the wiser." In this way Confucius shows them how to take into consideration the overall situation.

Confucius did not accept blindly every legend, but examined facts such as with the famed paragon of truthfulness. "How can we call even the great Wei-sheng Kao upright? When someone asked him for vinegar he went and begged it from people next door, and then gave it as though it were his own gift." Each of these examples from legend and history gave the students ethical questions to consider and discuss, so they themselves would know better how to behave.

Confucius also discussed contemporary issues. He suggested the possibility that the neighbouring state and his own state could be improved. "A single change could bring Ch'i to the level to Lu; and a single change would bring Lu to the Way." Such a vague statement would probably stimulate the disciples to think how this could be done. Is it necessary for everyone to be educated in order to realize the Way in a state? Actually most people are followers. "The common people may be made to follow the Way, but may not be made to understand it." Understanding requires making an effort to learn, and who can force anyone to do that? However, the actions of good men tend to influence others.

Confucius often pointed to certain men's qualities as object lessons for his students. He cites Tzu-chien, one of is disciples, to illustrate the mutual influence of men upon each other. "A gentleman indeed is such a one as he! If the land of Lu were indeed without gentlemen, how could he have developed his character." The master might even use himself as an example if it was appropriate. After Confucius had gone into the Grand Temple and asked questions about everything there, someone wondered if he really was an expert in the rules of propriety. When the master heard this, he said, "Just so! Such is a rule of propriety." He did not go out of his way to use himself as an example, but quickly made the point when it came up spontaneously.

Confucius could be skeptical about what someone said if he had reason to be. When Tsang Wu Chung went into exile for conspiracy to revolt, he seized the fief of Fang. Then he sent a message to the duke that he would go into exile if Fang was given to his brother; the request was granted. Confucius perceiving manipulation, commented, "It is said that he applied no pressure upon his prince; but I do not believe it." Here was a subtle political lesson for his students.

We have seen how Confucius pointed out areas in which the bold Tzu-lu (Yu) could improve, but he also used his positive qualities as an example. It was said that the impetuous Tzu-lu "never slept over a promise," and Confucius said of him, "It is Yu who could settle a lawsuit with half a word." Having shown where he needed improving by a quote from literature, he also used the same means to set forth his good points. "'Wearing a shabby help-quilted gown, yet capable of standing unabashed with those who wore fox and badger.' That would apply quite well to Yu, would it not?

Who harmed none, was foe to none,

Did nothing that was not right."

So taken up with this praise was Tzu-lu that he kept on continually chanting those lines to himself until finally Confucius had to awaken him again to higher wisdom. "Come now, the wisdom contained in them is not the full extent of excellence."

Confucius mentioned a Ch'i minister who was famous as a wise advisor, to illustrate friendly behavior. "Yen P'ing Chung was a good example of what one's intercourse with one's fellowmen should be. However long he knew anyone, he always maintained the same scrupulous courtesy." He pointed to a Cheng minister who died in 522 BC as an exemplar of four of the virtues which belong to the Way of the true gentleman: in his private conduct he was humble; in serving his superiors he was respectful; in nourishing the people he was kind; in ordering the people he was just. Yet there were some qualities which no one seemed to fulfill completely. Confucius said, "I have never yet seen a man who was truly steadfast." Someone suggested Shen Ch'eng. The master replied, "Ch'eng! He is at the mercy of his desires. How can he be called steadfast?" By this oblique reference, the students could learn to become more steadfast by watching their desires.

Cogent Sayings

Perhaps Confucius is most famous for his aphoristic sayings, many of which became well-known proverbs of the master. He seemed to have a way of making a moral statement which could inspire one to virtue without it seeming like he was preaching or telling them what to do. He expressed his wisdom as instruction for anyone who wished to take advantage of it rather than as direct commandments. Let us look at some of the statements he made to inspire and enlighten his listeners toward a better life.

On the steadiness of governing virtuously, he uses a natural metaphor. "A ruler who governs his state by the power of virtue is like the north polar star, which remains in its place while all the other stars revolve around it." How is this done as compared to how rulers usually attempt it? "Lead the people by governmental measures and keep order by laws and punishments, and they will try to avoid them, and will lose all self-respect. Lead them by virtue and keep order by the rules of propriety, and they will keep their self-respect and set themselves right." Strong laws and harsh punishments had not worked well in the long run. Confucius believed in and recommended the influence of moral goodness; for once a person attained it, he could regulate himself.

In human relations, if one tried to take advantage of another what will be the result? "If one's acts are motivated by profit, he will have many enemies." Confucius does not say "Do this" or "Do not do this," but rather elucidates the consequence of various actions, negative and especially positive. He describes how a true gentleman behaves, inspiring others to freely decide to become what seems so admirable. What about competition, as in sports, for example? "Gentlemen never compete. You will say that in archery they do so. But even then they bow and make way for one another when they are going up to the archery-ground, when they are coming down and at the subsequent drinking bout. Thus even when competing, they still remain gentlemen."

Is not good sportsmanship a sign of a cultured person? In these situations it is often the motive which indicates the person's character. "In ancient times men studied for the sake of self-improvement; nowadays men study in order to impress other people." Such a statement might bring an inner realization to a student and lead him to change his attitude for the better. Confucius encouraged his students to consider long-range problems, which some try to ignore. Why? Because it was practical. "He who is not concerned about what is far off will soon find something worse nearby."

Although courage is not one of the highest Confucian virtues, it is still essential in action. "To see what is right and not do it is cowardice." Once an action has taken place, however, what good does it do to cast blame? When one of his disciples brought such a charge against Duke Ai's ancestors while talking with the duke, Confucius made the following suggestion: "What is over and done, one need not discuss. What has already taken its course, one need not criticize; what already belongs to the past, one need not censure." Wisdom often involves discernment of when to speak and when not to. Confucius tells us one reason why. "When a man may be spoken with, not to speak to him is to waste a man. When a man may not be spoken with, to speak to him is to waste one's words. The truly wise never wastes a man; but on the other hand, he never wastes his words either." The reference here is probably to the discussion of the Way, which everyone is not ready to hear.

As a teacher Confucius was always encouraging his students to learn. Here he uses an everyday metaphor. "Learn as if you were following someone you could not catch up to, as though it were someone you were frightened of losing." No matter how much one knows, there is always more to learn; and no matter how advanced one becomes, there is always room for improvement. Yet for Confucius it was a joyful process to know that one was doing his best. "Is it not pleasant to learn continually and put it into practice? Is it not delightful to have friends coming from afar? Is one not a gentleman if he does not feel hurt even though he is not recognized?" Regardless of how the world treated him, Confucius could still maintain a positive attitude and go on learning and teaching.

From the material that is available to us, we have examined several of the techniques which Confucius utilized in order to lead others toward greater wisdom. Before we look at whether they were successful or not in terms of actual results among his students, we need to investigate the subject matter which Confucius emphasized.

Since Confucius was perhaps the first professional teacher of adults, or what we call higher education, there must not have been organized curriculum in his time. Although Confucius did discourse on definite subjects repeatedly and also recommended that his students study specific pursuits, it appears unlikely that these subjects were categorized or isolated from each other anywhere near like they are today. The continual purpose of Confucius' teaching was practical and designed to help each person improve his character and conduct, and perhaps become prepared for an official position in the government.

Although Confucius encouraged his students to learn about many things, he suggested that they be very selective and careful in what they said and did. Since Tzu-chang was studying to attain an official salary, the master recommended, "Hear much and put aside what is doubtful while you speak cautiously of the rest. Then few will blame you. See much and put aside what seems perilous while you are cautious in carrying the rest into practice. Then you will have few occasions for regret. When one's words give few occasions for blame and his acts give few occasions for repentance, he is on the way to receiving a salary." Actually Confucius was not as concerned about the quantity of one's knowledge, but emphasized what he considered to be the essence of it all.

Once when talking with Tzu-kung, Confucius perceived that his student was getting the wrong impression and said to him to clarify the situation, "I believe you look upon me as one whose aim is simply to learn and remember as many things as possible." Tzu-kung replied that this is what he thought, and asked the master if it was so. Confucius responded, "No; I have one thread which runs through them all." We hope to discover this underlying unity which pervades Confucius' teachings as we examine their content.

However, the golden rule does stand out as the most important rule of conduct. When Tzu-kung asked if there was a single saying which one could practice all the time, Confucius said, "Perhaps the saying about consideration: 'Do not do to others what you do not want them to do to you.'" Stated in the negative this way, the golden rule allows each person more freedom. Instead of telling a person how to act toward others, which could be an infliction of one's personal values or tastes upon the other, it says only not to do those things which one feels would be an infliction, leaving the other choices of conduct free.

Before we catalog the various topics of Confucius' teaching, there is one pre-requisite he emphasized for there to be any clear communication, and that was the correct use of language. When Tzu-lu asked Confucius what would be his first measure in administering the government for the prince of Wei, he answered with certainty that it would be to correct language. Tzu-lu could not believe it and scoffed at such an idea. So Confucius explained why: "Yu! How uncultivated you are! A gentleman, in regard to things he does not know, maintains a cautious reserve. If language is incorrect, then what is said is not in accordance with the truth of things.

If language is not in accordance with the truth of things, affairs cannot be carried on to success. When affairs cannot be carried on to success, proprieties and music will not flourish. When proprieties and music do not flourish, punishments will go astray. When punishments go astray, the people do not know how to move hand or foot. Therefore the gentleman uses only such language as is proper to speak, and only speaks of what it would be proper to carry out.

The gentleman, in what he says, leaves nothing to mere chance." We see here the importance of a close correlation between reality and knowledge, between knowledge and words, and between words and deeds. The correct understanding of language, then, plays a key intermediary function. The final quote in The Analects emphasizes this for human understanding. Confucius said, "He who does not understand the will of Heaven cannot be regarded as a gentleman. He who does not know the rules of propriety cannot establish his character. He who does not understand words, cannot understand people."

Subjects of Study

According to one passage in The Analects, Confucius taught four things: culture, conduct, loyalty, and truthfulness Culture consisted of literature, music, and perhaps propriety, though it is also a part of conduct. Confucius indicated the value of each: "Let a man be stimulated by poetry, established in character by the rules of propriety, and perfected by music." These pursuits were means by which one may achieve the higher ideal of following the Way. "The gentleman extensively studies literature and restrains himself with the rules of propriety. Thus he will not violate the Way."

Although these may be aids to the Way, the higher ideals come before the arts of culture in importance. "Set your heart upon the Way. Support yourself by its virtue. Rely on goodness. Find recreation in the arts." Actually the moral duties were considered essential and came before the arts which were almost like extra-curricular activities. "A young man's duty is to behave well to his parents at home and to his elders abroad, to be cautious in giving promises and punctual in keeping them, to overflow in love to all, and to cultivate the friendship of the good. If, when all that is done, he has any energy to spare, then let him study the cultural arts."

The Classics

What was the literature? Even in Confucius' time there existed six classics on poetry, history, music, changes, propriety, and the annals, which were all studied in depth by the master, as he often referred to them.

> Confucius said, "When I enter a country, I can easily tell its type of culture. When the people are gentle and kind and simple-hearted, that shows the teaching of poetry. When people are broad-minded and acquainted with the past, that shows the teaching of history. When the people are generous and show a good disposition, that shows the teaching of music. When the people are quiet and

> thoughtful, and show a sharp power of observation, that shows the teaching of the philosophy of change. When the people are humble and respectful and frugal in their habits, that shows the teaching of propriety. When the people are cultivated in their speech, ready with expressions and analogies, that shows the teaching of prose, or Spring and Autumn Annals. The danger in the teaching of poetry is that people remain ignorant, or too simple-hearted. The danger in the teaching of history is that people may be filled with incorrect legends and stories of events. The danger in the teaching of music is that the people grow extravagant. The danger in the teaching of philosophy is that the people become crooked. The danger in the teaching of propriety is that the rituals become too elaborate. And the danger in the teaching of Spring and Autumn Annals is that the people get a sense of the prevailing moral chaos. When a man is kind and gentle and simple-hearted, and yet not ignorant, we may be sure he is deep in the study of poetry. When a man is broad-minded and acquainted with the past, and yet not filled with incorrect legends or stories of events, we may be sure he is deep in the study of history. When a man is generous and shows a good disposition and yet not extravagant in his personal habits, we may be sure he is deep in the study of music. When a man is quiet and thoughtful and shows a sharp power of observation, and yet is not crooked, we may be sure that he is deep in the study of philosophy. When a man is humble and polite and frugal in his personal habits and yet not full of elaborate ceremonies, we may be sure he is deep in the study of propriety. And when a man is cultivated in his speech, ready with expressions and analogies and yet is not influenced by the picture of the prevailing moral chaos, we may be sure that he is deep in the study of Spring and Autumn Annals."

We see from this that more than a mere acquaintance with the classics was recommended, but the quality of study and practice which goes beyond the superficialities.

Confucius is often quoted in The Great Treatise on the I Ching. In one passage ne explains why the book was devised in the first place. He said, "Writing cannot express thoughts completely." Someone then asked if we are then unable to see the thoughts of the holy sages. Confucius replied, "The holy sages set up the images in order to express their thoughts completely; they devised the hexagrams in order to express the true and the false completely. Then they appended judgments and so could express their words completely." It is likely that Confucius extensively used not only the I Ching but the other classics as well in his instruction of students. Ssu-ma Ch'ien records that Confucius read the I Ching so frequently that the leather strap which held the bamboo "pages" together was worn out and replaced three times.

As we have seen, Confucius was a traditionalist who claimed only to be a transmitter of the ancients, which explains his great reverence for the classics. He said he followed the traditions of the Chou dynasty particularly the Duke of Chou, one of its founders. However, his ancestors were from the state of Sung and were probably of the Shang nobility. This may account for why he followed the three-year mourning period which was a Shang custom. Also the legendary emperors he revered above all were from the earliest Hsia dynasty. He explains this eclectic approach as being due to the Chou's accumulation of culture from these previous dynasties. "Chou could survey the two preceding dynasties. How great a wealth of culture! We follow upon Chou." In the biography of Confucius by Ssu-ma Ch'ien written about 100 BC we have a more elaborate description of how Confucius related to the three dynasties.

In the time of Confucius, the power of the Chou Emperors had declined, the forms of worship and social intercourse had degenerated, and learning and scholarship had fallen into decay. Confucius studied the religious or ceremonial order and historical records of the three dynasties, and he traced the events from the times of the Emperors Yao and Shun down to the times of Duke Mu of Ch'in and arranged them in chronological order. And he once said, "I should be able to talk about the feudal order of Hsia, but there are not enough surviving customs in the city of Chi. I should be able to discuss the feudal order of the Shang dynasty but there are not enough surviving customs in the city of Sung.

If there were enough surviving customs, I should be able to reconstruct them with evidence." And he surveyed the changes of customs between the Hsia and Shang dynasties, and after noting how these customs ran on into the Chou period with modifications, he said, "I can even predict how the future historical development will be for a hundred generations." He noted how one dynasty represented a culture with a wealth of ceremonial forms, and how the other dynasty represented a culture of the simple life, and how the Chou dynasty had combined and merged the two previous cultures into a perfect, beautiful pattern, and he therefore decided that he would choose the Chou culture as the ideal. Therefore, Confucius handed down a tradition of historic records of the various ancient customs.

Although there is probably some later projection here and we can see why Ssu-ma Ch'ien is called the father of Chinese historians using already Hegel's dialectic, still the tradition of Confucius as a transmitter of historical tradition is probably not unfounded. We mentioned earlier how Confucius practiced archery, and although it may not have been taught by Confucius himself, the gentleman's education was probably expected to include athletics, especially this art of the bow.

Poetry and Music

Poetry, of course, was an important subject of study. Confucius particularly used it to stress moral values. "All three hundred odes can be covered by one of their sentences, 'Let there be no evil in your thoughts.'" However, poetry had broader humanistic value for understanding oneself and other people, and even increased one's awareness of the natural world. "My children, why do you not study the Book of Poetry? The Odes serve to stimulate the mind. They may be used for purposes of self-contemplation. They teach the art of sociability. They show how to regulate feelings of resentment. From them you learn the more immediate duty of serving one's father, and the remoter one of serving one's prince. From them we become largely acquainted with the names of birds, beasts, and plants."

Confucius was also a great lover of music and played some himself. However, the teaching of this art was apparently handed over to the Grand music master to whom Confucius gave his ideas on how music should follow the ideal of the ancient pattern and then allow for some improvisation while still maintaining harmony. "Their music in so far as one can find out about it began with a strict unison. Soon the musicians were given more liberty; but the tone remained harmonious, brilliant, consistent, right on till the close." Ssu-ma Ch'ien quotes this exact passage, but then goes on to give more information in regard to Confucius' use of poetry and music.

> He once also said, "After my return to Lu from Wei, I have been able to restore the musical tradition and classify the music of sung and ya and restore the songs to their respective original music." In the ancient times, there were over three thousand songs, but Confucius took out the duplicates and selected those that were suited to good form. The collection began with the songs of Ch'i and Houchi, covered the great period of the Shang and Chou kings and carried it down to the times ot the tyrants Yu and Li. It begins with a song of marital love, and therefore it is said "the song Kuan-ch'ih heads the collection of Feng; Luming heads the collection of the 'Little ya'; and Ch'ingmiao heads the collection of the Sung." Confucius personally sang all the three hundred and five songs and played the music on a string instrument to make sure that it fitted in with the score of hsiao, wu, ya, and sung. Through his efforts, the tradition of ancient rites and music was therefore rescued from oblivion and handed down to posterity, that they might help in the carrying out of this ideal of a king's government and in the teaching of "the Six Arts."

Lin Yutang tells us that "the six Arts" could not only refer to the six classics mentioned above but also to the six branches of study practiced during these times, namely propriety, music, archery, carriage-driving, reading, and mathematics. Also in considering these later accounts, we must be aware of the tendency to glorify and expand on what Confucius did. Although Ssu-ma Ch'ien often went against orthodox Confucian beliefs, he was susceptible to exaggeration, as can be seen from this: "Confucius taught poetry, history, propriety, and music to 3,000 pupils of whom 72, like Yen Tutsou, had mastered "the Six Arts."

There is one more marvelous anecdote from Ssu-ma Ch'ien concerning Confucius' playing of music.

> Confucius was once learning to play on ch'in (a string instrument) from the music master Hsiang-tzu, and did not seem to make much progress for ten days. The music master said to him, "You may well learn something else now," and Confucius replied, "I have already learned the melody, but have not learned the beat and rhythm yet." After some time, the music master said, "You have now learned the beat and rhythm, you must take the next step." "I have not learned the expression," said Confucius. After a while, the music master again said, "Now you have learned the expression, you must take the next step." And Confucius replied, "I have not yet got an image in my mind of the personality of the composer." After some time the music master said, "There's a man behind this music, who is occupied in deep reflection and who sometimes happily lifts his head and looks far away, fixing his mind upon the eternal." "I've got it now," said Confucius. "He is a tall, dark man and his mind seems to be that of an empire builder. Can it be any other person than King Wen himself?" The music master rose from his seat and bowed twice to Confucius and said, "It is the composition of King Wen."

Propriety

As moderns, Confucius' emphasis on ritual ceremonies according to the rules of propriety is probably more difficult for us to relate to than any other aspect of his teaching. However, in the ancient times when "civilized culture was by no means universal, the danger of falling back into a primitive "barbarism" was probably very real. The rules of propriety offered a code of accepted conduct and behavior which they knew would work from past experience. These were the traditions and customs which demonstrated to themselves and others that they were cultured and proper gentlemen.

For Confucius, the gentleman knew and behaved according to the rules of propriety. In the first chapter of The Analects, Yu Tzu gives an account of their value. "Among the functions of propriety the most valuable is that it establishes harmony. The Way of the ancient kings from this harmony got its beauty. It is the guiding principle of all things great and small. If things go amiss, and he who knows the harmony tries to achieve it without regulating it by the rules of propriety, they will still go amiss."

Confucius himself explains what can happen if conduct is not guided by propriety. "Courtesy not bounded by the rules of propriety becomes tiresome. Caution not bounded by the rules of propriety becomes timidity, daring becomes insubordination, straightforwardness becomes rudeness." As much as he loved them, Confucius did not believe in over-indulging in ceremonies, and the feelings should be proper to the circumstances. "In ceremonies it is better to be sparing than extravagant. Funeral ceremonies should be observed in deep sorrow rather than in fear."

Often what was appropriate was a kind of golden mean. "When substance exceeds refinement, one becomes rude. When refinement exceeds substance, one becomes pedantic. When substance and refinement are properly blended, then one is a gentleman." Confucius was aware that the ancient ways had been moderated in his own time, and that such moderation was politic. "Were anyone today to serve his prince according to the full rules of propriety he would be thought a sycophant."

Politics

As many of Confucius' students were anxious to obtain positions in the government and also as Confucius himself hoped for an opportunity to advise rulers, it is natural that the art of politics was a favourite topic of conversation. The goal for Confucius was not merely to be learned in many subjects, but to be able to put one's knowledge into practice. Otherwise, what good is it? He said, "A man may be able to recite the three hundred Odes; but, if when given a post in the government, he does not know how to act, or when sent on a mission to far parts he cannot answer specific questions, however extensive his knowledge may be, of what use is it to him?"

However, a person first must improve himself and regulate his own conduct before he could hope to rule over others. Thus self-improvement was pre-requisite to engaging in politics. "If a minister makes his own conduct correct, he will have no difficulty in assisting in government. But if he cannot rectify himself, how can he possibly rectify others?" Although Confucius describes wisdom and goodness as essential to ruling, they still must be carried out with dignity, and according to propriety. He explains why.

> He whose wisdom brings him into power, needs goodness to secure that power. Else, though he get it, he will certainly lose it. He whose wisdom brings him into power and who has goodness to secure that power, if he has not dignity to approach the common people, they will not respect him. He whose wisdom has brought him into power, who has goodness to secure that power, and dignity to approach the common people, if he handles them contrary to the rules of propriety, full excellence is not reached.

Confucius believed that one's political action should follow the Way, as a higher ideal than whatever happens to be occurring in a particular government. One's actions, therefore, will vary depending on whether the government is following the Way or not. He gives this advice for the different circumstances:

> Have sincere faith and love learning. Be not afraid to die for pursuing the good Way. Do not enter a state that pursues dangerous courses, nor stay in a chaotic one. When the Way prevails under Heaven, then show yourself; when it does not prevail, then hide. When the Way prevails in your own land and you are poor and in a humble position, be ashamed of yourself. When the Way does not prevail in your land and you are wealthy and in an honorable position, be ashamed of yourself.

Confucius shows here political acumen and flexibility without compromising moral principles. He expresses similar political wisdom in these statements: "When the Way prevails in the land, be bold in speech and bold in action. When the Way does not prevail, be bold in action but conciliatory in speech." Without giving up courage in action, Confucius still recommends verbal discretion. Confucius knew how to hold his tongue, knowing not only when it was wise not to speak but also when it was not proper to speak. "He who holds no office in a state does not discuss its policies."

There was always someone who might misunderstand how to put the Way into practice. Chi K'ang-tzu asked Confucius if it would be a good idea to kill those who had not the Way in order to help those who had the Way. The master used the opportunity to describe the influence of a good ruler on the common people. He said, "You are there to rule, not to kill. If you desire what is good, the people will be good. The essence of the gentleman is that of wind; the essence of small people is that of grass. And when a wind blows over the grass, then it bends."

The proper relation between a ruler and his minister or between a parent and child, while not being reciprocal as between equals, still benefited by the proper attitude and conduct in each case. The political and family situations were treated as being analogous. The ruler or parent should love his people or children, while the minister or son should be loyal to the ruler or parent. Confucius explains the proper behavior of each. "How can he be said truly to love, who exacts no effort from the objects of his love? How can he be said to be truly loyal, who refrains from admonishing the object of his loyalty?"

Confucius summarizes the art of the ruler as follows:

> A country of a thousand war-chariots cannot be administered unless the ruler attends strictly to business, punctually observes his promises, is economical in expenditure, loves the people, and uses the labour of the peasantry only at the proper times of year.

For a moralist Confucius was quite down-to-earth and practical, and in an age of aristocracy he shows a remarkable humaneness toward the common people. But maybe this should not be so surprising since humanity and goodness were at the heart of his philosophy.

Religion

Although Confucius himself was a religious man in that he followed the religious practices of his time, he did not dwell on those issues in his instruction. It is pointed out several times in The Analects that Confucius rarely discussed spiritual matters. Tzu-kung said, "We can hear our master on culture and its manifestation, but we cannot hear his views on human nature and the Way of Heaven." One reason may be that the more sacred teachings were not for every man's ears, and thus were kept esoteric among those who were ready to hear them. Or, perhaps Confucius did not consider rational discussion relevant or appropriate to transcendental and mystical questions.

As we have seen, "destiny" as the will of Heaven was central in his personal beliefs, but The Analects states, "Confucius seldom talked about profit, destiny, and goodness." Actually there were many sayings about goodness recorded in The Analects which we will discuss later in this chapter. We should keep in mind that The Analects certainly represents only a small selection of Confucius' conversations over a period of many years, and that discussions about goodness were probably considered to be very important to the disciples; thus, though they may have occurred infrequently, many of them found their way into the written documents. It should be obvious why an ethical teacher like Confucius did not talk about profit as often as some of his listeners might have wished.

Even more so did Confucius stay away from mentioning the supernatural phenomena. "Confucius never discussed strange phenomena, physical exploits, disorders of nature, or spirits." For Confucius, none of these issues were to the point, but tended to side-track people from knowing and improving their own character. Since serving the spirits of the dead was the most important thing in the contemporary Chinese religion, the following statements show Confucius as a radical humanist. When Tzu-lu asked how one should serve ghosts and spirits, Confucius replied, "Till you have learned to serve men, how can you serve ghosts?" Tzu-lu then ventured to ask about the dead, and Confucius said, "Till you know about the living, how can you know about the dead?" Yet Confucius did practice the traditional religion with sincerity and reverence. In fact he considered his own attitude to be the most important factor in the sacrifices.

When Confucius offered sacrifice to his ancestors, he felt as if his ancestral spirits were actually present. When he offered sacrifice to other spiritual beings, he felt as if they were actually present. He said, "If I do not participate in the sacrifice, it is as if I did not sacrifice at all."

Perhaps the higher religion for Confucius was for a man to follow the Way. The following statement expresses an idea very similar to the philosophy of Lao Tzu, about whom legend says Confucius talked with one time. "Who expects to be able to go out of a house except by the door? How is it then that no one follows this Way of ours?" For Confucius the sure way was to follow the steps of the ancients. When asked about the Way of the good man, Confucius replied, "He who does not tread in the footprints cannot expect to find his way into the

Inner Room." Thus he felt that the goal or perfection of man was found within oneself as symbolized here by the inner sanctuary.

The inner nature rather than the outward appearance of a man were what concerned Confucius. If these impoverished aristocrats so prevalent at the time were ashamed of their outer circumstances, then their inner attitude was not correct; thus their advice could not be trusted. "A knight whose heart is set upon the Way, but who is ashamed of wearing shabby clothes and eating coarse food, is not worth calling into counsel." Confucius felt that there were different levels of the Way as far as men are concerned. Knowing what the Way is was only the first step. If one loves the Way, he will also follow it; but this is not as good as following it enthusiastically. "To know it is not as good as to love it, and to love it as not as good as to take delight in it." Are these stages of wisdom?

Virtue

One of the central concepts for both Lao Tzu and Confucius was teh, which is being translated here as "virtue" in the ancient sense of a power or ability.for goodness. The Chinese term has the connotation of spiritual power or moral power which people can "build up" within themselves. Confucius saw that it took love and desire to build up this virtue, but he was also aware of the power of sexual attraction. "I have not seen one who loves virtue as he loves beauty." Another translation reads: "I have never yet seen anyone whose desire to build up his moral power was as strong as sexual desire."

Virtue, for Confucius then, is developed through love or desire for goodness, but it must compete with the more powerful sexual urges. Thus becoming virtuous was no easy task. Once Tzu-chang asked about a rhymed couplet mentioning "piling up virtue" and "deciding when in two minds." Confucius said, "By 'piling up virtue' is meant taking faithfulness and sincerity as one's guiding principles, and moving continually to what is right. Again, to love a things means wanting it to live; to hate a thing means wanting it to perish. But suppose one wants something to live and at the same time wants it to perish; that is 'being in two minds.'"

Confucius was able to give more than one answer to the same question to help explain it so his students could understand. While the master was walking with Fan Ch'ih under the trees at the Rain Dance altars, he was asked about the same two lines of verse plus another rhyming line on "repairing shortcomings." Confucius responded, "An excellent question! 'Doing the work first, and considering the reward afterwards;' is that not piling up virtue? 'Attack the evil that is within yourself, rather than attacking the evil that is in others;' is this not repairing shortcomings?

'Because of a morning's blind rage

To forget one's own safety

And even endanger one's kith and kind.'

is that not a case of a divided mind?" We see here again the possibility of an inner conflict in motivation, with one being clearly a greater good than the other.

One key to the practice of virtue was the golden mean. The Doctrine of the Mean, one of the great Confucian classics which was written within a few generations of Confucius, is a beautiful treatise on this subject. Although the mean is not elaborated upon in The Analects, it is mentioned by Confucius: "How transcendent is the virtue of the middle conduct! Rare for a long time has been its practice among the people." Virtue, for Confucius, was action, something which was practiced. The greatest danger to it was incorrect speech. "Clever talk can confound the workings of virtue, just as small impatiences can confound great projects." The Way of Confucius was a way of virtue, of inner spiritual power expressed through deeds. How does one become virtuous, and how does a virtuous person act? These were the most important studies for Confucius' students. Let us examine character development and self-improvement in Confucius' teachings and then explore his descriptions of goodness and the true gentleman.

Character Development and Self-improvement

The dominant subject matter in Confucius' teachings was how to become a good and virtuous person by improving one's own character. There are several Confucian virtues; here he indicates the results or criteria of goodness, wisdom, and courage. "He who is really good can never be unhappy. He who is really wise can never be perplexed. He who is really brave is never afraid." Although courage is a commonly valued virtue of the ancient times, Confucius believed it must be subordinate to justice, another cardinal virtue. When Tzu-lu asked if courage was to be esteemed by the gentleman, Confucius qualified it, "The gentleman holds justice to be of highest importance. If a gentleman has courage but neglects justice, he becomes insurgent. If an inferior man has courage but neglects justice, he becomes a thief."

Confucius also give us a remarkably Socratic description of human wisdom. Again, Tzu-lu (Yu) who excelled in courage and daring needed to be reminded not only of justice but also of what wisdom or "meta-knowledge" is. Confucius said to him, "Yu, shall I teach you what knowledge is? When you know a thing, to recognize that you know it, and when you do not know a thing, to recognize that you do not know it. That is knowledge." Thus this higher-level knowledge of recognition becomes a check on the everyday knowledge and ignorance.

Confucius' main methods for attaining these virtues was, of course, learning. However, rote memorization was not at all sufficient; one must also be able to think. "He who learns but does not think is lost; he who thinks but does not learn is in danger." What are the dangers when one does not learn? Confucius asked Yu if he had heard the Six Sayings about the Six Degenerations. Tzu-lu had not, so Confucius explains what happens when love for each virtue is obscured because of lack of love for learning. Here again we see the role of love in the direction of motivation.

> Love of goodness without love of learning degenerates into simple-mindedness. Love of knowledge without love of learning degenerates into utter lack of principle. Love of faithfulness without love of learning degenerates into injurious disregard of consequences. Love of uprightness without love of learning degenerates into harshness. Love of courage without love of learning degenerates into insubordination. Love of strong character without love of learning degenerates into mere recklessness.

The learning which Confucius implies seems to be a wholistic knowledge of human character. The main emphasis is to know oneself, but by studying key signs one can also evaluate the character of another. The indications include, one's goals, motives, methods, and what gives him satisfaction. "Look closely into his aims, observe the means by which he pursues them, discover what brings him content - and can the man's real worth remain hidden from you?" However, the most advantageous use of studying others is to learn how to correct and improve ourselves; regardless of the man's character we can learn a lesson, positive or negative. "When we see men of worth, we should think how we may learn to equal them. When we see men of a contrary character, we should turn inward and examine ourselves."

Even so, it is difficult to recognize one's own failings and accuse oneself, but this fact indicates that there is always room for improvement. "In vain I have looked for a single man capable of seeing his own faults and bringing the charge home against himself." The important thing is at least to be working to improve oneself. The worst error is not to even make the attempt. "To have faults and to be making no effort to amend them is to have faults indeed!"

Confucius also mentions this in connection with friendship and the virtues of faithfulness and sincerity. "First and foremost, be faithful to your superiors, keep all promises, refuse the friendship of all who are not like you; and if you have made a mistake, do not be afraid of admitting the fact and amending your ways." Confucius pointed out to his students which kinds of friends are beneficial and which may prove harmful to one's character. "There are three sorts of friendships which are advantageous, and three which are injurious. Friendships with the upright, friendships with the sincere, and friendships with the well informed are advantageous. Friendships with those who flatter, friendships with those of weak principles, and friendships with those who talk cleverly are injurious." Likewise it is beneficial for one to be discriminating in his choice of pleasures, so as not to be harmed by dissipation.

There are three sorts of pleasures which are advantageous, and three which are injurious. Finding pleasure in the discriminating study of ceremonies and music, finding pleasure in discussing the good points in the conduct of others, and finding pleasure in having many wise friends, these are advantageous. But finding pleasure in profligate enjoyments, finding pleasure in idle gadding about, and finding pleasure in feasting, these are injurious. Confucius recommends a mean between extravagance and stinginess, though to err on the side of thrift is not the normal tendency and is less harmful. "Just as lavishness leads easily to presumption, so does frugality to meanness. But meanness is a far less serious fault than presumption."

However, excessive pride and stinginess can overshadow and nullify many good attributes. Confucius illustrates this with the hypothetical example of the Duke of Chou who represents an ideal. "Even if a man had abilities as admirable as those of the Duke of Chou, if he is arrogant and mean, all the rest is of no account." In answering a question about what is enlightenment, Confucius describes it as a detachment in the face of verbal attacks, probably a necessary virtue for one involved in politics! "He who is influenced neither by the soaking in of slander nor by the assault of denunciation may indeed be called enlightened."

He goes on to say that this could also be called "transcendence." We have seen how important words were to Confucius in the virtue of sincerity, or the keeping of promises. Here the enlightened man must be able to withstand false charges. In addition a man must live up to his inherent honesty or uprightness if the continuation of his life is to depend upon anything other than good fortune. "Man is born with uprightness. If one loses it, he will be lucky if he escapes with his life."

Goodness

Of all the qualities and virtues of men Confucius esteemed as greatest what he called jen, translated here as goodness, but also interpreted as humanity, humaneness, human-heartedness, benevolence, etc. For Confucius this term represents the essence of being a good person. Although it was a noble ideal to the master and not easily realized, it still can be found very close at hand if not within oneself. "Is goodness far away? If we really wanted goodness, we should find that it is right here." Being good was the basis of character and pre-requisite to other subjects of study because of its importance. "If a man is not good, what has he to do with the rules of propriety? If he is not good, what has he to do with music?"

Knowledge and wisdom are closely related to goodness. Also it is more important to increase one's own awareness than to be recognized by others. "A good man does not worry about not being known by others, but rather is concerned about not knowing them." He is also able to discern the qualities in people and act appropriately. "Only the good man knows how to like people or knows how to dislike people." This may be an old adage clarified by the statement which immediately follows it. "He whose heart is set upon goodness will dislike no one."

This latter idea appeals to the goodness of our hearts, yet Confucius indicates it is also necessary to have the wisdom to discern the good. "It is goodness that gives to a neighborhood its beauty. One who is free to choose, yet does not prefer to dwell among the good---how can he be accorded the name of wise?" Goodness is also a stabilizing yet an adaptable quality within man enabling him to overcome difficulties and sustain success; therefore it is wise to pursue goodness. "Without goodness a man cannot endure adversity for long, nor can he enjoy prosperity for long. The good man is naturally at ease with goodness. The wise man cultivates goodness for its advantage."

Confucius describes how men lacking in goodness tend to respond to hardships. "One who is by nature daring and is suffering from poverty will not long be law-abiding. Indeed, any men, save those that are truly good, if their sufferings are very great, will be likely to rebel." Confucius explains logically that goodness includes courage, but courage does not include goodness; just as virtue includes eloquence, while eloquence does not include virtue. "One who has accumulated virtue will certainly also possess eloquence; but he who has eloquence doe not necessarily possess virtue.

A good man will certainly also possess courage; but a brave man is not necessarily good." The virtues are related to each other in an organized pattern, the goal of the whole being goodness. By analyzing individual faults and correcting them, one can approach closer to goodness. "Every man's faults belong to a set. If one looks for faults it is only as a means of recognizing goodness."

Confucius encouraged his students to strive toward goodness in the belief that everyone has the energy to do so. By directing one's energy toward the good, the negative will have no opportunity to corrupt the person.

> I have never seen one who really loves goodness or one who really hates wickedness. One who really loves goodness will not place anything above it. One who really hates wickedness will practice goodness in such a way that wickedness will have no chance to get at him. Is there anyone who has devoted his whole strength to doing good

> for even as long as a single day? I have not seen anyone give up such an attempt because he had not the strength to go on. Perhaps there is such a case, but I have never seen it.

The caution in Confucius' speech can be seen in his not going beyond what he has observed while allowing for other possibilities.

The good man is trusting to a point, but is wise enough not to be made a fool. Tsai Yu tested Confucius on this point, asking him if a good man, if told there was a man in a well, would go in after him. The master replied, "Why should he do so? A gentleman may go to it, but cannot be made to go down into it. He may be deceived, but cannot be led astray." It is one thing to believe someone's words, but quite another to enter into a wrong action.

Although a person who has accumulated virtue is also eloquent, as we saw above, Confucius did not consider clever speaking to be necessary to a good man. This is indicated by an incident when someone said Jan Yung was good, but that he was a poor talker. Confucius responded, "What need has he to be a good talker? Those who put down others with smartness of speech usually find themselves hated. I do not know if he is good, but I see no need for him to be a good talker." Confucius rarely called anyone good.

In fact Confucius believed one might better approach goodness by being cautious in speech. "Imperturbable, enduring, simple, slow to speak - such a one is near to goodness." Above all, goodness was correct conduct and behavior whether in private or public life. To express this Confucius mentions familiar occasions of special behavior and states again his golden rule.

> Jan Jung asked about goodness. Confucius said, "Behave when away from home as though you were in the presence of an honored guest. Employ the people as though you were assisting at an important sacrifice. Do not do to others what you would not like yourself. Then there will be no feelings of opposition to you, whether it is the affairs of a state that you are handling or the affairs of a family."

Jan Jung said, "I know that I am not clever; I will make it my business to practice this lesson."

Confucius, of course, intended that his students should put his recommendations into practice. When Fan Ch'ih asked about goodness, he gave a more abstract summary, but equally applicable. "In private life, be courteous; in public life, be diligent; in relationships, be loyal. Even if you are living amidst the barbarians of the east or north, these principles may not be set aside." His advice was usually universal enough to apply everywhere.

Ultimately goodness can go beyond improving oneself to actually helping others to improve oneself to actually helping others to improve themselves, but it must begin within oneself in order for one to know how to help others. The following conversation shows that, Confucius could envision a level even beyond goodness - that of the divine sage.

Tzu-kung asked, "If a ruler extensively confers benefits on the people and can bring salvation to all, what do you think of him? Would you call him good?"

> Confucius said, "Why only good? He would without doubt be a divine sage. Even Yao and Shun fell short of it. A good man, wishing to establish his own character, also establishes the character of others, and wishing to be successful himself, also helps others to be successful. To be able to see others by what is within ourselves may be called the art of realizing goodness."

Here is a great key! By knowing what is within ourselves we can know others; knowing ourselves, we can improve ourselves and then benefit others also.

Before we move on to examine Confucius' concept of the gentleman, let us first note that he believed that goodness made a gentleman, but a gentleman was not necessarily good. "It is possible to be a gentleman and yet lack goodness, but there has never yet existed a good man who was not a gentle- man." This is a strong statement indicating the priority of goodness.

Although not necessarily all-inclusive of all positive values in every context in which Confucius used the term, goodness does, however, appear to be the supreme value and the one most emphasized in his instruction.

The Gentleman

The term chun-tzu originally meant the "son of a ruler" and up to the time of Confucius was used to refer to a member of the upper class. Confucius may very well have been the first one to use this term extensively to mean a man of virtue and principle. Cho-yun Hsu in a recent history of ancient China wrote, "The Analects appears to be the earliest work in which chun-tzu was used to imply high moral standards in a person; here it denotes the ideal man whom all men should cultivate their characters to imitate.... Such a man, noble in virtue, was not necessarily a noble in social status." This is an indication of the tremendous influence Confucius must have had, that in his disciples' minds at least he could so change the meaning of this socially-laden term and liberate it from class notions to apply to one of moral principles. We are using the word "gentleman" here as an English equivalent although the common translation "superior man" is certainly valid.

Many of the same ideas about the good man are used to describe the gentleman as well. The following description indicates that the virtues enable the gentleman to command the respect of others: "If the gentleman is not serious, he will not be respected, and his learning will not be on a firm foundation. He considers loyalty and faithfulness to be fundamental, has no friends who are not like him, and when he has made mistakes, he is not afraid of correcting them." Although the gentleman may not have attained goodness, he acts in such a way so that he might become good.

Ssu-ma Niu once asked Confucius what the term "gentleman" meant. Confucius said that a gentleman has no anxiety or fear. Ssu-ma Niu then asked rhetorically if this is what is meant by being a gentleman. The master then elaborated, "On looking within himself he discovers nothing wrong. What is there for him to be anxious about or fear?" Here again self-examination and self-improvement are the keys.

A gentleman is not worried by what others think of him, only that he correct himself. "A gentleman is distressed by his own lack of capacity; he is never distressed at the failure of others to recognize his merits." However, eventually he should be able to bring his good points to light; if he is never recognized at all, it may be an indication that he has not accomplished anything worthwhile. "A gentleman has reason to be distressed if he ends his days without making a reputation for himself."

At three different stages of life, Confucius observes that the gentleman must watch out for certain prominent tendencies. "There are three things which a gentleman guards against. In his youth when his physical powers are not yet settled, he guards against lust. In his prime when his physical powers are full of vigor, he guards against strife. In old age when his physical powers are decaying, he guards against avarice." A keen student of human nature, Confucius is able to admonish his students to be aware of certain propensities of the life process. Confucius gives his students an elaborate catalog of the concerns of a gentleman as guidelines for their behavior.

> The gentleman has nine cares. In seeing he is careful to see clearly; in hearing he is careful to hear distinctly; in his looks he is careful to be kind; in his manner to be respectful, in his words to be sincere, in his work to be diligent. When in doubt he is careful to ask for information; when angry he has a care for the consequences; and when he sees a chance for gain, he thinks carefully whether the pursuits of it would be right.

These may seem like common sense, but how often are these basic fundamentals of conduct neglected or ignored? By delineating them Confucius at least makes sure that his students have been made aware of them. If they were put into practice, how valuable they could be!

Confucius knew that wise words were not nearly as important as wise or good deeds. "The gentleman prefers to be slow in word but diligent in action." In fact the correlation between them was very important to the gentleman of Confucius' philosophy. "A gentleman is ashamed to let his words outrun his deeds." Such reminders were probably very helpful to his students who must have spent much time in conversation. A gentleman should also have the wisdom not to evaluate a man solely on his words, nor to reject a good idea because of who said it. "A gentleman does not promote a man on account of what he says; nor does he reject sayings, because the speaker is what he is."

To make his points regarding better behavior and conduct, Confucius used to contrast the gentleman with the small man. In this way the students could recognize the mediocre or usual behavior and could seek to replace it with the higher ideal. For example, "The gentleman sets his heart on virtue; the small man sets his on comfort. The gentleman thinks of sanctions; the small man thinks of favours." Confucius recommends a more universal perspective. "The gentleman can see a question from all sides without bias. The small man is biased and can see a question only from one side."

The broader view enables one to be guided by the higher standard of justice. "A gentleman in dealing with the world is not for anything or against anything; he follows what is right." The higher viewpoint begins from neutrality in order to see objectively. What is it which leads most people away from justice? "The gentleman understands what is right; the lesser man understands profit." Confucius recommends a positive attitude toward others rather than negative fault-finding. "The gentleman calls attention to the good points in others; he does not call attention to their defects. The small man does just the reverse of this." Continually Confucius emphasizes self-improvement and being responsible for oneself rather than inflicting on others. "The demands that a gentleman makes are upon himself; those that a small man makes are upon others."

The influence of a gentleman, however, is not limited by his social position. "The gentleman can influence those who are above him; the small man can only influence those who are below him." The gentleman can also be distinguished by his disposition. "The gentleman is calm and at ease." Some of this difference may be the result of whether the conscience is clear or not. The inner attitude also carries over into one's manner. "The gentleman is dignified but not proud; the small man is proud but not dignified."

Confucius' gentleman is an idealist rather than one merely striving to make ends meet; besides, the economy may go up or down anyway. "A gentleman, in his plans, thinks of the Way; he does not think how he is going to make a living. Even farming sometimes has a shortage; and even learning may incidentally bring a salary. A gentleman is concerned with the progress of the Way; he is not anxious about poverty." For Confucius, ethics always came first. There is human value beyond being able to work, and Confucius would avoid dehumanization. "The gentleman is not an implement."

The gentleman is a creative and active being who knows how to get things accomplished in the correct way. "A gentleman considers justice to be essential in everything. He practices it according to the principles of propriety. He brings it forth in modesty and faithfully completes it. This is indeed a gentleman." Thus we find the model which Confucius placed before his students for them to study and learn to emulate. His curriculum is wholly concerned with the subjective development of the human being.

Although some humanities such as literature, history, and philosophy were used as aids, the overall emphasis is on the improvement of each person's character so that he may be a good gentleman. If he were able to gain a political appointment as the result of his education, as several did, this was only an incidental consequence as far as Confucius was concerned. His absense was to help people to become good.

INDEX